CW01466759

SYRIA AND THE NEU͏

"A masterpiece, this book is a riveting call for action to prevent governments that massacre their own citizens from directing who shall, and who shall not, receive donor-funded life-saving emergency help."

—Jeffrey Feltman, UN Under-Secretary-General for Political Affairs 2012–2018

"This in an extraordinary book on humanitarian law and practice in the Syria conflict. By a scholar-practicioner with many years of experience studying Syria and acting as advisor to the UN mediator on the country, it is a model of how theoretical concerns and practical experience in policy making can cross fertilize each other."

—Raymond Hinnebusch, professor of international relations,
University of St Andrews Centre for Syrian Studies

"The road to hell is paved with good intentions. Carsten Wieland masterfully paints a gloomy picture of an international community's attempt to help suffering civilians in the Syrian hell. And how their pretensions of neutrality ended up benefitting the perpetrators of those civilians. Neutrality can be a deadly trap. Wieland accurately describes that trap and ways how to get out of hell."

—Omid Nouripour, Foreign Policy spokesman of the Green
Parliamentary Group in the German Bundestag

"The most convincingly argued call yet to take international humanitarian aid out of the control of unaccountable governments that use sovereignty as a pretext – the ultimate exposure of sovereignty as fake neutrality."

Eberhard Kienle, Research Professor at the Centre des recherches
internationales —(CERI), Centre national de la recherche
scientifique (CNRS) / SciencesPo, Paris

"A highly interesting and original study based on many years of practical and intensive experience. It clearly lays out the complicated juridical, humanitarian and political dimensions of the dilemmas of delivering humanitarian aid during wars. An authoritative guide, highly recommended for politicians, humanitarians and other decision-makers."

—Nikolaos van Dam, former Dutch diplomat, scholar and Syria expert

SYRIA AND THE NEUTRALITY TRAP

Dilemmas of Delivering Humanitarian Aid through Violent Regimes

Carsten Wieland

I.B. TAURIS

LONDON • NEW YORK • OXFORD • NEW DELHI • SYDNEY

I.B. TAURIS
Bloomsbury Publishing Plc
50 Bedford Square, London, WC1B 3DP, UK
1385 Broadway, New York, NY 10018, USA
29 Earlsfort Terrace, Dublin 2, Ireland

BLOOMSBURY, I.B. TAURIS and the I.B. Tauris logo are trademarks of
Bloomsbury Publishing Plc

First published in Great Britain 2021
Reprinted in 2021

Copyright © Carsten Wieland, 2021

Carsten Wieland has asserted his right under the Copyright, Designs and Patents Act,
1988, to be identified as Author of this work.

Cover image: Residents wait in line to receive food aid distributed in the Yarmouk
refugee camp on January 31, 2014 in Damascus, Syria. (© United Nation Relief
and Works Agency/Handout/Getty Images)

All rights reserved. No part of this publication may be reproduced or transmitted in any
form or by any means, electronic or mechanical, including photocopying, recording,
or any information storage or retrieval system, without prior permission in writing
from the publishers.

Bloomsbury Publishing Plc does not have any control over, or responsibility for, any
third-party websites referred to or in this book. All internet addresses given in this
book were correct at the time of going to press. The author and publisher regret
any inconvenience caused if addresses have changed or sites have ceased to
exist, but can accept no responsibility for any such changes.

A catalogue record for this book is available from the British Library.

A catalog record for this book is available from the Library of Congress.

ISBN: HB: 978-0-7556-4138-3
        PB: 978-0-7556-4139-0
        ePDF: 978-0-7556-4140-6
        eBook: 978-0-7556-4141-3

Typeset by RefineCatch Limited, Bungay, Suffolk
Printed and bound in Great Britain

To find out more about our authors and books, visit www.bloomsbury.com
and sign up for our newsletters.

For my daughter Amélie and the children of Syria.
For their future in a less violent world.

Carsten Wieland is a German diplomat, senior UN consultant, Middle East and conflict expert with high-ranking mediation experience. He has served with three UN Special Envoys for Syria as Senior Expert for Intra-Syrian Talks and political advisor. He has also worked on political responses to the Syrian conflict for the German Foreign Office. In his diplomatic capacity he was also Director of the German Information Center for the Arab World in Cairo. Currently, he works as Senior Middle East Advisor for the Green Party Parliamentary Group in the German Bundestag.

Wieland is also a lecturer at New York University (NYU) Berlin, Associate Fellow at the Geneva Centre for Security Policy (GCSP), guest professor at the University Rosario in Bogotá, and previously a fellow at the Public Policy Institute at Georgetown University, Washington DC, USA. He worked also as director of the Konrad Adenauer Foundation (KAS) in Colombia.

A journalist by training, he reported from the United States, the Middle East and Latin America as a foreign correspondent for the German Press Agency (DPA). His academic publications include *Syria: A Decade of Lost Chances* (2012), *Syria – Ballots or Bullets* (2006) and *Syria at Bay: Secularism, Islamism, and "Pax Americana"* (2006).

Wieland studied history, political science and philosophy at Humboldt University in Berlin, Duke University in North Carolina and at Jawaharlal Nehru University in New Delhi.

CONTENTS

Cover Image: Residents of the Damascus neighbourhood of Yarmouk desperately wait to receive food aid in January 2014. At this time, an estimated 18,000 people were besieged inside this area by government forces and lacked medical supplies and food.

FOREWORD

In a small Geneva hotel room, overnight from 30 to 31 January 2016, I sat together with a member of the Syrian opposition and tried to find ways to motivate them to come to the negotiating table. For almost two years, the UN peace process in Geneva had been dead. But the international dynamic turned more positive at the end of 2015 with the formation of the International Syria Support Group (ISSG) in Vienna. Thanks to the Nuclear Deal with Iran (officially known as the Joint Comprehensive Plan of Action), the US and Iran were able to sit down at one table and in one format again also in other contexts, like on Syria. At the end of January, then UN Special Envoy Staffan De Mistura had invited both the Syrian government and the High Negotiation Committee (HNC) to come to Geneva's Palais des Nations for the Geneva Talks. The government had arrived and was received by the Envoy, thus demonstrating its willingness to engage in front of the world media that had gathered in their hundreds at the lakeside hotels. But the opposition was reluctant. As the weaker party to the conflict, they were were hedging their bets. That night in January, most of them had remained in a meeting in Doha, bickering about whether or not they should travel to Geneva. What kept them from engaging was mainly the escalating violence: shelling and barrel bombs falling on civilian neighbourhoods, on medical facilities – in short, a humanitarian disaster and human rights violations on a massive scale. Most of the moderate opposition was in favour of the peace talks, but many of them felt they were unable to join the talks under such circumstances. Their demands at that point were basically humanitarian: they asked for the release of a number of detainees, at least women and children, and access to some of areas besieged by the Syrian government in which people were starving, having eaten all the nearby birds, cats and even grass.

The brutality of the Syrian conflict was omnipresent in every moment of the events in Geneva. Even in the later phases of the peace efforts, violence surged periodically just before new rounds of talks were supposed to resume in order to achieve this exact result: that the opposition felt the heat from their contacts on the ground, saw the gruesome pictures from their constituencies and were tempted not to engage. Furious Syrians in Aleppo, Daraa or Douma asked them not to embark on diplomacy while women and children were running for cover from the approaching helicopters that dropped the make-shift bombs on their neighbourhoods, on their schools or hospitals, or while their neighbours were being buried under the rubble of their collapsing houses.

At 2am on that night of 31 January, after several phone calls I made with De Mistura at one end and calls between my counterpart and the opposition leader in Doha at the other, we managed to build a bridge for the Geneva Talks – or Geneva III – to start the very next day. I had negotiated some smaller confidence-building measures for the morning and convinced the few opposition members present in Geneva not to be held hostage and blackmailed by the spiral of violence. They finally understood that it was much more effective to join political talks on eye level with the Syrian government and the UN, and thus shift the daily brutality in Syria into the spotlight of the world media as a negotiating party rather than a bunch of dispersed protesters rattling at the fence in front of the Palais des Nations.

Having worked on Syria for some twenty years as a journalist, scholar and diplomat, I was familiar with the country's history, with many personalities in its civil society and those who had turned to politics in challenging times. I had got to know their families, their fears, their way of thinking and the pressure that they were under from those compatriots under fire on the ground that the opposition representatives were supposed to represent at the table in the idyllic setting of Lac Leman. I also had deep, and sometimes emotional, conversations on countless Geneva nights with representatives from *both* sides of the divide. Still, it was very difficult to try to ignore the daily violence and death toll in Syria on each day that we failed to advance a political solution. Nevertheless, we attempted to focus on diplomatic exchanges. This was all we could do, even though this often did not lead to anything concrete but was rather a form of playing for time, mostly caused by the government side. If nothing else, the start of the Geneva Talks in January 2020 after that fateful night in the lakeside hotel made a subsequent ceasefire possible that lasted reasonably for several months. Some lives were spared, for sure. But afterwards, developments in Syria turned increasingly towards a military solution, with diplomatic windows of opportunities missed, the UN-mediated process struggling for relevance, regional and international political climates deteriorating, and humanitarians squeezed between a resentful and cynical regime and an ever more radicalized armed opposition on the ground, traumatized, demoralized and morally numb by the enormous scale of both violence and suffering.

When I left the UN at the end of 2019, after having served under three UN Special Envoys for Syria, from Lakhdar Brahimi to Geir Pedersen, I did not want to let this rich experience pass by without carving out at least some critical and self-critical lessons for the future from one of the worst conflicts of this century. I decided to write *not* about my main file, the political talks, but about something that had become a personal and moral concern during those intensive months and years. We worked on a political track while humanitarian issues constantly influenced the overall developments and our discussions, sometimes to the extent that they overshadowed the political process altogether. Also this might have been well intended by some of the relevant actors.

As diplomats – but also as human beings – we were appalled by the fact that in the twenty-first century, people were being deliberately starved to death in a combat tactic taken straight from the Middle Ages, that bombs hit women and children queuing up for bread, that medical personnel were tortured to death because they treated people who had peacefully demonstrated in the streets, that the industrial-style, systematic torture of thousands was a daily routine, that schools and hospitals were targeted from the air, that a second load of barrel bombs would be sent to hit an area again just a few minutes later to kill the rescue teams who had arrived subsquently, that chemical weapons were used against civilians who huddled in basements for shelter, that all the presumed 'red lines' of our civilization – developed by a large corpus of international humanitarian and human rights law – seemingly counted for noting, and were reduced to dry and obsolete theory. And all the while, millions of dollars and euros were spent on humanitarian assistance that was mostly channelled through a regime which was, to a very large extent, responsible for the humanitarian disaster in the first place.

When is the right time to learn and draw conclusions? During a conflict? After it? Before the next one? Since conflict and emerging post-conflict scenarios are ongoing in parallel in Syria, in large parts of the Middle East and beyond, this book may come at a right time to foster – or at least to accompany – a critical debate about some lessons learnt. Now since most violent frontlines in Syria have stabilised, a new phase of this protracted conflict has set in. What has occurred in Syria throughout these years has been more complex than 'yet another' humanitarian catastrophe with a high civilian death toll and harrowing TV images. The Syrian example has also displayed structural deficits in how our international system works, how money is spent, negotiations are led, political decision-makers and humanitarians work and act, and how international law is being silently changed.

I regard this book as a humble contribution to an ongoing debate at the interface of legal and political discussion. I'm conscious of the fact that such a hybrid endeavour also bears risks. But I hope that practitioners and decision-makers may welcome a more profound understanding of the legal context in order to better shape their arguments and actions, and that scholars may profit from practitioners' experience from the political machine room of a large international vessel.

Finally, I would like to thank all Syrians who have taken risks and efforts to tell me their stories, using their own name or anonymously, and all other interlocutors who have shared their candid reflections on this difficult subject. I am also grateful to those diplomatic colleagues in foreign ministries and inside the UN system who have shared information and their assessments with the aim of advancing the informed debate about this dilemma that will remain a crucial challenge for international politics far beyond the Syrian war.

In particular, I am deeply indebted to Prof. Dr. Eibe Riedel, professor emeritus of German and Comparative Public Law, European and International Law at the University of Mannheim (Germany). A judge at The Hague Permanent Court of Arbitration, former Swiss Chair of Human Rights in Geneva, and a member of the UN Committee on Economic, Social and cultural rights, he has readily provided guidance on legal groundworks and scholarly discussions on international law and humanitarian principles in theory and practice. Thanks to my dialogue with him, I have hopefully stayed on track regarding the difficult issues that are, as we know, ever moving targets.

Berlin, January 2021

ABBREVIATIONS

ACU	Assistance Coordination Unit
AP	Additional Protocol (to the Geneva Conventions)
CIL	Customary International Law
ELN	National Liberation Army (Colombia)
FAO	Food and Agriculture Organization
FARC	Fuerzas Armadas Revolucionarias de Colombia
FSA	Free Syrian Army
GC	Geneva Convention
HLP	Housing Land and Property
HNC	High Negotiation Commission
HRP	Humanitarian Response Plan
HRW	Human Rights Watch
HTF	Humanitarian Task Force in Geneva
HTS	Hayat Tahrir al-Sham (Committee for the Liberation of the Levant)
ICC	International Criminal Court
ICRC	International Committee of the Red Cross and Crescent
IDP	Internally Displaced Person
IHL	International Humanitarian Law
IHO	International Humanitarian Organization
IHRL	International Human Rights Law
IL	International Law
IOM	International Organization of Migration
JRS	Jesuit Refugee Service
LACU	Local Administration Council's Unit
LAS	League of Arab States
LTTE	Liberation Tigers of Tamil Eelam (Sri Lanka)
NATO	North Atlantic Treaty Organization
NDF	National Defence Forces
NIAC	Non-international armed conflict
OSE	Office of the UN Special Envoy for Syria in Geneva
SAMS	Syrian American Medical Society
SARC	Syrian Arab Red Crescent
SEMA	Syrian Medical Association for Syrian Expatriates
SHARP	UN Syria Humanitarian Assistance Response Plan
SNHR	Syrian Network for Human Rights
SNC	Syrian Negotiation Commission
SOC	Syrian National Coalition of Revolutionary and Opposition Forces
SRTF	Syria Recovery Trust Fund
UOSSM	Union of Medical Care and Relief Organizations
UN	United Nations

UNICEF	United Nations Children's Fund (till 1953: United Nations International Children's Emergency Fund)
UNHCR	United Nations High Commissioner for Refugees
UNMM	UN monitoring mechanism
UN-OCHA	United Nations Office for the Coordination of Humanitarian Affairs
UN-OHCHR	Office of the High Commissioner for Human Rights
UNPROFOR	United Nations Protection Force in Bosnia-Herzegovina
UNSC	United Nations Security Council
WFP	World Food Programme

Chapter 1

INTRODUCTION TO A TOUGH DILEMMA

Humanitarian assistance should reach the most vulnerable and needy, and be distributed to as many of them as possible. It must be impartial and neutral in a conflict in order to achieve this aim. This is the underlying theory of humanitarian efforts. In practice, however, taking the appropriate decisions to facilitate those ambitions is far more complex and difficult, especially when specific patterns of conflict apply.

This book is about a tough policy dilemma that may end up in a trap: how can political and humanitarian decision-makers alleviate human suffering to the largest extent possible in a brutal, asymmetric and intricate war without betraying the principles of impartiality, neutrality and of postulates of international legal frameworks in general? This contribution to the wider debate looks at the case of Syria in particular. Since the beginning of the popular uprising in 2011, within the wave of the Arab Spring protests, governments have struggled for answers on how to cope with this vast challenge on political, humanitarian and ethical levels.

On the conflict's ninth anniversary in March 2020, the anti-government Syrian Network for Human Rights (SNHR) announced that 226,247 civilians had been killed in the Syrian conflict, almost 30,000 of whom were children.[1] According to this report, more than 88 per cent of those civilians had been killed by the Syrian regime[2] and Iranian militias on the ground, and another 3 percent by Russian forces. Many of the victims were casualties of air raids; none of the armed opposition groups or even Islamist rebels ever held a plane or helicopter. By comparison, the so-called Islamic State (IS) killed 2.2 per cent of the civilian victims in Syria, and factions of the armed opposition, some 1.8 per cent.[3]

Over the same period to March 2020, the SNHR counted there had been 14,221 cases of torture, 98.8 percent of which had been perpetrated by the regime. Many Syrian citizens were tortured excruciatingly to death at the hands of their own government in a systematic manner, as evidenced by the Caesar Files of 2014, which contained photographic documentation of the cruelties, supplied by a defector from the military police.[4] According to further SNHR data from March 2020, 146,825 people were listed as still detained or forcibly disappeared, exposed to horrendous conditions and torture, of whom 88.5 percent for account of the government side.[5] In 2017, the UN High Commissioner for Human Rights, Zeid Ra'ad Al-Hussein, noted that: "[t]oday in a sense the entire country has become a torture-chamber; a place of savage horror and absolute injustice."[6]

Due to the conflict, around 15 million Syrians have been forcibly displaced, seven to nine million of whom inside Syria, according to UNHCR or SNHR numbers.[7] SNHR further reports that 853 medical personnel have been killed since 2011, mostly by regime forces and its allies Russia and Iran; 713 journalists have also died, with 80 per cent of these deaths being attributed to the regime. The human rights organization also found that 222 chemical attacks, 492 cluster bomb attacks, and 81,916 indiscriminate barrel bomb attacks had taken place. These are the most comprehensive statistics available to date.

It was not only the sheer quantity of death and suffering in Syria that challenged anybody's imagination. *How* people died was also staggering. In terms of legal and political repercussions, the extent to which long-held principles of international humanitarian law (IHL) and international human rights law (IHRL) have been breached is extraordinary. The general rules for the treatment of civilians in wars, the Geneva Conventions, that most countries have signed up to (even Syria in 1953, although without the Additional Protocols), have been spurned either by those who have violated their content and spirit almost daily or by those whose imagination, energy or interest have become exhausted to adequately criticizing or sanctioning this behaviour. In addition, independent, impartial and neutral humanitarian assistance faced tremendous obstacles during the Syrian conflict, which in turn has triggered a highly controversial political debate about how to avoid blatant abuse in this and other conflicts to come.

"I have been working for more than twenty years in the humanitarian sector, in NGOs and then in the government, but I have never seen such a politicized humanitarian situation and complex challenge like that in Syria," a German diplomat acknowledged to the author. "The Syrian conflict has left a strong imprint on humanitarian discussions in general."[8] A similar picture is conveyed by UN colleagues who concede that their humanitarian and protection mission in Syria is the most expensive, challenging and complex the United Nations has ever undertaken.[9] Other international humanitarians – who had worked in various challenging contexts, including Sudan, the Democratic Republic of Congo and Yemen – say that the situation in Syria was among the worst in terms of restrictions on ability to operate.[10] Another German diplomat who worked on humanitarian affairs in Geneva adds: "Human rights violations have always existed. But some twenty years ago in Sudan or Congo, the bombardment of hospitals, refusal of humanitarian access and so on were condemned much more harshly than today. IHL is on the retreat. This is a shocking development, and Syria is the main example."[11] In addition, the Norwegian Refugee Council and Oxfam, both of which have ample experience on the ground as registered international humanitarian organizations in Syria, conclude: "Syria is one of the most difficult contexts in the world in which to deliver principled humanitarian assistance."[12] And the French diplomat and think-tank member Charles Thépaut writes: "The humanitarian response in Syria is both a logistical masterpiece and an ethical conundrum."[13]

It is particularly noteworthy that this development has occurred just when the growing pretensions of international human rights and humanitarian law have been regarded as far developed. However, after the disastrous US-led attack on Iraq, its equally disastrous post-war management from 2003 onwards and the controversial international intervention in Libya in 2011, the notion of an international Responsibility to Protect (R2P) has finally been buried under the Syrian rubble. For many Syrians, this was more than bad timing. Many of them originally took to the streets striving for dignity, personal freedoms, an end to arbitrary arrests and torture, and for better life perspectives, perhaps even democracy. International intervention to end the massive violence against civilians in a timely manner to protect human life before the crisis spread, radicalized and intensified, remained a pipe dream.

All of these dynamics evolved in a political macro-scenario in which the appetite of governments to become politically or militarily involved in the Syrian conflict to save lives was strongly limited for several reasons among European countries and the United States, under both the Obama and Trump administrations. The question that remained to be resolved inside Western foreign ministries was how to aptly respond to an escalating conflict with a high human toll within self-imposed limits of non-military action. In particular, Western decision-makers were split on what constituted legitimate and legally adequate means to alleviate human suffering but which would not be instrumentalized by parties to the conflict, including by a government that had violated its responsibility towards its own people to the worst possible extent.

Heated debates took place between those departments inside the foreign ministries that worked with a political focus on the Syrian conflict and those who were responsible for humanitarian issues. The same happened inside the UN itself. The respective camps had very different approaches given that their perspectives were often irreconcilable, almost by definition. This led to a great amount of frustration on both sides and to sometimes incoherent policy outcomes, especially when a third set of actors became active as well, namely those who approached the matter from a purely developmental and stabilization perspective. Thépaut points to a contradiction in this context:

> The paradox is that U.N. assistance to Syrians is mostly funded by countries opposed to Assad. With a total contribution of $19 billion and $11 billion respectively since 2011, Europe and the United States provide around 90 percent of U.N. funding. However, key donors such as the U.S. Agency for International Development and the European Commission have been reluctant to push back against diversions of U.N. support to regime cronies and loyalists. They have likely feared being accused by humanitarian actors of politicizing assistance and did not want to weaken U.N. agencies further. They may have also feared the regime could react by further blocking assistance to non-loyalists.[14]

The traditional firewall between political and humanitarian decision-makers in ministries and international organizations exists for good reason. It is meant to prevent the risk of instrumentalizing and discrediting humanitarian principles. But the Syrian case has raised questions around whether this firewall was appropriate at all times and under all circumstances, and whether it really proved to be a bulwark for humanitarian impartiality and neutrality, all things considered. Alternatives are not easy to find and can be extremely risky while dealing with unscrupulous counterparts and when tough decisions must be taken on the ground. Protecting humanitarian principles and activities has become increasingly difficult in today's complex and asymmetric wars.

The humanitarian Neutrality Trap means that decision-makers in donor governments may have good intentions when funding humanitarian assistance and when they insist on shielding this decision from political contexts and political deliberations. But if this humanitarian assistance, the way it is handled, ends up being distorted or abused on a large scale and if it actually turns into a convenient political and economic weapon used by a government at war against its people, that well-meant decision may do more harm than good. The trap snaps shut when: a) the concepts of impartiality and neutrality become a farce; b) purely humanitarian goals are not reached; c) the interventions end up prolonging the war and overall suffering; and, in the end, d) what was supposed to be an altruistic decision becomes merely dogmatic or even political in its own right in the absence of genuine neutrality in practice.

During the first years of this asymmetric conflict in particular, small NGOs tended to be dismissed by humanitarian decision-makers in Western ministries as 'political' actors since they were regarded as cooperating with insurgents. Somehow they managed to sneak into destroyed opposition areas in clandestine cross-border operations and constructed makeshift hospitals in basements on which bombs rained down. Meanwhile, UN organizations were by default regarded as neutral and impartial actors delivering assistance to Damascus – from where the helicopters, jets and missiles were launched. Such an approach had a legal foundation and followed international practice. However, this very practice came to be heavily tested in the Syrian conflict, and its legal foundations can be challenged, as we will see in the following chapters.

When an authoritarian regime loses control over its people and territory, one typical strategy it tends to apply is to insist even more on absolute national sovereignty in its external relations and – as we will see– with regard to the modalities of delivering humanitarian assistance. In such cases, the postulation of hard sovereignty compensates for the actual deficiency of sovereignty and bad government. Some elements of traditional international law can be used to support this claim, in theory. In practice, it also depends on the extent to which international supporters of a government as a warring party toe the line in this discourse or even shore up this claim by their words and deeds.

It was in this context of asymmetry of warfare and asymmetry of suffering that questions about cross-border delivery became increasingly urgent from a humanitarian perspective. Delivering aid *cross line* – i.e. from government-held territories to opposition territories – was frequently blocked by regime-backed authorities who had no interest in helping foster resilience in the areas they bombed. Equally difficult and controversial was the delivery of aid *cross border* – i.e. into Syrian territory from a neighbouring country. In certain periods, much of the destruction and humanitarian suffering occurred in areas close to neighbouring countries, especially Turkey, which itself had become party to the war and was far from neutral.

It was only after three years of conflict that some progress was made. In 2014, cross-border deliveries became politically and legally possible for large-scale UN operations through a limited number of border-crossings. Damascus was not asked for permission, since it was home to the same authorities who hindered cross-line deliveries by creative bureaucratic harassment and thus made a cross-border resolution necessary in the first place. The first cross-border resolution lasted only until January 2020, by which time the international climate had deteriorated. Russia and China prevented the prolongation of this resolution through their respective vetos in the UN Security Council. Follow-up resolutions hammered out in January and July 2020 were reduced in time and scope, while Russia and China did not scruple to hide that their ultimate intention was to stop UN cross-border deliveries altogether.

The quandary of access to the most needy has been the overarching problem of humanitarian operations in Syria. Instead of seeking political accommodation, in 2011 the government opted for a full-scale war of attrition against its citizens with all means available. Right at the start of originally peaceful protests, it applied a narrative of its fighting sectarianism, extremism and terrorism, which de-humanized the other party or parties with the aim of rendering unscrupulous warfare more justifiable and easier to digest. But from a humanitarian perspective, help was urgently needed in real time wherever destruction was wreaked, mostly from the air. If this was the case, why did the UN and other humanitarian organizations accept the strict conditions, limits of movement and operations imposed by the Syrian government? Should the UN have more strongly conditioned or even severed its cooperation with an obstinate regime that denied access as a means of warfare? By doing so, it would have neglected its other humanitarian duty to help *all* people in need, including those in government areas and those that could be reached cross-line only through tough negotiations with the government as a partner. But challenging circumstances also led to some creative approaches that tried to reduce the asymmetry between humanitarian deliveries in government and non-government areas. The dilemma also increased the importance of non-humanitarian assistance as a tool under various labels such as resilience, stabilization or conflict-prevention measures.

As a complicating factor, the UN consists of agencies with a wide spectrum of different tasks, all of which have their own interests and organizational behaviour: some focus on humanitarian issues, for example, while others look at matters through the development lens. Still others specialize in justice issues and war crimes, or who work on ending conflict by mediation. The latter two tasks are essentially incompatible. A mediator needs to be impartial – although not neutral, as stipulated by the norms laid out in the United Nations Charter – and is well advised not to engage in a discussion about justice and accountability while the conflict is still in full swing, since she or he will diminish the prospects for peace by deterring parties to come to the table. All this is often very difficult to understand for a suffering population that cries out for help, addressing its pleas to a general concept of 'the United Nations'.

Different missions and priorities of UN organizations and of donor countries' ministries or departments inside ministries exist by default. Still, a public debate becomes necessary when policy outcomes diverge too widely from international norms and values, such as the mark of the UN Charter and fundamental principles of IHL and IHRL, or when policy outcomes fuel a conflict instead of alleviating suffering, when moral and professional standards are obviously neglected or when individual agendas distort institutional causes. In a nutshell, the policy dilemma in the Syrian case is such a difficult one because of a challenging confluence of factors:

1. In an age of growing bilateralism, the binding force of universal norms and international legal positions have been weakening. This became particularly evident in the Syrian scenario both in the active sense (norms were violated) and in the reactive sense (violations of red lines were not met with adequate responses).
2. Key political actors had no consensual and coherent reading of international law, international humanitarian law, and international human rights law. They used their arguments selectively in order to advance national interests.
3. It had become gradually cultivated international practice that humanitarian assistance would be channelled through government cooperation and with government consent.
4. The main cause of human suffering and source of indiscriminate destruction were air raids ordered by the very government through which humanitarian assistance was channelled.
5. UN agencies and other international organizations were caught in a difficult dilemma: should they should work as well as possible with the incumbent government under its conditions? Work without the government's consent? Or cease all operations in the country? Each option carried dire implications for the civilian population.
6. The United Nations and its staff, by name and definition, are composed of all member states, including those who are party to the conflict. Conflicting loyalties and ideological leanings have been at play constantly during practical operations.
7. UN agencies and offices – often with diverging missions – have been poorly coordinated, to such an extent that sometimes they hindered each other in the overall purpose of promoting peace and justice, and alleviating suffering.

To avoid misunderstandings, it must be made clear that this book does *not* cast any judgement on the warring parties with regard to the legitimacy or non-legitimacy of their political demands, strategies of upheaval or survival. If the Syrian Revolution – indeed, the Arab Spring – was legitimate, or whether its ends justified its means, is discussed elsewhere.[15] Whether or not the Syrian regime had and has a legitimate claim to power, and whether it took right or wrong decisions when facing the challenge from the street, is not up to this book to judge (though President Assad once conceded that 'mistakes' were made when he opted for the 'security solution').[16] What matters here is that the actions of the government of the Syrian Arab Republic are evaluated through the lens of IHL and IHRL as a government in the family of the United Nations that bears *particular responsibility* for the people who live within the boundaries of the government's sphere of control. At the same time, the Syrian government is measured by its own strongly asserted claims of state sovereignty and of being a responsible, law-abiding member of the world community. Damascus has often used legal argumentation to assert itself internationally while violating international legal standards domestically in its struggle for survival. It is this discrepancy that matters here and not a political assessment of the struggle itself. In more legal terms, this book is not about any side's right to launch a struggle or war (*ius ad bellum*) but on the behaviour within this conflict (*ius in bello*).

After this introduction to the Neutrality Trap and initial reflections on the humanitarian dilemma in Syria, Chapter 2 of this book discusses the problem of humanitarianism and the system that is supposed to uphold a universal standard of human rights. Contemporary literature tends to view the real-world architecture of human rights as being on the decline, despite an ever-developing corpus of international law, particularly humanitarian and human rights law, and their institutionalized capacities. A global humanitarian regime with their own bureaucracies and organizational behaviour has replaced the idealized vision of a committed and empathetic defence of humanitarian principles, above all, neutrality and impartiality, and the defence of human rights. The discussion goes well beyond Syria and touches upon examples of humanitarian dilemmas from other contexts. Reactions of donor states, the UN or aid agencies in those situations are briefly compared, such as in Sri Lanka, Sudan, Somalia, Bosnia-Herzegovina, Afghanistan or Yemen.

An understanding of the relevant foundations and principles of IHL and IHRL is necessary in order to approach the overall theme of this book and the Syrian case in particular. Chapter 3 discusses the Geneva Conventions that the state of Syria has also signed, reiterating the most relevant principles for the case study. They constitute a bitter contrast given the brutal reality on the ground. By and large, Syria maintained most criteria required of a state despite the devastating war, and therefore, according to international law, its government has a special responsibility towards its people – a responsibility that it violated to the worst possible extent. At the same time, the chapter sheds light on the legal argumentation of the Syrian government, equally drawn from the acquis of UN resolutions. This legal reading supports Damascus' claim of untouched sovereignty and territorial integrity of a state during humanitarian assistance. Juxtaposed with these claims, the principles of humanitarian neutrality and impartiality are introduced here. Against this background, the controversial argument is sketched as to whether consent needs to be given to humanitarian aid being delivered, especially cross border, in light of a massive humanitarian crisis or human rights violations.

Chapter 4 focuses on the validity of international legal principles, and how validity claims have varied, changed or weakened throughout times. International law (IL) is approached as work in constant progress in an environment of high interdependence with political actions that can in turn have law-shaping repercussions. Today, just as IL and its sub-fields have reached to almost every sphere of international and domestic decision-making, its cohesive capability in practice and normative binding force seem to be weakening. War makes law, as it has done in the Syrian case. Diplomats who work on the humanitarian file conclude that today's IHL is on the defensive. Traditionally consensual principles are being questioned and weakened. Without the cover of Russia and China, this development would not be possible. Particularly obvious is the retrogression of national sovereignty towards a Westphalian ideal type of untouchable and unconditioned state sovereignty. This has direct implications on options for and the effectiveness of humanitarian assistance, especially with an obstinate and brutal host government in place.

In Chapter 5, erosions of IHL and IHRL are exemplified in the debate of combating terrorism or what is called such. The terrorism narrative has lived prominently in our collective consciousness since the 9/11 attacks in New York and Washington DC in 2001 and has caused severe collateral damage: it tends to dehumanize the other, stripping them of their fundamental human rights. As in Syria, it is often used by authoritarian governments to justify oppression or unscrupulous means of warfare. Such a discourse conveniently puts forward the notion of an 'unlawful combatant', which negates any need to treat opponents with the minimum rights stipulated by IHL and IHRL. Thus it unleashes not only poisonous rhetoric, but also shapes a conflict's course with unlimited use of violence.

Chapter 6 elaborates on the intricate system via which the Syrian government influenced, bullied and utilized humanitarian presence and projects on its territory. Squeezed between the government and international actors, the Syrian Arab Red Crescent (SARC) became both a victim and a collaborator in this system of intimidation and corruption, while the majority of its field staff worked hard to reach the needy. This situation provoked policy dilemmas on how best to deliver and improve the access of humanitarian assistance. Donors found themselves in a bind and some of them even brainstormed how a complete halt on humanitarian delivery would play out in practice. Such a radical option looked too risky, but a more vigorous push towards cross-border operations widened the scope of action, at least temporarily. Practical challenges are described using first-hand experiences of local staff on the ground or of diplomats in headquarters where difficult decisions had to be taken.

Criticism mounted with regard to how some UN staff and agencies were handling the crisis on the ground, as discussed in Chapter 7. This section reflects upon reports and studies published in this regard and puts the heavy allegations into a dilemmatic perspective from a diplomatic angle, adding examples from first-hand sources. This includes UN officials' strong emphasis on the Syrian government's sovereignty despite its massive violations of IHL and IHRL, an at least partial identification of the regime's ideology and struggle, its rhetoric and push for even more aid decoupled from political reforms. Such attitudes also manifested itself in the hiring of regime family members into crucial UN positions and in the contracting of agencies that camouflaged themselves as charities but were in reality extensions to regime militias. The UN lost credibility, in particular with NGOs who were asked to share sensitive coordinates of humanitarian sites with the UN with the aim of shielding them from air raids. But many of the sites were targeted nevertheless.

These mounting problems have triggered reactions within the world body and outside it, as discussed in Chapter 8. One political measure taken by the UN itself was to establish particular Parameters and Principles adapted for the challenge in Syria. In fact, they were derived from old material provided by the legal corpus of IHL and IHRL. The necessity to remind the own organization and its member states, especially Syria and its allies, once again of those principles shows how seriously the situation had slipped out of control. It is still too early and difficult to assess if those steps and other, more operative adjustments, will prove sufficient to avoid future traps of this kind.

Chapter 9 describes one consequence of problematic humanitarian practice and the UN's severe credibility crisis: several donor governments diversified financial allocations away from the humanitarian sector to a more hybrid approach that linked up with funding from non-humanitarian resilience, early recovery and other sources, something that has often been lumped together under the heading of 'humanitarian plus'. This approach certainly deviated from working within the strict frame of humanitarian neutrality and impartiality. But it attempted to reach the neediest with alternative means and to reduce the flow of resources into the regime's war coffers as collateral damage from conventional paths of humanitarian delivery. These creative ways of avoiding strict humanitarian procedures ran into their own problems, however, since political considerations were married with a humanitarian motivation into a quasi-humanitarian approach.

Chapter 10 broadens the focus to a wider discussion on the political circumstances that have contributed to the Syrian quagmire and the problems that have ultimately led into the Neutrality Trap. It becomes obvious how difficult, if not impossible, it is to reconcile the different positions across the political divide. While one side cites moral reasons when calling for a halt to misguided humanitarian assistance in order to prevent fuelling the conflict further, the other side claims that a continuation of such aid – which is reaching at least some of the needy – is a moral imperative. In the end, humanitarian funding became a moral substitute for donor governments in the face of political failure to deal with the violence and put an end to human suffering through diplomatic and political means, or even combining it with military instruments. Russia did intervene on various levels but, despite of its pretentions, failed to develop a credible agenda of conflict resolution that would have enjoyed wider legitimacy and support. Instead, it has on various fronts discredited UN work and, together with its ally in Damascus, shown contempt for multilateral efforts.

Chapter 11 puts forward arguments for change after the dire experiences in Syria. Avoiding the Neutrality Trap is not easy. But some recommendations are offered for possible lessons or guidelines for future crises. Radical options with a larger political impact, such as humanitarian withdrawal, are juxtaposed against more practical steps that can be undertaken within the current practice and system. More collective action and bargaining, better recruitment and training, improved coordination of humanitarian actors on the ground and of donors, a revision to donors' internal procedures and behaviour are some of the main ways to avoid traps of this kind. However, all this shows again how closely related political and humanitarian strategies and goals can be and, in some circumstances, must be. The challenge of maintaining the firewall between both realms without falling into the Neutrality Trap is immense. The moment when it is time to carve holes into the wall to catch a glimpse from the other side is a risky one and difficult to determine. But in such extreme cases like in Syria, efforts to mobilize a political corrective in donors' and humanitarians' behaviour may be necessary when principled aid becomes impossible.

Chapter 2

EXPECTATIONS AND DISILLUSIONS BEYOND SYRIA

The gap between expectations and disillusionment tends to be particularly wide in an age of increasing humanitarian and human rights legislation as well as its institutionalization: the most recent boost to such law-making occurred in the 1990s after the fall of the Berlin Wall. Academic literature from the past decade often asserts a decline of universal norms, although some international legal experts, activists and practitioners are attempting to stem the tide and uphold a progressive reading of international law in all its aspects. However, violations of human rights and humanitarian principles are widespread, in particular in today's new asymmetric wars. Moreover, they seem to be met with diminishing outrage, resistance and consequences by external actors, as the Syrian case exemplifies.

Abuse and diversion of humanitarian assistance has often been described as being as old as the Geneva Conventions; neither is this phenomenon restricted to one country or region. As Donini concludes, after having conducted an overview of abuse and flaws of humanitarian efforts worldwide, "although humanitarian thinking and practice have evolved significantly over the past 150 years, there never was a 'golden age' when core humanitarian values took precedence over political considerations", thus "challenges to the values of humanity, impartiality, neutrality, and independence, are not new."[1] Writing under the impression of the Bosnian War, Rieff states that despite the post-World War II documents such as the Universal Declaration of Human Rights, the Genocide Convention and the four Geneva Conventions that have transformed international law and the normative bases of international relations, "the murderous twentieth century remained just as murderous."[2] An equally sober summary is offered by Smillie: "Humanitarianism is under threat, under siege, in peril. Humanitarianism as we knew it is dying". In other words, the old humanitarian values and norms are "ripe targets for manipulation."[3]

Taking a historical perspective on humanitarian interventions, Simms and Trim contradict this pessimistic view. They look into the enforcement of humanitarian principles and hold that "in an interdependent global community, the concept of intervention on humanitarian grounds is not moribund; rather, it remains the subject of vigorous debate among military, policy and development practitioners, academics, and peace and human rights activists, with the media and the public keen followers."[4] The authors point to the fact that humanitarianism – and reasons for intervention on humanitarian grounds – have undergone several changes since the sixteenth century, but that the moral impetus and political idea behind them still exist, despite numerous challenges.

Above all, Simms and Trim contend that the idea of humanitarian intervention is not, in any case, a new one. What has developed over time are rather terminologies on the one hand and concepts on the other. Only if one uses the term 'humanitarian' with an exclusive reference to human rights and international human right law, is one referring to humanitarian intervention as something carried out since the mid- to late nineteenth century, when the concept of 'human rights' emerged. "Yet this cuts it off from the concepts and praxis that gave rise to it – acceptable for a political scientist, perhaps, but not for an historian." In the past, interventions arose from concerns that today would be termed 'humanitarian', or relate to what now would be called 'human rights' or 'crimes against humanity', but which went by other names at that time.[5]

The concepts of who or what should be protected have also evolved. "Ethical concern for the sufferings of people of other nationalities or ethnicities started as a primarily confessional solidarity, and then expanded to encompass ever broader groups. [. . .] The effect of the Enlightenment probably was to secularise solidarity and see the emergence of a 'humanitarian sensibility'", according to Simms and Trim. Those first thought in need of protection were mostly confessional co-religionists, but later that group would be extended to all fellow Christians, and then all human beings – strangers, in fact. Also the concept of what was illegitimate shifted over time: "starting with 'tyranny' and religious persecution, it then encompassed slavery (once a staple of civilised commerce) and 'uncivilised' governance, and then focused on war crimes, before expanding to crimes 'against humanity'. The concept of what the international system ought to support and maintain evolved too: from Christendom; to liberty, liberalism and civilisation; to universal human rights."[6]

Taking the more pessimistic view that describes the current state of affairs as a decline of values and their enforcement, not to mention humanitarian interventions, Hopgood argues that dying humanitarianism goes hand in hand with dying global humanism. In his view, the world is witnessing the end times of a universal and human rights regime:

> Whether it is the increase in deadly attacks on aid workers, the torture and 'disappearing' of al-Qaeda suspects by American officials, the flouting of international law by states such as Sri Lanka and Sudan, or the shambles of the Khmer Rouge tribunal in Phnom Penh, the prospect of one world under secular human rights law is receding. What seemed like a dawn is in fact a sunset. The foundations of universal liberal norms and global governance are crumbling, creating a vacancy where sovereignty and religion now make dramatic inroads in the post–Cold War world.[7]

Multipolarity, he writes, will mean "gridlock over norms at the global level, with sovereigns and religious authorities increasingly able to block progress in civil liberties and gender and sexual orientation."[8] This is the development of increasing bilateralism as described in this book with regard to a variety of cross-cutting bilateral deals on Syria, the shattered Middle East region and beyond. A genuine humanitarian stance with multilateral foundations has become rare – and weak if it does exist. Even a comprehensive and multilateral approach on conflict resolution has become somewhat of a by-product to 'the real game' that is going on between two or a few stakeholders with a national agenda. One real-life example has been the Geneva process on Syria run by the UN that was almost marginalized by the Astana format of the three key foreign players on Syrian turf: Russia, Turkey and Iran. The outcomes of their deals had little to do with advancing or even respecting human rights, but rather with safeguarding their national interests in Syria and distributing the cake. "Law for a flat system – reciprocity law – will increasingly replace that for a hierarchy: Global Human Rights," writes Hopgood. "The implications for the United Nations are profound: more of the Security Council, more Permanent Five, less Human Rights in New York, and less of a role for UN operational agencies spreading global secular norms." The picture becomes even worse when the Security Council is in a state of auto-paralysis, as it is with regard to Syria. "The ICC [International Criminal Court] and R2P [Responsibility to Protect] are the last stand of a European imperial vision of one world united around impartial, neutral, and apolitical norms," is Hopgood's apocalyptic projection. "The view from nowhere, always an aspiration, is soon to be a relic of a bygone era we can visit only in museums."[9]

Critical debates in the humanitarian sector have intensified in recent years and have even at times called into question the very viability of the humanitarian project, as Andrew Cunningham writes in his study about the delicate international NGO–state relationships:

> The sanctity of the humanitarian principles – humanity, independence, neutrality and impartiality – has been questioned; the relationship with governmental and intergovernmental donors is often politically and ethically problematic; the Western identity of the majority of the large international agencies is commonly seen as a liability; and the contexts within which humanitarian actors work are perceived to be increasingly more dangerous than in years past.

Moreover, multi-mandate organizations – those that implement both humanitarian and development aid projects – "are seen by some to be muddying the pure waters of humanitarianism." And finally, the issue of politicization of humanitarian assistance has become a major subject or even 'aid criminalization' as Cunningham calls it.[10] Often, host countries reassert their own sovereignty and push back against international NGOs, as we will see in the Syrian case study. In humanitarian literature, this is also known as the 'strong states' thematic.[11] In particular, authoritarian states tend to view international NGOs and the UN itself as a threat, especially when they come along with a discourse of 'universal values', militarized humanitarian interventions and notions like the Responsibility to Protect.

Another angle of criticism in the humanitarian literature is the dependency of the human rights system on resources and (mostly liberal) power. Work on human rights has been structured more or less in large organizations with their intrinsic organizational behaviour that may deviate from what the fight for human rights was really once about. As a consequence, the 'moral authority' of the human rights concept is being challenged. Hopgood writes: "The classic humanist space of impartiality – of a space that was not politics, money or power – has foundations that will crumble regardless of how deep they pour the concrete for humanity's new palace in the sand dunes of The Hague."[12] Donini and his research team similarly conclude that the humanitarian establishment, with its media discourse and extensive resources, has become a powerful player that can shape realities on the ground: "[...] humanitarian action has crossed the threshold of power. It has transitioned through growth and institutionalization from a powerful discourse to a discourse of power, from mobilizing myth to overpowering enterprise." Since humanitarianism is – ideally – a 'relationship without reciprocity', instrumentalization is inherent in this relationship: "[...] there is a disconnect (and a growing one in the context of globalization) between the lofty universalist and principled goals of humanitarianism and the messy reality on the ground."[13]

Assertive views from an academic or scholarly perspective meet political reality where humanitarian staff have to work in a grey zone. In difficult situations on the ground, humanitarians may not meet their own standards and the high bar of humanitarian principles of humanity, impartiality, neutrality and independence.[14] Probably, this is a natural part of their job description. The humanitarians' task consists of challenging – and constant – negotiations. The imperative to define 'red lines' of their engagement, needs, at the same time, to be coupled with their readiness to work in those painful grey zones of a reality that is not ideal, or on the 'fringes of the humanitarian space',[15] if they want to work and deliver at all. As the humanitarian diplomat Jan Egeland put it: "If you are there to help the victims from the depths of hell, you have to speak to the devil."[16] The normative reasoning behind such constraints and compromises in humanitarian negotiations have been discussed since the 1970s, triggered by painful experiences in various cases of conflict.

As we will see, Syria may be the largest and most sustained example of systematic violation and manipulation of humanitarian norms of them all. The extreme tension between pragmatic and principled aid delivery caused controversies in political, humanitarian and legal circles about radical steps needed to correct the course. But if and when humanitarians draw red lines and stop engaging, this comes at the cost of not helping people in desperate need, at least in the short term. In the long run, establishing clear boundaries to a humanitarian mission may prevent it from being manipulated to the point of complicity. Red lines can also increase negotiation power. But in this regard any theory will not match the complex reality on the ground; furthermore, each case is different, from country to country and from village to village.

Humanitarian negotiations exemplify what has been discussed as moral dilemmas, tragic choices, 'dirty hands' problems, emergency ethics and non-ideal theory.[17] Recent investigations into the rise of humanitarian action as a mode of global governance since the end of the Cold War and during the global 'War on Terror' have shed light on the contemporary political character of humanitarian negotiations.[18]

Obviously, the gap between theory and practice concerning the consequent implementation of humanitarian principles and protection of human rights – independent of political interests, organizational behaviour and individual biases – is not unique to Syria, though it is a particularly blatant example. Achieving a somewhat acceptable balance between humanitarian values and political agendas has been an ongoing challenge in humanitarian assistance since its beginnings.[19] Still, the political developments and humanitarian behaviour in the Syrian case have also had a significant legal aspect. Syria – and the timing of the conflict in the setting of the overall international climate – has had and will continue to have a strong influence on the development of concepts and content of certain aspects of international law. One aspect is an accelerating trend with regard to state sovereignty that accelerated in the first ten years of the twenty-first century, as Leenders and Mansour observe:

> Perhaps the Syrian crisis can be viewed as part of a trend in which state sovereignty is reclaiming its significance in war-induced humanitarian crises. Indeed, the Syrian regime's bureaucratic obstruction and manipulation of humanitarian aid echoes similarly assertive government action elsewhere, including in Darfur at the end of the first decade of the twenty-first century and in Sri Lanka at the final stages of its civil war, in 2008–2009. In both cases, regimes also embraced loud narratives on state sovereignty to control and curb humanitarian agencies. Yet in Darfur and Sri Lanka, the state pushed its control over humanitarian agencies to the extent that the latter were expelled or felt compelled to leave.[20]

Looking beyond Syria, the tug of war between political agendas and humanitarian and human rights imperatives is mindboggling and seemingly endless. The first dilemmatic situation of modern humanitarian history is generally traced back to the war in Nigeria and the declaration of the independent Republic of Biafra by rebels in 1967. Just one year later, the Biafra rebels were militarily squeezed into a land-locked province without any prospect of survival. The war could have been over, and regular supplies for the civilian population that was suffering mass starvation could have started. Many analysts hold that it was the massive influx of humanitarian assistance into Biafra, mostly by air, that helped the Biafran Army survive another two years, until 1970. Thus, the argument goes, humanitarian assistance prolonged the suffering of civilians in a simmering war between the Nigerian government and the secessionists. Even worse, mostly Christian relief organizations were charged with arms smuggling to the Christian rebels who fought against the mostly Muslim Nigerian government. Since then, relief has become a contentious issue and an interesting example of how humanitarian organizations took the issue into their own hands since no global thinking in the vein of Responsibility to Protect existed at that time. In addition, Biafra brought to prominence a young doctor who was working for the Red Cross at that time. He refused to keep silent, impartial and neutral, and thus violated the rules of the ICRC by propagating the narrative of a Muslim genocide against Christians in French media and politics. The doctor was Bernhard Kouchner, later Foreign Minister of France, who left the Red Cross at this point and founded the organization Médecins Sans Frontières (MSF, or Doctors without Borders).[21]

After Biafra, several instances occurred, particularly in Africa, that followed a similar pattern of relief organizations supporting rebels, willingly or unwillingly, directly or indirectly. Or of rebels starving their own people in order to attract humanitarian assistance and international support. Ethiopia, Somalia, Southern Sudan, Liberia, Sierra Leone, Rwanda and the Democratic Republic of Congo are mentioned in the humanitarian literature in this context.[22] This accumulation of incidents made authors like Alex de Waal, now executive director of the World Peace Foundation, state in 1997 that "most humanitarian aid in Africa is useless or damaging and should be abandoned."[23] Others thought that relief operations should be stopped when they are attacked or put under pressure by rebels. What happened in Biafra is something that the Syrian government may regard as a convenient narrative of humanitarians helping rebels to succeed. The difference, however, is that the Syrian government started to kill unarmed civilians in massive numbers who had no intentions to take up arms initially, who were even hesitant to call for Assad's resignation in the first months of the protests, and who had no wish to secede from Syria (unlike the Biafran situation). During these developments, the government in Damascus was the actor mainly responsible for the high civilian death toll. Humanitarian organizations operating cross-border in Syria were not supporting any secession or secessionist army but rather seeking to help mostly civilians, which had been targeted by their own regime, that denied cross-line humanitarian assistance.

A decade or so after Biafra, another milestone in modern humanitarian history was reached in Sudan. At the end of the 1980s and during the early 1990s, a host country's sovereignty was restricted externally for the first time in favour of humanitarian access: the UN broke new ground in operating across front lines. This represented a break with the old Westphalian notion of absolute state sovereignty that will be discussed later in this book. Operation Lifeline Sudan (OLS) started in 1989 with the aim of tackling the famine that was compounding war-related suffering. The operation, led by UNICEF, created a humanitarian space in southern Sudan, where the government in Khartoum had lost control to rebels. This established a precedent for many subsequent humanitarian interventions, like those in Angola, Iraq, Somalia, Rwanda and Bosnia in the 1990s. In the case of Sudan, humanitarian access was largely dependent on the application of international pressure on both warring parties. Nevertheless, the sovereignty of the government in Khartoum was not ultimately challenged. As an independent 1996 review of OLS explains, it was a "temporary ceding of sovereignty to the UN of parts of South Sudan that are outside government control."[24] Thus the situation was regarded as an informal or negotiated safe area programme. An operational division of Sudan into government- (north) and non-government-controlled areas (south) was created. In the first legitimate cross-border operation for the delivery of humanitarian assistance, non-government held areas were serviced from Nairobi. A problem developed, however, in that humanitarian assistance was not distributed equally in both areas: the south profited from the UN's humanitarian presence, while civilians in the north suffered under the aegis of a government that actively hindered aid work. "In effect, the equivocal autonomy of the Southern Sector has been purchased at the expense of war-affected populations in the North," the 1996 review concludes. "In this regard, UN humanitarian policy has failed." The north–south arrangement also created a quandary around coherence within the UN organization. A UNDP-appointed Resident Representative in Khartoum was formally also in charge of OLS. This created a fundamental conflict of interests. "One cannot work with the government as a development partner and, at the same time, relate to it as a warring party for humanitarian purposes," the review concluded.[25] Particularly problematic was the fact that the development process in Sudan was linked to the military goals of the government in Khartoum.

Sudan has remained a difficult terrain for humanitarian work ever since. The Darfur conflict that started in 2003 in Sudan's south-west province, is another example. The humanitarian relief effort launched at that time was the largest in the world, and had more than 16,000 staff. The security situation worsened considerably for the humanitarian workers on the ground after the Darfur Peace Agreement of May 2006: its approval – and the process leading up to it – had been controversial. Some rebel groups did not sign the Agreement and consequently became suspicious of the international humanitarian staff, assuming that they were biased against them. To a certain degree, rebels behaved like bandits, attacking humanitarian missions and stealing supplies. After the Agreement, rebel groups splintered into many smaller factions, which made the security situation even worse. However, it was the government side that dealt the humanitarians the worst blow. In 2009, the government expelled thirteen international humanitarian organizations and revoked the licences of three local ones, leaving 1.5 million people without assistance. Khartoum historically used humanitarian assistance as a bargaining chip to advance other ethno-political goals, and held the view that norms related to humanitarian access and civilian protection were obstacles to those goals. International assistance ran counter to national ideology and the government's self-definition. The drastic measure taken in 2009 had another specific political reason, though: it coincided with the day the International Criminal Court (ICC) issued its arrest warrant for Sudan's then president, Omar al-Bashir. The government alleged that the humanitarian organizations were collecting evidence against the government that the ICC would use against President Bashir. Expelling international aid workers was clearly an act of revenge. At the same time, it dangerously blurred lines between political and humanitarian issues. Nevertheless, the government was able to use the following months to its advantage, using high-level exposure at the UN and diplomatic efforts to engage with key states. As a result, a new US strategy emphasized diplomacy and increased humanitarian access instead of confrontation. Sudan had successfully utilized its leverage of denying humanitarian access to advance its policy goals. However, humanitarian access did not improve long term.[26]

In Sri Lanka, the problem of constrained humanitarian access bore some similarities to the Syrian situation, and existed throughout the thirty-year war between the Sinhalese government and the Liberation Tigers of Tamil Eelam (LTTE). In the final phase of the war in 2008–09, access denial was strongly linked to the government's national goal of defeating terrorism. The government prohibited nearly all UN humanitarian actors from delivering assistance to areas of heavy fighting, and restricted the status and movement of local aid workers. Only the ICRC and Caritas Internationalis, a confederation of Catholic relief agencies, were allowed to continue their operations. In the final months of the conflict, the government indiscriminately shelled densely populated civilian areas. It also confiscated goods from aid convoys. In the period after the conflict, the government continued barring humanitarian assistance to many internally displaced persons (IDPs). It also restricted human rights under the continued narrative of fighting terrorism and of consolidating domestic security. The international community did not challenge these IHL and IHRL violations.[27] This has been criticized as choosing the 'lesser evil' that could have been intended as mitigation but actually ended up as complicity.[28]

Charles Petrie, who authored the UN Secretary-General's internal review on the mission in Sri Lanka, told this author that the UN had become a "politically averse body" and "government-sovereignty-focused." He said the UN self-censored their reports to the UN Security Council believing that "the truth would be uncomfortable for them."[29] According to his report, the UN lacked monitoring capabilities after its withdrawal from the Tamil areas and left the population unprotected. It also failed to verify killings and other human rights violations by the Sri Lankan government and therefore left them out in their reports. By contrast, the UN *did* cite violations by Tamil LTTE rebels that could be more easily verified. If the UN did report government killings, then only unassertively to lower-ranking officials at the Sri Lankan Ministry of Foreign Affairs. Government denials of killings were not rebutted. The report also points to a lack of vision from, and coordination between, the UN entities involved. Moreover, the leadership of the UN Country Team in Colombo had insufficient political expertise and experience in armed conflicts, not to mention in human rights and humanitarian law issues, to deal effectively with the extraordinary challenge that Sri Lanka presented. The UN Regional Coordinator was overtaxed, understaffed and not adequately supported by UN headquarters in New York. Among other things, the UN system displayed a lack of "an adequate and shared sense of responsibility for human rights violations" and "an incoherent internal UN crisis-management structure which failed to conceive and execute a coherent strategy in response to early warnings and subsequent international human rights and humanitarian law violations against civilians." All in all, the report speaks of a 'systematic failure' by the UN in Sri Lanka.[30] Many of the report's findings sound very familiar when looking at the Syrian case a decade later.

Asked to write an internal report by the incoming Secretary-General António Guterres in 2017, Petrie – who left the UN in frustration in 2010 after a thirty-year stint – also criticized the UN's ongoing mission in Myanmar. He concluded that the "United Nations in-country presence in Myanmar continues to be glaringly dysfunctional. Strong tensions exist within the UN Country Team, the humanitarian parts of the UN system finds itself having to confront the hostility of the development arm, while the human rights pillar is seen as complicating both. Compounding the dysfunctionality is the lack of accountability at the highest levels of the UN system to ensure the overall coherence of the UN response." Apart from personnel failures, he indicated functional and structural problems. As had been the case in Sri Lanka, the UN was unable to come up with a coherent strategy in Myanmar. There was a lack of "comprehensive ownership or responsibility for their impact." Also, the lines of responsibility between the UN presence in Myanmar and different UN headquarters were unclear. An overall consequence "is a growing irrelevance of the UN in guiding and defining the international community's efforts to address the challenges confronting Myanmar." In Petrie's opinion, the position of a UN Country Representative in Myanmar was strongly political and he suggested that it should therefore be upgraded to a be the first level representation of the Secretary-General instead.[31] The post of a new UN Special Representative of the Secretary-General with direct lines of communication to him (rather than through UNDP) was indeed established in 2018. The Myanmar host government continued to obstruct and manipulate much of the UN's work on the ground, however, rejected visas for UN staff, and trust levels between the two parties remained low. Most of these problems are echoed in more detail in the Rosenthal Report of 2019, including the immense challenge that the UN faced in addressing the massacre and expulsion of large parts of the Muslim Rohingya minority in 2017. "The United Nations is armed with its moral authority, its values and principles, and its ample range of capabilities," the report states, "but it has limited political space in countries whose Governments forcefully invoke sovereignty and non-intervention in their internal affairs as a cover for not meeting their commitments to abide by international humanitarian and human rights laws and norms."[32]

In the Balkans, during the Bosnian war (1991–95), UNHCR developed into the biggest aid organization on the ground, and a plethora of international NGOs were treading on each other's toes: by 1995, there were 250 of them. Aid convoys were frequently stopped and humanitarian supplies stolen, mostly by Serb military and paramilitaries. One major problem in Bosnia was a lack of clarity around the UN's political mission and its humanitarian agenda. The UNPROFOR mandate given by the UN Security Council in 1992 included "creating conditions for the effective delivery of humanitarian aid." However, Rieff writes, "the peacekeepers were forbidden from using force to push the aid through. Thirty thousand UN troops were deployed by the time the mission ended, and yet they were not authorized to use their weapons in defence of anyone except themselves or any principle except that of the need to continue the mission." As a consequence, aid was distributed unequally. While some enclaves hardly received anything (such as Srebrenica, Goražde and Žepa), UNHCR managed to assist many of the needy in other areas, despite the obstacles.[33]

In February 1993, the UN High Commissioner for Refugees, Sadako Ogata, took a remarkable but lonely decision. To the surprise of many inside and outside the UN, she decided to suspend UNHCR operations in Bosnia and Herzegovina in protest at the blocking of humanitarian access to besieged Muslim enclaves by Serb separatists and other obstructions posed by Croatian forces. In addition, the Bosniak side in besieged Sarajevo had begun to reject, or would not even unload, aid convoys in solidarity with the other besieged Bosnian-Muslim enclaves. Ogata's decision to halt operations affected 1.6 million people, 380,000 of whom lived in Sarajevo, hungry, exposed to diseases and to the bitter Balkan winter. Since UNHCR was by far the largest relief organization, this sent a strong political message to the warring parties, too. This episode is interesting from two angles. First, within a few days it had brought about a political reaction from both Serb separatist leader Radovan Karadžić and the Croatian president Franjo Tuđman, who pledged support for free passage and access. In addition, the Bosnian presidency under Alija Izetbegović promised to stop the boycott of aid deliveries. Second, Ogata's decision caused consternation inside the UN system. It seemed that neither UN headquarters had been informed in advance, nor was the UNPROFOR peacekeeping force whose task was helping convoys get through the frontlines. Political pressure mounted from all sides, and a few days later UN Secretary-General Boutros Boutros-Ghali overturned Ogata's decision. But the goal was met: humanitarian access was secured again, if only temporarily.[34]

In Ethiopia, where droughts caused suffering in the 1970s and onwards, the state has considered its relationship with international humanitarian actors as highly paternalistic. As a result, the state, which had not internalized norms of access and protection, introduced bureaucratic hurdles for international and national humanitarian actors. At the same time, the UN agencies dealt solely with the government in Addis Ababa while a few NGOs ran clandestine operations across the border in the form of camouflaged relief convoys into rebel-held territories where the majority of the famine-afflicted population was living, something very similar to the early years of the Syrian crisis.. The Ethiopian government even bombed cross-border relief routes. Paradoxically, although Addis Ababa rejected or manipulated humanitarian assistance in principle, it became even more dependent on it as time went on, as its own bad governance rendered it unable to respond effectively to crises. This dependency on foreign assistance, in turn, spurred more resentment. After the 2003 famine – and in another parallel to Syria – the state tightened restrictions even more and interfered with aid organizations' internal procedures.[35]

In the cases of Somalia and Afghanistan, patterns emerged where aid agencies, including the UN, became part of donor countries' wider political and military agendas. Here, some humanitarian organizations' approaches dovetailed with the US agenda on how to create progress in Afghanistan. Among other things, this led to high-profile efforts that often prevailed over real humanitarian needs as in 2001–02.[36] Sometimes, though, major donors asserted themselves, as happened in Somalia in 2009, when the US shut down all food assistance on the grounds that significant quantities of food aid were being diverted from humanitarian purposes. Somalia is an example where the political agenda of a western government – in this case, the US – in its 'war against terrorism', halted aid deliveries in light of new anti-terrorism legislation. The decision exacerbated the suffering of the needy. The long-simmering conflict in Somalia returned to the international spotlight because of the anti-terrorism discourse after 9/11, not because of human suffering on the ground. A series of anti-terrorism resolutions in the UN and legislation in member states changed the legal context within which aid agencies operated. In the US context, aid agencies had to certify that their money would not end up with entities or individuals that could pose a danger to US national security. Strengthened anti-terrorism laws after 9/11 applied to the Somalian Islamist rebel group, Al-Shabab. On the grounds of preventing funds being diverted to this organization, the US and other Western states like the UK, Canada, Australia, Norway and Sweden restricted or suspended humanitarian assistance to Somalia in 2010.[37]

In Yemen, UN humanitarian actors have pulled out temporarily several times in protest at restricted access and obstacles posed by the Iranian-backed Houthi rebels who, at the same time, represented a quasi-government, although not internationally recognized, in the capital of Sana'a and in large parts of the country's territory. One of those examples occurred in February 2020, when UNHCR again reduced some of its activities on the ground. A UN official was quoted in the media as providing the following reasons: "We don't go to an area and just give assistance; we do an assessment to know who needs that aid, and we are blocked from doing that. We also have to monitor the work that we do, and this is blocked, too. And if we can't assess and if we can't monitor, then we can't manage the risks of operating in areas like northern Yemen."[38]

This experience, and that of Bosnia, sound quite different from the Syrian situation, where the UN and other humanitarian organizations attempted to stay on the ground at – it seems – almost at any cost. Certainly, in Yemen and Bosnia some civilians suffered additionally due to the UN's temporary withdrawals. But on the other hand, the UN defended its humanitarian principles of impartiality and neutrality. It upheld its aspiration to help the neediest without succumbing to the political interests of one party of the conflict. In the long run, the parties may recognize how a lack of international relief can turn into their disadvantage, and thus become more accommodating. Still, systematic lessons have not yet been learned. But sadly enough, those who have worked on the reviews of numerous humanitarian problems, have come to the conclusion that key players in the humanitarian community, even those with leadership and management responsibilities, have shown "limited commitment to learning and being accountable."[39]

As we will see in the following chapters, despite a long and sad history of manipulation from all sides in all places – by donors, governments, rebels and all kinds of interested parties in a war – the Syrian case is and will remain a particularly blatant example of well-planned and *systematic instrumentalization* of humanitarian efforts that, in addition, has been echoed and supported by strong international allies.

Chapter 3

CONTAINING THE HUMAN BEAST: FUNDAMENTALS OF INTERNATIONAL HUMANITARIAN LAW AND INTERNATIONAL HUMAN RIGHTS LAW

The purpose of this chapter is to cut through the jungle of international humanitarian law (IHL) and international human rights law (IHRL) while continuing to focus on our policy dilemma in Syria.

The most important IHL instruments date back to the First Geneva Convention, signed in 1864, and the 1868 Saint Petersburg Declaration. The first codifications of IHL were made in the Hague Conventions as early as 1899 and 1907. They all referred to conventional international war until non-international armed conflict was addressed first in Article 3 common to the four 1949 Geneva Conventions. IHL consists of treaties like the Geneva Conventions (GC) and their Additional Protocols (AP) and customary law. The latter is especially relevant as Syria is a party to the Geneva Conventions but not to the Additional Protocols; nor is Turkey, an important neighbouring state. Legal opinion exists that customary humanitarian law may provide a better protection to the victims of non-international armed conflicts than Common Article 3 or even AP II.[1]

IHRL was developed much later than IHL, mainly in reaction to the barbarous acts committed by the Nazis during World War II culminating in the Holocaust. These atrocities convinced ever more political leaders that genocide – and similar crimes against a state's own population – were a matter of legitimate international concern.[2]

Among the few human rights that are absolute and non-derogable are those regarding slavery and torture. As the Caesar Files and other evidence have made clear, torture has been used systematically by the Syrian regime against its own citizens as a tactic of war despite the fact that Syria ratified the UN Convention against Torture in 2004. Such serious violations of human rights constitute, by definition, crimes against humanity "when committed as part of a widespread or systematic attack directed against any civilian population, with knowledge of the attack."[3] The absolute prohibition of torture plays a central role in both IHL and IHRL frameworks[4] and applies to states and non-state actors alike.[5] More recently, an attempt was made to add the 'powerlessness of the victim' as an additional element in the definition of torture, which would also apply to the wounded in Syrian state hospitals where they feared mistreatment by the secret services.[6]

Given the flagrant violations of the most basic humanitarian and human rights laws in the Syrian conflict, the Convention (IV) relative to the Protection of Civilian Persons in Time of War reads as a bitter reminder of how governments *should* act:

(1) […] To this end the following acts are and shall remain prohibited at any time and in any place whatsoever with respect to the above-mentioned persons:

    (a) violence to life and person, in particular murder of all kinds, mutilation, cruel treatment and torture;

    (b) taking of hostages;

    (c) outrages upon personal dignity, in particular humiliating and degrading treatment;

    (d) the passing of sentences and the carrying out of executions without previous judgment pronounced by a regularly constituted court, affording all the judicial guarantees which are recognized as indispensable by civilized peoples.

(2) The wounded and sick shall be collected and cared for."[7]

According to Article 12 common to the first two Conventions that relates to wounded, sick and shipwrecked combatants, "any attempts upon their lives, or violence to their persons, shall be strictly prohibited; in particular, they shall not be murdered or exterminated, subject to torture or to biological experiments; they shall not wilfully be left without medical assistance and care, […]."[8]

Moreover, the International Court of Justice describes clearly the connection between IHL and IHRL: "[…] the protection offered by human rights conventions does not cease in case of armed conflict."[9] The interrelationship of both legal systems is regarded as well established today.[10] The pretext of being in a war does not diminish state actors' responsibilities vis-à-vis the fundamental principles of human life. In 2012, at the beginning of the military escalation in Syria, the ICRC stated in its operational update:

The ICRC concludes that there is currently a non-international (internal) armed conflict in Syria opposing Government Forces and a number of armed groups operating in several parts of the country … Thus, hostilities between these parties wherever they may occur in Syria are subject to the rules of international humanitarian law. These rules impose limits on how fighting can be conducted, with the aim of protecting the civilian population and persons not, or no longer, directly participating in hostilities.[11]

It is important to note that rebel groups or other non-state actors cannot be held accountable for torture and ill-treatment under IHRL, nor can states be held accountable for the acts of insurgents.[12] Indeed, IHL offers irregular combatants few incentives to adhere to the rules and respect the laws of war. When they hide among civilians or even launch attacks from civilian areas, they violate IHL but they also play out a comparative advantage since they place their state opponents in a catch-22: should the national army attack and cause extensive civilian casualties, or should it abstain from action altogether?[13]

The Government's Particular Responsibility

The reason why this book focuses on the state as an actor that interacts with international humanitarian organizations during a protracted war is because, according to IHL and IHRL, a state and its government have a *particular responsibility* and *obligation to protect* their citizens both in international and in non-international armed conflicts.[14] This is true, however, only as much as the state government exerts control over its territory and thus fulfils the classical definition of a state as a subject of international law according to the Montevideo Convention of 1934: it must have a permanent population, a defined territory, a government, and the capacity to enter into relations with other states.[15] While the last point is only necessary to define a state as a legal entity in international law, the first three are considered core pillars of a state's definition until today, based on Georg Jellinek's (1851–1911) *Allgemeine Staatslehre* from 1900.[16] Government as *Staatsgewalt* does not define how the state's powers are organized (authoritarian state, democratic state etc.) nor which purpose the state's organization follows (e.g. welfare versus predatory state), although some later state philosophers have added more aspects to the three core elements, such as a state constitution.

The Syrian Arab Republic and its government have, by and large, upheld these criteria throughout the crisis despite a large part of its population being displaced inside and outside its borders and parts of the state's territory being seized temporarily by others. In particular, the last condition – i.e. interaction with other states on eye-level – has been a crucial way for the government in Damascus to assert itself internationally and in the UN peace process, precisely when its loss of control over territory, population and even parts of its borders during the most difficult periods of the conflict threatened the very existence of the state. Also, despite the diplomatic isolation of the Syrian government by many Western states, there were friendly or neutral states, even inside the European Union, such as the Czech Republic, that maintained diplomatic relations with Damascus.

The fact that the Syrian government fought for its survival and felt under siege at particular moments of the crisis does not diminish its legal obligations, however. Riedel concedes that the scope to which human rights, including economic, social and cultural rights, can be upheld by a state in a protracted conflict may be objectively limited. This, of course, also applies to Syria. "But such inability has to be distinguished from unwillingness to comply; the burden of proof rests squarely on the state party under review [...]."[17] Like other governments in this situation, Damascus was reluctant to recognize the level of hostilities as a non-international armed conflict, particularly given that acknowledging the insurgents as a party to a conflict would result in the non-state group being accorded legal status and legitimacy.[18] Instead, Damascus declared that their enemies were simply 'terrorists' or foreign fighters. One striking example is a leaked audio recording (published in

December 2019) of a commander of the Syrian Arab Army during the assault on the north-western province of Idlib, which was packed with refugees:

> Oh Fighters of the Syrian Army. There are no civilians left. There are no elders left. There are no children left. There are no women left. In front of you are only foreign fighters. And you need to kill those all. No mercy, no compassion. March ahead, have no mercy. Quick, go, go! Continuous shelling. Continuous airstrikes. We need to recapture the area, no matter what. Enter, enter, quick, go, go burn, burn. Don't leave any tree, stone or human. Quick boys, go![19]

This – and numerous other patterns of rhetoric and action – make clear that the Syrian government was unwilling to recognize that the most important rules and principles applicable in situations of international armed conflict are today understood as having attained customary status with respect to non-international armed conflict as well: 'The parties to the conflict must at all times distinguish between civilians and combatants. Attacks may only be directed against combatants. Attacks must not be directed against civilians.'[20] Moreover, the Geneva Conventions are applicable in IHL and IHRL "during all 'armed conflicts' *irrespective of whether the states involved formally recognize a state of war*."[21] But armed opposition can no longer evade its responsibilities either: contemporary human rights law increasingly recognizes that where non-state actors exercise de facto control over territory, they are also bound by international human rights obligations.[22]

Accordingly, and rightly so, non-state actors in the Syrian conflict have been subject to regular scrutiny and criticism. This came to the fore after the once-peaceful street protests escalated into a complex, violent conflict. For example, in one of its 2020 reports, entitled 'No clean hands', the UN Commission of Inquiry (CoI) documented continuing "violations and abuses by nearly every conflict actor controlling territory in Syria," including government forces, the Syrian National Army (SNA), the Syrian Democratic Forces (SDF), Hayat Tahrir al-Sham (HTS) and other parties. The report also highlighted an increase in patterns of targeted abuses such as assassinations, sexual and gender-based violence against women and girls, and looting or appropriation of private property, with sectarian undertones. The report stressed that civilian suffering was a constant and personal feature of this crisis.[23]

Nevertheless, since the Syrian state government with its claims to absolute sovereignty and other legal and resource related advantages enjoys important privileges – not to mention the advantage of access to existing military equipment and infrastructure – it is also bound to *particular* obligations vis-à-vis its population. Therefore, most humanitarian principles that serve as a foundation of today's practice, refer in a particular manner to the responsibility of the state.

State-centred International Practice

Even though actors may blatantly violate international law, and IHL or IHRL in particular, they often take a positivist position within the context of international law in order to justify other aspects of the international legal corpus that may be suitable for their purposes. The Syrian government has a strong point when referring to UN Resolution 46/182 (1991), on which the United Nations Office for the Coordination of Humanitarian Affairs (OCHA) was founded. It serves as a blueprint for today's international humanitarian system and at the same time is regarded as the incarnation of the state-oriented approach of humanitarian assistance. The relevant guiding principles codified in this Resolution read as follows:

[...] 2. Humanitarian assistance must be provided in accordance with the principles of humanity, neutrality and impartiality.

3. *The sovereignty, territorial integrity and national unity of States must be fully respected* in accordance with the Charter of the United Nations. In this context, humanitarian assistance should be provided *with the consent of the affected country* and in principle on the basis of an *appeal by the affected country*.

[...] 6. *States* whose populations are in need of humanitarian assistance are called upon to *facilitate the work* of these organizations in implementing humanitarian assistance, in particular the supply of food, medicines, shelter and health care, for which access to victims is essential.

[...] 35 (c) Organizing, *in consultation with the Government* of the affected country, a joint inter-agency needs-assessment mission [...].

(d) Actively *facilitating*, including through negotiation if needed, the *access* by the operational organizations *to emergency areas* for the rapid provision of emergency assistance by obtaining the consent of all parties concerned [...].[24]

While Article 3 goes down well with governments, they find Article 2 more uncomfortable, especially when they see humanitarian assistance as potential additional leverage in a political and military struggle. Conversely, rebel groups might regard Article 2 as supporting the cause of the weaker actor with high humanitarian needs, while they might view Article 3 as a biased principle that makes humanitarian delivery difficult or impossible to the needy if cross-line or cross-border access is blocked by the government they are fighting against.

International practice derived from one source of international law – in this case a resolution of the UN Assembly – is not more and not less than a practice. It can be qualified by other legal sources and/or change through other practices that gradually become customary law.

Neutrality and Impartiality

In times of crisis, an important focus lies on the relationship between the state and international humanitarian actors, which gives the state an important leverage that it may use (or abuse) as in the Syrian case. UNHCR Humanitarian Principles, for example, serve as a high yardstick for humanitarian operations:

Because UNHCR's mandate is *non-political, humanitarian and social,* the organization is guided by *humanitarian principles* in its response to all humanitarian crises, whether caused by conflict, violence or natural disasters. [...]

[...] *States have the primary responsibility to protect and assist persons in their territories* who are affected by disasters, armed conflicts or violence. *Humanitarian action* is designed to complement and support States in fulfilling those responsibilities; it *should neither undermine nor supplement state responsibility.*"

[...] At the same time, humanitarian actors distinguish themselves from other actors responding to a crisis by their **impartiality.** This means that *humanitarian action is based solely on need,* with *priority given to the most urgent cases irrespective of race, nationality, gender, religious belief, political opinion or class.*

The **neutrality** of humanitarian action is further upheld when *humanitarian actors refrain from taking sides in hostilities or engaging in political, racial, religious or ideological controversies.* At the same time, independence requires *humanitarian actors to be autonomous. They are not to be subject to control or subordination by political, economic, military or other non-humanitarian objectives.*"[25]

Similarly, the Code of Conduct for the International Red Cross and Red Crescent Movement and Non-Governmental Organizations Disaster Relief, states:

[...] As members of the international community, we recognise our obligation to provide humanitarian assistance *wherever it is needed.* Hence the need for *unimpeded access* to affected populations is of fundamental importance in exercising that responsibility. The prime motivation of our response to disaster is to alleviate human suffering *amongst those least able to withstand the stress caused by disaster.* When we give humanitarian aid it is *not a partisan or political act* and should not be viewed as such.

[...] Aid is given regardless of the race, creed or nationality of the recipients and without adverse distinction of any kind. Aid priorities are calculated *on the basis of need alone.*

[...] Human suffering must be alleviated whenever it is found; life is as precious in one part of a country as another. Thus, *our provision of aid will reflect the degree of suffering it seeks to alleviate.*

[...] Aid will not be used to further a particular political or religious standpoint.

[...] We shall endeavour *not to act as instruments of government foreign policy.*

[...] We therefore formulate our own policies and implementation strategies and do not seek to implement the policy of any government, except in so far as it coincides with our own independent policy. *We will never knowingly – or through negligence – allow ourselves, or our employees, to be used to gather information of a political, military or economically sensitive nature for governments or other bodies that may serve purposes other than those which are strictly humanitarian,* nor will we act as instruments of foreign policy of donor governments.

[...] Relief supplies and equipment are brought into a country solely for the purpose of alleviating human suffering, *not for commercial benefit or gain*. Such supplies should normally be allowed *free and unrestricted passage* and should not be subject to requirements for consular certificates of origin or invoices, import and/or export licences or other restrictions, or to importation taxation, landing fees or port charges. [...][26]

Other organizations have adopted these fundamentals, including OCHA.[27] These are important texts because the terms 'humanitarian' and 'impartial' as such are not clearly defined in IHL. However, Pictet's commentary to the Geneva Conventions of 1958 defines humanitarian as "being concerned with the condition of man, considered solely as a human-being, regardless of his [her] value as a military, political, professional or other unit."[28] The above-mentioned humanitarian principles maintained by the Red Cross and the UN all express the clear notion that "assistance offered by third states or international organizations can only be considered 'humanitarian' when it is provided equally to all affected civilians of both parties to the conflict."[29]

The differentiation between impartiality and neutrality is important to bear in mind. Neutrality, for example, is not applicable to UN peace operations. In other words: "A neutral person refuses to make a judgment whereas the one who is impartial judges a situation in accordance with pre-established rules."[30] In IHL, 'impartial' is described by three interrelated elements: non-discrimination; proportionality; and the requirement that there be no subjective distinctions, such as making judgments about who is good or bad, guilty or innocent etc.[31] Impartiality's primary goal is to ensure that the "equality of the victims is recognized, that assistance is allocated in accordance with need, and the humanitarian agenda is not used for ends other than the prevention and alleviation of suffering."[32] Neutrality is defined by the Red Cross/Red Crescent Movement as a principle that humanitarian actors do "not take sides in hostilities or engage at any time in controversies of a political, racial, religious or ideological nature." Neutrality derives from the principle of impartiality.[33]

There are obvious conflicts, for example, between the principle of accountability of IHRL and neutrality of IHL. Humanitarian actors cannot and should not be concerned with who has done what wrong but who needs what most. In political mediation, mediators need to be impartial – i.e. they will treat both or more opposing parties on equal terms and fairly – so that they can build trust with all of them and get them to the table. At the same time, mediators are not necessarily neutral because they will be bound by and convinced of the basic values of their organization like, for example, the UN Charter.

In the humanitarian field, the functional advantage of the two principles of neutrality *and* impartiality is that their strict observation offers clear guidance to humanitarian personnel and creates a comfort zone of action by eclipsing many other – and in this sense distracting –factors beyond their scope and purpose of work.

In fact, there is no legal requirement in IHL that humanitarian organizations or states offering humanitarian assistance have to be neutral. The principle of neutrality is more an operational notion that derives from the essential concepts of humanity and impartiality. It is a means of creating trust between the parties. By contrast, IHL requires that assistance be 'humanitarian' and 'impartial' and, in turn, protects all impartial humanitarian assistance.[34]

Some view neutrality merely as a lofty principle that is never really reflected in actions on the ground. For example, from a military perspective in crisis operations, former Lieutenant-General Roméo Dallaire states that in many settings, "neutrality is but an 'aspiration', a 'myth', and an 'impossibility'." It has always been subjective and context specific. Dallaire describes it even as an 'extreme position' that can maintained by only a handful of actors, such as the ICRC – but even then, as this book shows, it is far from guaranteed. Dallaire writes: "[T]he sacrosanct principles of neutrality and humanitarian space have been used and abused by many ways that ultimately benefit killers rather than victims of armed conflict."[35] Charles Petrie, former UN Assistant Secretary-General, is critical of the fact that neutrality became an aspiration that was not reached. Humanitarian assistance was often distributed under political influence in the worst crises and the UN's integrity suffered. "After Rwanda, neutrality and impartiality drifted apart. Impartiality trumped neutrality."[36]

Countries' Controversial Consent

Under current interpretations, humanitarian law implies important conditions for states as cooperation partners of humanitarian assistance. States are seen as obliged to accept offers of, or seek, humanitarian assistance. This rule applies in international and non-international armed conflicts, it is formulated in treaty law (art. 70 AP I and art. 18 AP II) and also constitutes a rule of customary law. It means different specific obligations for different states (or other parties in non-international conflicts):

- states that are in a position to do so must provide or support and promote relief actions
- states through which relief efforts pass must allow and facilitate such transit;
- states physically controlling the destination area for relief efforts must accept that relief, i.e. allow that aid supplies to be distributed and related services rendered.[37]

At the same time, the law also addresses states' concern that humanitarian activities could be misused for political purposes. Therefore, states are obliged to accept offers when: a) the civilian population is suffering undue hardship that threatens its survival; and b) when the assistance offered (or requested) is "exclusively humanitarian and impartial in nature" and relief actions are "conducted without any averse distinction." The threshold of this provision is met when the refusal of relief would cause the civilian population to starve or otherwise threatens its survival. It is not entirely clear whether a state (or non-state actor) is obliged to accept international offers of humanitarian assistance before a refusal leads to the extreme cases of starvation or otherwise threatens its survival.

As a logical consequence to obstructionist state behaviour, the very requirement of a state to consent to humanitarian deliveries has been questioned among IHL scholars. However, the rather sobering conclusion is that humanitarian deliveries in practice rarely work if a state rejects them. The ICRC observed that 95 per cent of humanitarian needs could be met only with the consent of authorities if a forceful humanitarian intervention is not an option.[38] It may be doubted whether this figure still holds true with regard to the Syrian conflict, given the restraints on access imposed by the government, the gradual fragmentation of territory and the (temporarily) frequent practice of cross-border operations as a last resort.

Of particular importance regarding the nature of the Syrian conflict is the prohibition of starvation of civilians as a method of warfare (art. 14, AP II) and the prohibition of 'violence to life' against persons 'taking no active part in hostilities' or persons *hors de combat*.[39] Starvation as a method of warfare also blatantly violates the state's obligation to provide humanitarian assistance to the *entire population*. This means that the state which receives international humanitarian aid must allow cross-line deliveries to pass, which has been a major problem in Syria.

By contrast, according to international law and to obvious constraints, non-state armed groups are bound to provide aid only to people under their control, for example, by letting humanitarian organizations enter their territories.[40] But, strictly speaking, there is no legal requirement to ask non-state armed groups for consent to deliver humanitarian assistance in contrast to states qualified as the High Contracting Party (art. 18/2 AP II).[41]

There are further compelling arguments that oblige states to consent to cross-line humanitarian assistance. In today's understanding of IHL, citizens have the right to health and other social, economic and cultural rights. This strengthens the argument that states must approve – or at least not interfere with – international actors delivering impartial and humanitarian assistance to civilians who have come under rebel control. The state must also accept that, as part of this process, international organizations will enter into a dialogue with insurgent groups to negotiate access.[42]

Important other obligations for the state under IHL follow once consent is given and the international organizations are operating on the ground. A key point is the respect for and the protection of humanitarian relief personnel and objects.[43] Therefore, attacks on hospitals, ambulances and humanitarian convoys are a blatant violation of this obligation. One of the gravest cases during the Syrian war was the aerial bombardment of a Syrian Arab Red Crescent (SARC) warehouse and an aid convoy in Orem Al Kubra, some 15 km west of Aleppo in September 2016. Around twenty civilians and one SARC staff member were killed as they were unloading trucks carrying vital humanitarian aid. Much of the shipment was destroyed too. Only the Syrian regime and its Russian ally possessed airpower. Such an attack is classified a war crime in the Statute of the International Criminal Court. The ICRC lists various forms of prohibited actions against relief personnel and facilities: direct attacks, harassment, intimidation, arbitrary detention, mistreatment, physical and psychological violence, murder, beatings, abduction, hostage-taking, kidnapping etc. Facilities must not be destroyed, misappropriated or looted. Such prohibitions are strengthened since an individual's right to health exists in parallel.[44]

Another obligation of the state consenting to international humanitarian assistance is to "facilitate rapid and unimpeded passage of all relief consignments, equipment and personnel." Furthermore, the freedom of movement of authorized humanitarian relief personnel must be granted. This includes rapid visa processing and customs clearance.[45] In Syria, the government frequently denied or restricted the passage of humanitarian actors or withheld visas for their staff. Red tape routinely delayed authorizations. Another common practice was to strip authorized convoys of certain items that were considered to be of 'dual use' nature. Indeed, according to IHL, state authorities do have the right to control the delivery of humanitarian assistance, supervise their distribution and to instruct the use of certain routes. The state has a legitimate interest in making sure that only truly 'humanitarian' and 'impartial' assistance is delivered and that the goods do not fall into the enemy's (insurgents') hands.[46] However, even though vegetable seeds destined for besieged areas where people were starving were definitely not dual-use items, the regime's military or militias removed them from convoys since systematic starvation was part of the perfidious warfare tactics pursued by Damascus. Similarly, baby milk, surgical kits, insulin and dialysis equipment were confiscated from aid convoys.[47]

Brutal conflicts like that that in Syria make the schism between theory and practice painfully obvious. In legal theory at least, situations in which parties to a conflict can lawfully reject offers of humanitarian assistance are very limited. Clear restrictions exist on imposing undue harassment on humanitarian operations on the ground. In a situation in which a state has lost parts of its territory, often the only way in which it can fulfil its obligations under IHL is to let humanitarian organizations provide cross-line or cross-border assistance – if not both.[48]

Robertson traces his argument in favour of such humanitarian action against the consent of an affected state back several hundred years to John Locke's justification of executing a head of state who commits war crimes against his people, and to Hugo Grotius and Emer de Vattel who justified the role of external actors in overthrowing tyranny at the request of an oppressed people as a logical development of Locke's theory of government by consent. "If tyrants can be overthrown when they abuse their power and destroy the people they are obliged to protect," writes Robertson, "then it follows that other governments may lawfully render 'humanitarian' assistance to those battling for their lives."[49] This is a common theme in contemporary humanitarian literature, and is echoed by those with practical humanitarian experience. Donini concludes:

> If the state is predatory, if the systems are so broken or so corrupt that they present a real barrier to effective and efficient aid, then aid agencies have every reason to seek alternative ways to assist. Even in predatory states, however, responding to crisis and protecting citizens is a fundamental sovereign duty, and aid agencies as well as donors, if they are to be anything other than providers of band-aids, need to find ways of working with the state to help and if necessary denounce it into meeting its responsibilities.[50]

Chapter 4

A MOVING TARGET: THE DYNAMICS OF INTERNATIONAL HUMANITARIAN AND INTERNATIONAL HUMAN RIGHTS LAW

Law or War?

Debates on our policy dilemma oscillate within two camps that have often been at loggerheads with each other: those who argue politically and those who argue legally. Broadly speaking, the former camp argues that it has been politics (and even military activity) that have shaped international law and all its sub-fields, such as international humanitarian law, international human rights law, etc. Therefore, it is legitimate that politics adapts this international law whenever political conviction and determination is forceful enough to set a precedent. In a worse case, politicians may use international law selectively, since it is they who shape normative power through facts (in Georg Jellinek's words: *Normative Kraft des Faktischen*). A prominent example of this line of argumentation is that of former British prime minister, Tony Blair. Justifying the unilateral British intervention in Sierra Leone in 2000, grounded in humanitarian and liberal policies, to end violence and restore democratic power, he said: "Global interdependence requires global values commonly or evenly applied. But sometimes force is necessary to get the space for those values to be applied: in Sierra Leone or Kosovo for example."[1] A similar line was taken for the 2003 intervention in Iraq, but this one famously turned into a blunder both in terms of justification and implementation.

By contrast, the legalistic camp is concerned with the fragility of international law. They see the risk that its foundations may collapse as unexpectedly as the 2,000-year-old pillars of the main arch of Syria's archaeological site at Palmyra if the existing framework of international law loses its normative – and practical – binding force. This might happen if the threshold to question it, when politically opportune, is set too low. In our case study on humanitarian assistance in Syria, this camp favoured the existing practice of delivering humanitarian assistance through a state government in the absence of any decision to the contrary by the UN Security Council. Decision-makers in the legalistic camp have striven to painstakingly maintain the firewall between political judgement and humanitarian impartiality and neutrality. Some diplomats who witnessed these debates add that as a last consequence, a firewall emerged even between human rights on the one hand and (intended) humanitarian neutrality and impartiality on the other. The legalistic camp is concerned that tearing down this wall would make humanitarian principles vulnerable, and that the protection of humanitarian work on the ground would become very difficult as a result. Disturbing the status quo would shake the foundations of tried-and-tested international crisis management and the legal fundaments of *ius in bello*.

Although the legalistic reading of IHL and IHRL has generally prevailed as the official policy of most donor states, its proponents have come under pressure as a result of the ever more obvious discrepancies between legal theory and humanitarian practice. In the case of Syria, most humanitarian assistance went through Damascus, and, at the same time, unscrupulous and indiscriminate warfare gave the impression that the Syrian government and its allies Russia and Iran clearly prioritized military efficiency over established standards of IHL. Moreover, in their use of unscrupulous combat tactics, they used this opportunity to shape new international and legal realities.

Whereas the Syrian regime's main goal was its sheer survival against a backdrop of limited resources (and therefore resorted to barrel bombs), Russia, among other geopolitical reasons, had an additional normative motivation to its political and military engagement in Syria. It has been aiming at preventing any consolidation of the principle of humanitarian intervention against a sovereign state's domestic business. In addition, Russia – and for that matter China, which mostly sided with it in a paralysed UN Security Council – have a dismal record on human rights themselves and are well aware of the danger of possible upheavals within their own borders. A ripening acceptance of, and strengthened right to, humanitarian intervention has not been in their interest.

Ultimately, though, the key authoritarian states in this discussion may have been successful in re-shaping the development of international law in a regressive fashion, although it may take a few years to see the full extent of which crystallize. This would entail in particular a reinforcement of the hard notion of sovereignty and growing obstacles to humanitarian assistance, not to mention humanitarian intervention.

In Geoffrey Robertson's words: "[. . .] international law has this curious capacity to pull itself up by its own bootstraps, by extrapolating new or developed principles from the practice of states (or at least from the subsequent justifications offered by states for their practices [. . .]." In short: "Making war means making law."[2]

Those who politically opposed the practice of the Syrian regime and its allies tended to refer rather helplessly to existing international norms and practice. They condemned the pro-Assad alliance for violating IHL and IHRL but did not offer an engaged diplomatic, political or even military counterweight that – if applied with restraint – could have shored up the resilience of existing norms and practice necessary for a multilateral world. As the Dutch diplomat and academic Nikolaos van Dam has argued, the West should not lament the outcome of this conflict when it shied away from efforts to offer an alternative.[3]

Both the political and the legalistic camps find support in different aspects, readings and schools of international law. The question of international law's binding power and legitimacy, especially in times of a strongly dynamic and expanding corpus and ambitions of international law, is part of a lively academic debate among legal experts. Major political and military events have consistently accompanied and at times shaped international law and practice. Syria – and one could add Libya and Yemen – may be the crystallization point of another such paradigm shift.[4]

An Octopus with Dwindling Force

The content, functions, aims and ambitions of international law have changed over time.[5] Its origin, however, can be found in the modern European state system. While its purpose since the Thirty Years' War was the coordination of power between sovereign states, during the twentieth century it moved more towards cooperation. Increasingly, international law has started to influence domestic decision-making or developed coercive functions for governments to do things they would have otherwise avoided. Another trend has been that particular (or mainly bilateral) international law has developed universal regulations and pretensions. Also its substantial functions have expanded towards areas such as securing peace, conflict resolution, economic regulations, more detailed human rights or climate protection (while humanitarian principles were a rather early phenomenon in IL evolution).

Thomas Franck remarked in 1995 that international law had entered its 'post-ontological phase', in which "it now impacts on virtually every area of public policy." In addition, an increasing number of international institutions and courts have emerged that interpret international law, in particular in the fields of international human rights law, international trade law, international criminal law, and the international law of the sea.[6] International law has reached out like an octopus towards ever more areas of life, and not just as a regulatory force in the challenging power relationships between states. Matthias Kumm writes:

> Contemporary international law has expanded its scope, loosened its link to state consent and strengthened compulsory adjudication and enforcement mechanisms. This partial emancipation from state control means that domestic accountability mechanisms are becoming ineffective as a means to legitimate international law. Correspondingly, the legitimacy of international law is increasingly challenged in domestic settings in the name of democracy and constitutional self-government.[7]

He even speaks of modern international law having a de-nationalizing effect.[8] This discussion obviously refers to debates within democratic settings. But the fact that international law may be going through a legitimacy crisis, encourages non-democracies and anti-multilateralists a fortiori to apply double standards or to remove the shackles of IL constraints, especially when an authoritarian regime is fighting for survival. Once more, the Syrian upheaval was badly timed in terms of the international backdrop against which the struggle has been taking place.

Kumm's concern is also directed towards the increasingly questioned and crumbling binding force of customary law, i.e. a rule gradually set by patience and long-standing practices in international relations. He writes:

> Customary international law (CIL), too, is no longer thought to require a long general and consistent state practice followed by states from a sense of legal obligation. Instead, so-called 'modern' CIL significantly discounts the requirement of general and consistent state practice in favour of an approach that focuses primarily on statements. Particularly in the area of human rights, declarations made by representatives of states either in international fora such as the General Assembly or in the context of multilateral treaty-making are central to the inquiry whether a rule of CIL has developed or not. Here too the effect is to further disconnect the creation of an international legal obligation from a state's specific consent.[9]

This development provides more argumentative leverage to authoritarian rulers wishing to dismiss at least those aspects of international law that they find inconvenient to follow in times of existential crisis.

In recent times, counter-reactions against this very claim of universality and ubiquity have been articulated more vividly in a period that is strongly marked by the paradigm of bilateralism. The binding force of multilateral norms has weakened in this context. Violations of international law, especially IHL, have become more frequent once more in the major conflicts of our times, such as those in Syria or Yemen (active aspect of violation). At the same time, the violation of red lines of IHL – for example, the indiscriminate or deliberate targeting of humanitarian and civilian facilities, the use of torture or starvation as a means of warfare – have not been responded to adequately either politically or militarily, and nor have they elicited sufficient public outcry to trigger decisive international or multilateral action (reactive aspect). One reason for this is that many parts of the world have witnessed a democratic backsliding and the rise of right-wing populism, which goes hand in hand with bilateral views and approaches.

A German diplomat in Geneva told this author that in everyday diplomatic practice, it has become obvious that IHL is on the defensive. Violations are increasing but the public outcry is dwindling away. "It is frightening that the possibilities of humanitarian action are getting ever more limited. Even standard formulations from the acquis of IL and IHL are being challenged in the discussions about the drafting of UN and other documents." The diplomat says that this is also a dangerous development for humanitarian actors on the ground, the legal base for whose intervention has become insecure. In the worst case, they may even end up doing something illegal. "Without the cover of Russia and China, this development would not be possible," according to the diplomat.

Often, the Syrian government has taken the role of a spoiler who mobilizes others like Venezuela or North Korea with the aim of challenging standard formulations. The diplomat recalls the discussions on the UNHCR omnibus resolution, the annual report of the High Commissioner on global humanitarian developments. "Syria has become active in the past years in trying to soften up humanitarian and protection standards," he says. In 2019, the Syrian government rejected the formulation that '*consent*' of the host country is needed to deliver humanitarian assistance and lobbied to replace it with '*full consent*'. "This makes no sense, since consent is consent, but the direction is clear," the diplomat explains. "The goal is to further raise the bar for humanitarian operations and to strengthen the notion of state sovereignty."[10] From IHL literature, it emerges that humanitarian access cannot be withheld for arbitrary reasons. In the end, however, the change of formulation to '*full consent*' was approved in the discussion of the UNHCR omnibus resolution. A high-ranking OCHA representative spoke about this example in an interview with the author and said that words were only the first step: "The next step will be practical obstacles for humanitarian action." One possibility for how this new formulation can influence humanitarian work is that a government's '*pro-active consent*' may be required. The OCHA representative said that in his work, in operational terms, consent is considered to be given when no outright objection exists. This may change in the future.[11]

The German diplomat in Geneva added that he had observed international humanitarian organizations, such as the ICRC, adopting a more cautious and almost defensive stance. Their discourse has changed. "They reduce their rhetoric to core elements of IHL without confronting anyone and would rather speak about other topics such as cooperation with the World Bank, but not how you can get Russia and China to adhere to IHL." This observation chimes with Hopgood's, who states that "in reality the ICRC has survived precisely by not speaking out about human rights, a path MSF [Médecins Sans Frontieres] has also taken in relation to recent crises, and R2P (to which it is opposed)."[12]

However, a watering-down of formulations regarding IHL has not been confined to just one side of the aisle. At the 33rd International Conference of the Red Cross and Red Crescent at the end of 2019, it was the US and the UK that rejected hitherto consensual language. In the context of reiterating the states' obligation "to respect IHL," the addition "to respect *and to ensure respect for* IHL" was taken out at both countries' insistence. Diplomats said that the informal justification suggested by US and British colleagues was that the previous formulation might result in legal difficulties with regard to their arms exports to countries where IHL violations take place. "This is yet another example of how recognized standards of international law and international humanitarian law are being lowered," the German diplomat in Geneva confirmed.

As these examples show, multilateral principles and commitments are under pressure and substantially challenged. The rise of bilateralism has almost been personified in the leadership figures of today's major powers. The protagonists are leaders of Western democracies like the US under ex-President Donald Trump and the UK under Prime Minister Boris Johnson as well as countries with more traditionally authoritarian leaderships such as Russia under President Vladimir Putin or Turkey under President Racip Tayyep Erdoğan.

Drawing on his first-hand experiences, Panos Moumtzis, UN Assistant Secretary-General and Regional Humanitarian Coordinator for the Syria crisis, who was based in Amman between 2017 and 2019, told this author in frustration:

> We live in a world where we do not have an international system to ensure compliance with respect to protection of civilians who are caught up in the middle of a war. Thousands of women, men, and children were caught up in the middle of a war and witness their homes, schools, residential neighborhoods, clinics bombed and destroyed. The trauma of these children will live with them for the rest of their lives. The Security Council has not been able to enforce protection of civilians. I recall having worked in Bosnia, there was a dramatic change in international mobilization after the Sarajevo market bombing. In Syria, no amount of bombing managed to shift the international community to join hands and say in one voice: enough is enough. [. . .] The politicization of the Syria conflict meant that that everybody, including outside powers, looked after their own interests, and the Syrian people are the ones who paid the price, sometimes with their own lives![13]

Due to this post-modern legitimacy crisis of international law, it makes sense to take a closer look at the normative foundations of IL and at the claims of validity that have been debated throughout its intellectual history. Different theories have aspired to explain – or to lend validity to – IL in a changing social, political and philosophical environment. Natural law was an early foundation that was itself based on a divine order, or one regarded as shaped by human reason. In an increasingly pluralistic environment, natural law has lost much of its binding force in modern times. However, remnants of it are still present in the debates about the universality of values that enjoyed a new boost in the late twentieth century following the fall of the Berlin Wall, and which has maintained some traction till today. When the young French president Emmanuel Macron announced a shift in France's Syria policy in summer 2017, and moved away from aspirations towards regime change, he underlined his U-turn with a remarkably pragmatic concession. Macron said that Assad may be an enemy of the Syrian people, but not of France. France's enemy were the terrorists of the so-called Islamic State.[14] Given the brutality of the war that Assad's regime had been waging against his own people, the French president triggered a fiery debate in the country of the very Revolution that had declared human rights universal back in 1789.

The classical counterpart to proponents of the natural law school is the positivist school that grounds legal validity in a legal act alone. The reason why something should be regarded as valid could be answered in various forms. One is simply the will of states to do so.[15] Another one is derived from societal norms such as the binding nature of law itself (*pacta sunt servanda*).[16]

Meanwhile, the consensus theory has prevailed where the consensus of actors is regarded as representing the foundation of the legal system. This model has more explanatory value because despite a changing 'will' of states (i.e. their respective governments), international law has proven to be structurally resilient, and states have even been bound to abide by legal obligations against their will. Critics have argued, however, that economically or politically stronger states tend to dictate this consensus. Taken to the extreme, this line of argument would water down IL to a mere mechanism of maintaining real power structures, rendering it therefore to limited use.[17] Others criticize the fact that consent is neither a necessary condition for all international laws, nor is it a sufficient condition for the authoritative quality of international laws that require consent. Contrary to the consent view, which assumes that the authority of international law consolidates over time (i.e. more consensual international law = more authority), an opposite view holds that the increase in the number of international laws has, in effect, undermined the authority of international law. Those concerned about developments in non-democratic states have articulated this criticism most forcefully.[18]

The opposite of consensus is coercion. Since International Law has very weak coercive mechanisms, a necessary and indispensable link between coercion and law would contest that international law is a law at all.[19] This consensus theory has been overcome in today's scholarly discussions of IL. One counter-argument is that national law with stricter coercive mechanisms is valid even without coercion following immediately after each and every action. Moreover, there are now more opportunities to implement international law than ever before, such as international courts or internationally enacted sanctions.

The realistic school of international relations, which follows a political approach rather than a legal one, is till now influenced by the legal theory of coercion. Blatant violations of IL in modern history, like the Nazi tyranny during World War II, raised doubts again about the sources of validity of IL. Hard-core realists hold that power and not international law is the determinant of international relations.[20] Those with softer views do not question the relevance of IL as such but relativize its significance.[21] According to this school, there is no primacy of IL but it is one of several elements of reasoning and assessment that shape policies. This may well characterize the foreign policy of certain states (among others the United States) but legal scholars hold that this theory cannot serve as a normative model of IL.

The sociological school derives IL's binding force from the social nature of man, who has a tendency to live in associations and societies with a certain amount of solidarity, something that Aristotle already had in mind when he described man as a 'social animal'. From this anthropocentric perspective, states are instrumental institutions only.[22] Clapham summarizes it as follows:

> The ultimate explanation of the binding force of international law is that individuals, whether as single human-beings, or whether associated with others in a state, are constrained , in so far as they are reasonable beings, to believe that order and not chaos in the governing principle of the world in which they have to live.[23]

The not-so-surprising conclusion of these debates by international legal scholars is an important one for the central dilemma discussed in this book: despite all attempts, in the end there is no final answer regarding the ultimate reason and original cause of validity of international law.[24] Even though this exercise resembles the Münchhausen Trilemma, IL is a social practice and an orientation guide for political decision-making and action, and a high amount of political effort and capital is invested in negotiating international treaties, regulations and in shaping international institutions. Therefore, international law is more than just a branch of 'international ethics', as some have pointed out, referring to the difficulty of establishing universally accepted obligations.[25]

The nature of international law may be best understood as "just a system of customary law, upon which has been erected, almost entirely within the last century, a superstructure of 'conventional' or treaty-made law," writes Clapham, "and some of its chief defects are precisely those that the history of law teaches us to expect in a customary system."[26] The key flaw is not frequent violations, since most customary rules and the majority of treaties are regularly observed in international law, in Clapham's view. The flaws are more of structural nature, although also the frequency of violations nowadays – as is so evident in our case study – has contributed to trigger the contemporary debate of the crisis of international law. Indeed, as early as 2012 Clapham spoke of a "weak cohesion of international society,"[27] and this may get weaker by the day in an age when unilateralism and bilateral approaches to conflict resolution gain ground.

We are facing an IL paradox here: through its development, IL has become more ubiquitous and "the scope for states to operate outside the reach of international las is rapidly diminishing," and in particular "international human rights law regulates many aspects of a state's treatment of its citizens."[28] On the other hand, through this very deepening and expansion, IL has estranged domestic actors and institutions and now faces a legitimacy gap or even crisis that authoritarian regimes may exploit more than democratic ones. Başak Cali defines international law as "our imperfect institution to regulate our co-habitation in the form of separate, but independent political entities." This brings with it a "prima facie duty of minimal deference to international law." He continues: "minimal deference involves the 'attribution of presumptive weight' to international laws that are duly consented or provisionally consented treaties, established customary international laws, and non-consensual systemic norms of international law, or general principles."[29] International laws are based on variable forms of authority relationships. Cali defines the capacity of a particular international law by the logic through which it instructs domestic authorities to act (or fails to do so).

Although IL can be regarded as legally binding, it may not necessarily enjoy authority in the sense that it does not have the capacity to impose a "specific pre-emptive duty or the duty it imposes could be rebuttable by other considerations," writes Cali. "The binding nature of international law, therefore, is a necessary, but insufficient condition for the authority of international law over domestic orders. Conversely, the authoritativeness of international law is not sufficient for compliance. States may violate international law or they may respect international law for other reasons – such as self-interest, for example."[30]

Such a scenario has clearly unfolded in Syria. International law has become a refuge when needed but is blatantly violated when opportune in other cases.

Interestingly enough, however, all actors still tend to defend their actions with reference to international law, even if they violate it, or they use other reasons in line with presumably internationally recognized principles such as the 'fight against terrorism', with its international and legal implications. The sanctioning of such behaviour is highly dependent on: a) political will and commitment; b) a consensus of the powerful, i.e. P5 voting behaviour in the UN Security Council; and c) a series of factors that include geo-political interests, constellations in the international macro climate, interplay with other crises and the trade-off of interests elsewhere, political and military capacities etc.

In this context, contemporary scholars have pointed out that the evolution of International Law should be seen more in the light of the facts on the ground in international relations and less as a positivist debate of relations between norms and questions of legal validity. Eibe Riedel writes: "a wider conception of law will embrace relevant factual bases of norms as an empirical basis of a social and political nature, thereby taking into purview the reality of the international community."[31] Such 'soft laws' are international standards that are often developed by the United Nations and that become influential as a matter of fact, less because they need to be referred to as sources of law in the strict sense.

In other words, the standards that are set through *practice* by the UN – such as delivering humanitarian assistance via state governments in the first place, no matter to what extent those states are parties of war – has set a standard that the government of Syria has repeatedly invoked to justify current practice as 'valid' and 'obligatory'. In this case, the UN practice has set a standard that in some way also supports the notion of a hard state sovereignty that eclipses any attention to the state's government behaviour towards its citizens.

Contested Notions of State Sovereignty

The evolving notion of state sovereignty is another ongoing transformation in the history of ideas, and within International Law, that has direct political implications for our policy dilemma. According to some international provisions and, above all, to international practice, state sovereignty is a crucial factor to consider when delivering humanitarian assistance into a crisis region.

The doctrine of state sovereignty emerged during the Renaissance. It was first mentioned in Jean Bodin's *De Republica* in 1576 and confirmed in an international legal document in the 1648 Peace of Westphalia. Since then, the notion of sovereignty has developed into a contested issue both concerning the nature of the modern state and in the development of international law.[32] Classical International Law has developed the hard notion of sovereignty, in which the state sovereign exerts absolute power. This concept did have some logic, since it aimed to prevent further wars caused by rulers meddling in the internal affairs of other rulers on the grounds of converting subjects or other interests. What was meant to be an attribute of a personal ruler within a state became later an attribute to the state itself in its relations to other states (according to modern state theory).

A plethora of literature exists on the principle of state sovereignty and the derived right to embark on wars with impunity. Nevertheless, that right has become highly qualified, and to a large extent is limited to self-defence. Since this book is not about *ius ad bellum* but rather *ius in bello*, the focus here is on the connection of sovereignty with responsibilities and obligations, especially towards the population that lives in that state.

One of the first philosophers who thought sovereignty not in terms of interaction of states or as a law-and-order doctrine (as in Thomas Hobbes' Leviathan) was Jean-Jacques Rousseau, for whom the people was the sovereign. This was a quite radical change of perspective. In a further development, the a priori law of nature to which also the sovereigns were restricted was conceived of an antipode of the doctrine of absolute sovereignty. In this context, natural law "denied the irresponsibility of states and the finality of their independence from one another".[33] What the law of nature really entails is dependent on prevailing conditions at a given time, and therefore will vary in content. In general, though, it gave birth to modern international law and the law of war.[34] Over time, the notion that some divine or not-so-divine natural law was the basis of a structured coexistence between states and societies has been gradually replaced with positivist ideas. As Clapham writes, this trend secularized the whole idea of law but somehow also weakened its moral foundations.[35] This is particularly problematic for the validity of international law, given that it has few enforcement mechanisms. As a result, state sovereignty has developed from a "principle of internal order [...] into one of international anarchy."[36]

Modern international law developed with the aim of correcting disproportionate state power, following the painful experiences of two world wars and their unscrupulous brutality. From the twentieth century onwards, state sovereignty has become more and more defined through the prism of obligations in the way described above. Various schools of thought exist from which this obligation can be derived, be it from consensus or natural law etc., but one thing is clear: all of those ideas have restrained state governments' free scope of action.

For the purpose of this book, I will use two terms when referring to sovereignty: *hard sovereignty* and *permeable sovereignty*. The former is an unconditional sovereignty or state immunity. It represents the highest and undisputed value in international interactions with little or no possibility of imposing external guidelines or restrictions on a government's or state's behaviour. The latter, coined by Eberhard Menzel,[37] is a porous sovereignty with loopholes that let in external influence, a state power that is bound to adhere to certain norms and standards of behaviour both in international affairs and in relation to its own people.

Hard and permeable sovereignty are used here as 'ideal types' in the Weberian sense in order to explain current political debates and controversies. There are caveats, however, from a historical perspective. In their research about the history of humanitarian intervention, Simms and Trim point out that the so-called Westphalian concept of absolute sovereignty was not so absolute after all. Throughout history, interventions and normative limitations of sovereignty have been common. The peace treaties of Westphalia even specifically included guarantees of freedom of conscience for some religious minorities within the Holy Roman Empire and made some states from outside the Empire guarantors of the rights of religious minorities in other locations. "What today is typically identified as the 'Westphalian model' emerged, but only later in the eighteenth century," Simms and Trim emphasize. "Even then it did not monopolise attitudes to sovereignty; the concept that how a government treated the governed ought to be a factor in sovereignty retained its influence." As a consequence with regard to current political debates, the authors uphold the legitimacy of interventions on humanitarian grounds derived from historical practice: "[t]he idea that the modern international system derives solely from Westphalia is, at best, highly dubious. This means that the presumption of some vocal scholars, policy practitioners and human rights activists, that humanitarian intervention is illegitimate simply because it contravenes Westphalian principles, is not so much erroneous as baseless."[38] With this historical perspective in mind, the claims of a government, like the one in Damascus, that derives its justification to be the absolute sovereign from 'the international law', even in matters of humanitarian access and even in light of massive human rights violations and great humanitarian need, look even thinner.

In the 1990s it looked as though the mainstream notion of sovereignty was gradually becoming more and more permeable – until the Syrian crisis occurred. Scholars of international law cited such examples as the fall of communism and of the Berlin Wall in 1989 as indications that the liberal democratic paradigm – including a more resilient focus on human rights – had prevailed in world politics. Other key events were the wars in Bosnia-Hercegovina during 1992–95 and in Rwanda in 1994 both of which had genocidal traits, and, in particular, the controversial bombing of Serb targets by a NATO alliance during the Kosovo war in 1999, a military intervention with limited international legitimacy but in the name of human rights. In the public debates in Europe and beyond, the genocides in Bosnia-Hercegovina and Rwanda were accompanied by a deep disillusion and disappointment that modern instruments of international law and politics were unable to prevent such a human catastrophe. The paradigm was obviously shifting towards protecting human rights and towards the legitimacy of humanitarian interventions under certain conditions. Consequentially, this was practised in Kosovo despite disagreement in the UN Security Council and the lack of a UN mandate in line with Chapter VII of the UN Charter.

In this context, the paradigm shift also reached domestic politics, as was the case in Germany where the traditionally pacifist Green Party made a U-turn under Joschka Fischer (who later became foreign minister), with the effect that the party decided to support NATO attacks against Serbia without a UN mandate. Ending large-scale violence against civilians had become more important than unconditional and ideological pacifism, and the hard notion of sovereignty of classical international law. Fischer was attacked with a paint bomb during the fateful Green Party congress that took this decision in May 1999, and was left with damage to his eardrum for having changed his party's political direction. With similar motivation, the Czech civil rights activist and later president, Václav Havel, stated in a speech to the Canadian parliament on the NATO bombing of the Federal Republic of Yugoslavia that:

This war places human rights above the rights of the State ... although it has no
direct mandate from the UN, it did not happen as an act of aggression or out of
disrespect for international law. It happened, on the contrary, out of respect for a
law that ranks higher than the law which protects the sovereignty of states. The
alliance has acted out of respect for human rights as both conscience and
international legal documents dictate.[39]

Robertson calls this an "exception to sovereignty" and an "evolving principle of
humanitarian necessity", whereby a "force of proportional kind may be used to
prevent a humanitarian catastrophe. This is the Good Samaritan paradigm writ
large: the obligation to stop mass murder of innocents must override the rule
about not intervening in the affairs of other states."[40] Robertson makes a strong
point in favour of this development but recommends caution at the same time:
"There is no court as yet to stop a state which murders and extirpates its own
people: for them, if the Security Council fails to reach superpower agreement, the
only salvation can come through other states exercising the right of humanitarian
intervention. Thanks to Kosovo, that right has re-entered international law, but
must be qualified in ways which will restrict its potential for abuse."[41] He lists nine
conditions that must be met for this purpose, in his view.

Progressive humanitarian optimists saw glimmers on the horizon of a new "global
domestic political order" that would display a novel "post-national politics of military
humanism," as Ulrich Beck put it in the late 1990s. For the twenty-first century, he
foresaw a rising number of pacifying wars or human-rights wars. At the same time,
he expressed his uneasiness at this development: "The good news is the bad news:
The hegemonial power determines what law is and what human right is. And the war
becomes the perpetuation of *morals* with different means. Precisely because of this, it
becomes more and more difficult to contain the escalating logic of war."[42]

Clearly, the discussions continued, and in the first decade of the millennium
they took the direction of what soon became known as the principle of
Responsibility to Protect (R2P). An early precedent existed as of 1989, when
humanitarian cross-border deliveries had taken place against the will of the host
government in Sudan. Similarly, in 1991, a de facto state crystallized in northern
Iraq through the collapse of central state control after the Gulf War and the
creation of a no-fly zone by the US, France and Britain in order to protect the
Kurdish population from attacks perpetrated by the Iraqi government under
Saddam Hussein.[43] Consequently, the lessons of the massacres and genocides in
Bosnia and Rwanda, as well as the humanitarian catastrophes averted in Kosovo,
paved the way for more courageous demands to qualify state sovereignty. This
encouraged legal efforts to strongly link sovereignty to responsibilities. A conducive
atmosphere emerged for calls for more robust interventions.

This drive was reflected in the 1992 Agenda for Peace that UN Secretary-
General Boutros-Ghali published. The proposal by the first African UN chief called
for proactive peace-making and humanitarian interventions. It outlined suggestions
for enabling intergovernmental organizations to respond quickly and effectively to
threats to international peace and security in the post-Cold War era. Four major

areas of activity were identified: preventive diplomacy (Responsibility to Prevent); peace-making and peacekeeping (Responsibility to React); and post-conflict peacebuilding (Responsibility to Rebuild).[44] Moreover, since the early 1990s, the UN Security Council has adopted several resolutions treating massive violations of human rights and of international humanitarian law as a 'threat to the peace' in the sense of Art. 39 of the UN Charter. The conflicts in the former Yugoslavia and Somalia are among the first examples. Between 1991 and mid-1993, the international system witnessed an eight-fold increase in the number of UN peacekeeping troops deployed and a quadrupling of the UN's peacekeeping budget. In addition, operations and notions of crisis prevention, peace enforcement and the idea of humanitarian intervention in an ongoing conflict boomed.[45] UNSC Resolution 1296, adopted in 2000, stated explicitly that denial of access of humanitarian personnel to victims of armed conflict constitutes a threat to the peace.[46]

The path towards R2P was also cleared by the Brahimi Report of 2000.[47] It adapted the three principles of peacekeeping – i.e. the consent of local parties, impartiality and non-use of force except in self-defence – and elaborated more complex conditions of internal conflicts in which the consent of local parties may be unreliable. The report also consciously blurred the lines between peacekeeping and peace enforcement.[48] The year 2000 also saw the African Union (AU) enshrine the R2P principle in its Constitutive Act. It was followed by an AU Peace and Security Council set up in 2004. The body can assess a potential crisis situation, send fact-finding missions to troublespots and authorize and legitimize AU intervention in internal crisis situations. In other words, the AU mandated to itself the right and the responsibility to protect. The limitations in practice, however, quickly became visible with new crises looming in Burundi, Sudan (Darfur) and later in Libya in 2011, over which AU member states were deeply divided.[49]

A further important step towards wider acceptability and international legitimacy of the principle of state-responsibility was the World Summit of 2005 at the UN headquarters in New York. The 191 assembled heads of state and government elevated R2P to the level of a component of the complex and evolving mosaic of international law. At the same time, those who pushed for such a progressive interpretation tried to accommodate concerns that the right to 'humanitarian intervention' would spin out of control or even that a new political wave of self-determination movements would use R2P as fresh cover for their old political aspirations. The World Summit agreed that state responsibility would rest on three pillars:[50]

1. The responsibility of the state to protect its population from genocide, war crimes, ethnic cleansing, and crimes against humanity including their incitement (*responsibility to prevent*).
2. The commitment of the international community to assist states in meeting these obligations through the UN in accordance with Chapters VI and VII of the Charter (*responsibility to react*).
3. The responsibility of states to take collective action in a timely and decisive manner through the Security Council, in accordance with the Charter,

including Chapter VII, on a case-by-case basis, and in accordance with regional organizations, should peaceful means be inadequate and national authorities are manifestly failing to protect their populations from above mentioned forms of violence (*responsibility to rebuild*).

The three principles were not so much new law but rather a different way of presenting some existing legal obligations and sound policy objectives in an alternative form. They also gained much stronger visibility among policy-makers and in the public debate, which was important for doctrine and practice alike. Of course, principle 2 is a more or less camouflaged indication of the last resort of military intervention for conflicts that cannot be resolved through diplomacy or mediation. The question is where the threshold lies. Since we do not live in an ideal world, despite declarations of altruism and humanism, the threshold will also be influenced by realpolitik to a lesser or sometimes larger extent. The latter is probably true for Syria, which left many human rights advocates and Syrians on the receiving end of violence at the brink of despair or fatalism. Talking about R2P while trying to play down the last-resort option, has never been honest since the initiation of the R2P concept. In this sense, it was at best evasive when former Irish President Mary Robinson declared in 2008 of the R2P doctrine: "We should be clear that it is not a justification of military intervention."[51]

Although R2P did not do away with the controversy about humanitarian intervention, and the concept's legal nature is open to question, there has been an ever more visible and commonly acknowledged notion of the unquestioned responsibility to protect populations from genocide, war crimes, ethnic cleansing and crimes against humanity, which the UN General Assembly and the UN Secretary-General have repeatedly evoked. The new quality in this era of debates may lie in what Fleck describes as: "State sovereignty is no obstacle for taking responsible action under Chapter VII, as sovereignty and responsibility are to be understood as mutually reinforcing principles."[52]

Many hopes were pinned on R2P by human rights activists and those in scholarship, diplomacy and politics who tended towards a progressive reading of international law and the permeable notion of sovereignty during its heyday in the first decade of the millennium – until the Arab Spring set in. When the wave of popular protests swept the streets in a domino effect from Tunisia, Libya, Egypt and Yemen towards Syria, universalists hoped that the common values of human freedom, dignity and perhaps also democracy would take hold in the Arab world. But at least as important was another aspect: the notion of *stability* that is also linked to the notion of state sovereignty. In the past, 'stability' in this region had typically meant the stagnation of government, oppression of public opinion and civil society. Western states had found accommodation with this trade-off. The level of difficulty involved in changing the established paradigms became obvious when former French foreign minister Michèle Alliot-Marie offered help to Tunisia's president, Ben Ali, as a first reflex when the protests broke out. As events unfolded, she was obliged to resign, and after some hesitation France's president, Nicolas Sarkozy, lent his weight to the movement for democratic change in Libya and beyond. Similarly, other Western states had to readjust their political compass for the Arab region. It remained a delicate trade-off between a new and uncertain dynamic and stagnation/stability.

Certainly, the old definition of stability as social, economic and even moral stagnation became untenable after the Arab Spring. It needed courage and foresight to redefine a new notion of stability in the region. This necessarily implied some kind of a free play of political forces that allowed a peaceful change of government through elections. This new notion of stability turned out to be short-lived. Still, Arab societies have changed irreversibly. The fruits of a new, popular self-consciousness may be harvested at later stages. Meanwhile, ostensibly a political restauration has taken hold to which the West has not yet found a real answer.

What a change this is compared to a few years earlier, when the initial changes in the Arab world were met in the West with an almost impulsive sympathy. This translated into determined political action in favour of human rights and against unconditional state sovereignty. The nineteen-state NATO-led Libyan intervention in 2011 was the practical expression of the evolving significance of R2P after the World Summit in 2005. The intervention's motive was – at its outset – the prevention of an imminent massacre of civilians in the city of Benghazi by troops of President Muammar Gaddafi. The humanitarian and human-rights impetus of this venture was clearly discernible. US President Obama declared that the impending threat was "a massacre that would have reverberated across the region and stained the conscience of the world."[53] In UNSC Resolution 1970, the Libyan government was called upon to not only protect its population but also to "fulfil the legitimate demands of the population" while threatening an intervention under Chapter VII of the UN Charter.[54] The subsequent UN Security Council Resolution 1973[55] legitimized the military intervention due to the Libyan government's non-compliance, established an arms embargo and a no-fly zone.

However, the controversial international and domestic debates that triggered this decision widened cracks in the pro-R2P front and displayed the limits of the concept. The five states that abstained in the UN Security Council were unusual bedfellows: Russia, China, Germany, India and Brazil. Heated domestic debates followed in Russia and Germany. The Russian debate is particularly interesting because it foreshadowed events in Syria and beyond. The Russian president at that time was Dimitri Medvedev, while Vladimir Putin was prime minister and had a 'personal opinion' on this international issue. While Medvedev defended Resolution 1973 as acceptable, Putin criticized it as a 'crusade' that reminded him of the Middle Ages.[56] When the Libya intervention finally led to regime change through the killing of President Gaddafi by Libyan rebels supported by Western air power, Putin regarded this as an unacceptable transgression of the Resolution's mandate covered by western powers. In this judgement he was not alone.

Libya would prove to be the straw that broke R2P's back. In particular, the leaders of China and Russia – soon ruled by Putin, once more President – affirmed that they would never let something like this happen again. External intervention in the name of human rights and prevention of a humanitarian catastrophe, particularly if it was perceived as overstepping its mandate in full military swing, threatened the very existence" of the authoritarian regime in China and the ever more authoritarian Russian government, both of which have imposed increasing limitations to freedom of expression and human rights on their populations. In addition, these great powers hold their own record for brutally suppressing upheavals – Russia in Chechnya during 1994–95 and China in Tiananmen Square in 1989, its discrimination and mass detention of the Muslim Uighur population or its suppression of the large popular protests in Hong Kong in 2019. Russia had no interest either that its bilateral interventions in Georgia and the Ukraine would one day be interpreted as reasons for international interventions on humanitarian grounds.

The false pretext of an imminent chemical weapons threat under which the United States, with support of the UK under Blair, had launched the military intervention in Iraq in 2003 to topple President Saddam Hussein, has become an additional, retrospective argument to point at the dangers of interventionist policies, be them of humanitarian or other preventive nature.

Therefore, the Syrian mass movement that rose against President Bashar al-Assad in 2011 took place in a distinctly altered international environment. The schism between Russia and the US widened (also as a result of the 2014 Orange Revolution in the Ukraine), the Security Council was mostly paralyzed on decisions concerning Syria and beyond, and no Western state felt any appetite to embark on yet another foray into the region with an uncertain outcome. Although the Syrian constellation was very different from Iraq, and a limited and timely intervention may have indeed served the purpose of preventing a great number of civilian deaths, this seemed out of question after the experiences in Iraq and Libya. This was a classic dilemma of realpolitik.[57] Making a case for humanitarian intervention became even harder over time as the Syrian upheaval militarized and radicalized due to the brutal suppression of civilian protests, and when this conflict became a playing field of proxy wars including Hezbollah, Iran and Putin's Russia, which emerged as the strongest protagonist from 2015 onwards. Any intervention in Syria thus meant a direct stand-off with Russia in particular, a country that sounded the death knell for R2P and defended a return to the notion of hard sovereignty decoupled from multilateral obligations.

Leenders and Mansour argue: "While the actual erosion of state sovereignty since the end of the Cold War remains a matter of dispute, we contend that the Syrian conflict can be viewed as an exemplary case supporting those who contended all along that reports of the death of state sovereignty were premature at best."[58] In this context, Syrian claims of state sovereignty were bolstered through: 1) the paralysis of the UN Security Council and the resulting impossibility to enforce a conditionality of sovereignty with humanitarian and human rights responsibilities; 2) the lack of political willingness to establish a counterweight and circumvent the Security Council through a coalition of the willing similar to NATO's intervention in Kosovo or through the General Assembly (Uniting for Peace); 3) the ready acceptance of the Syrian government as the High Contracting Party for humanitarian and other forms of cooperation despite its dismal human rights record; and 4) the frequently criticized behaviour of UN functionaries who too easily bought into the government's narrative and claim of absolute sovereignty.

Understandably, other academic or historically inspired approaches that questioned the government's claims for hard sovereignty had little practical effect. Leenders and Mansour, for example, remind us of the notion that "mutually exclusive claims on state sovereignty" may emerge in revolutionary situations and civil war. The authors considered the Syrian government's insistence on unconditional sovereignty "an illusory claim" that had little domestic support in the light of the regime's brutal repression of its own citizens. Therefore, the regime's claims "shifted to external audiences composed of UN humanitarian agencies and donor states as the latter have reinforced and sustained the Syrian regime's empirically implausible claims on state sovereignty."[59]

The Syrian opposition, in the form of the High Negotiation Commission (HNC), argued in the same vein during the Geneva Talks in 2016 and 2017. Their legal expert, Mohammed Sabra, in a meeting with the team of the UN Special Envoy, Staffan De Mistura, made a case for justifying the establishment of a Transitional Government Body in Syria (without President Assad) on the basis of 'revolutionary legitimacy' or 'overall legitimacy' derived from the will of 'the people'. His argument was that the government in Damascus had lost its legitimacy by killing its own people and by being faced with a large wave of unrest. To underline his point, Sabra cited the popular national movements in nineteenth-century Europe, framing the Arab Spring upheavals as part of that heritage.[60] However, by this time, international actors (including most Western states) had already given up the notion of regime change in Syria as unrealistic, no matter how bad the humanitarian and human rights situation in Syria continued to be and no matter how low the government's legitimacy was perceived to be. And even if there were a revolutionary spirit, at least at the beginning of 2011 and 2012, it was difficult to determine how strong the 'popular will' still was to topple the dictator, apart from lacking international support to pursue this goal.

An additional difficulty represented the ever-increasing fragmentation of the militarized confrontation with rebels, many of whom had radicalized and were financed by various foreign backers, especially Turkey, Saudi Arabia and Qatar. At points, over 1,000 factions and militias were engaged in the battlefields. In addition, five regional and great powers (Russia, Iran, Turkey, the US and Israel) were militarily present in Syria in one form or another harbouring diverging interests. The radical groups, including those remaining from the so-called Islamic State, have always been outside any political process in Geneva. This fragmentation has contributed to long-lasting instability and made a scenario of alternative and legitimate governance in Syria difficult to imagine – no matter how fragmented, illegitimate and brutal the regime in Damascus itself was considered to be. At least the latter still enjoyed legal – and to a large extent, political – international recognition, and membership in the United Nations.

The fact of military and territorial fragmentation on the ground was accompanied by an opposing development in 2017: the moderate political opposition that took part in the Geneva Talks united under a common umbrella, the Syrian Negotiations Committee (SNC). It was left mainly to the Turks to re-establish a connection between the mostly exiled opposition and the ground in Syria. After the Turkish

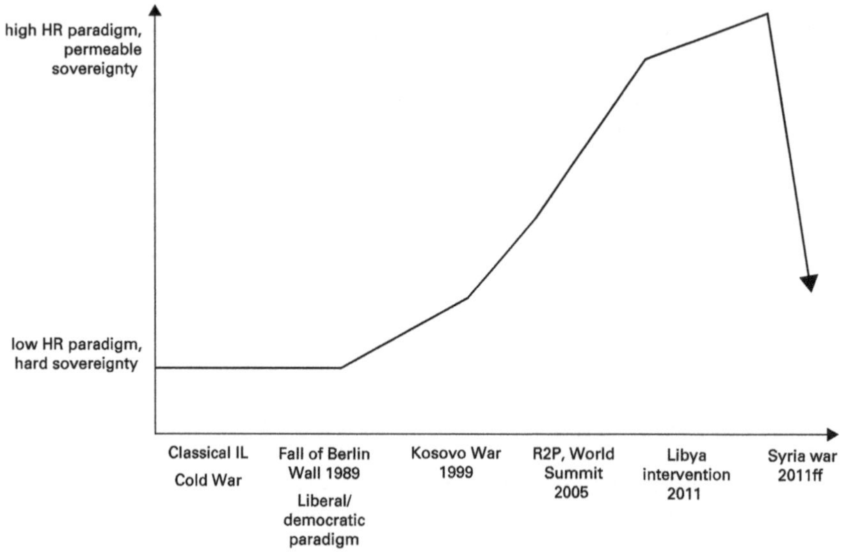
high HR paradigm, permeable sovereignty
low HR paradigm, hard sovereignty
Classical IL
Cold War
Fall of Berlin Wall 1989
Liberal/ democratic paradigm
Kosovo War 1999
R2P, World Summit 2005
Libya intervention 2011
Syria war 2011ff

Figure 4.1 The rise and fall of the humanitarian intervention and human rights paradigms.

occupation of large stretches of land in northern Syria in 2019, Ankara made heavy use of a major component of the SNC, the Syrian National Coalition (SOC) and its attached Syrian Interim Government, an organization with quasi-governmental or at least administrative service functions under Turkish control inside Syria. Since Turkey's steps were coordinated with Syria's ally Russia in the Astana format, this dent in the Syrian regime's sovereignty is likely to last for some time. This is the second 'exception' to fully fledged Syrian state sovereignty after Russian and Iranian presence by government invitation – at least originally.

Chapter 5

THE TERRORISM TOOL: DE-HUMANIZING THE 'OTHER'

One characteristic of the Syrian upheaval was that it was born out of a civil mass movement that protested against the behaviour of a government vis-à-vis its population. Initially, it was not quite the typical situation of a non-international armed conflict in which rebels merged with and were hiding among civilians, a situation in which international humanitarian law (IHL) still shows deficiencies.[1] It was rather an unarmed civilian movement itself that stood at the centre of events from which, gradually, militaristic and extremist elements emerged and span off. This posed significant challenges not only for international law and its application but also to political and humanitarian actors.

Ultimately, however, the problem in Syria lay less in the objective difficulty in distinguishing civilians from combatants but in the *deliberate annihilation of civilians*. One of the torturers employed by Assad in the secret services, Col. Anwar Raslan, admitted this in a media interview in 2013 after his defection: since early 2012, the goal of torturing prisoners was no longer gaining information but rather "killing civilians at massive scale who had absolutely nothing to do with armed opposition or terrorist groups."[2]

The Sin of Rage at Ground Zero

From the very beginning of the crisis, the government in Damascus used skilful legal argumentation to support its actions on the international stage. For this purpose, it proved to be 'helpful' that a major Western state had already paved the way in some regards by delivering argumentative ammunition that eroded IHL and IHRL through the justification of fighting terrorism. This development took its course after the 9/11 terrorist attacks on New York and Washington DC in 2001. The political reaction of the US Administration under President George W. Bush, and the subsequent argumentation against terrorism of numerous other political leaders, have become a great challenge to IHL and IHRL. Many of those leaders were autocrats in the Arab world and beyond who delightedly took up this opportunity and the new discourse to clamp down on civil society, political reformers or activists. A tendency was established to grant states more leeway in their efforts to counter security threats defined as terrorism, and to relax the restraints imposed on state action by international law.[3]

Between 2001 and 2009 the US government took the legally dubious view that 'terrorists' were neither combatants nor civilians, but 'unlawful combatants' – a term unknown to IHL.[4] This made 'special measures' possible and morally more plausible to respective political constituencies; they included practices such as waterboarding during investigations or the establishment of prison camps like that at Guantanamo Bay, Cuba, outside both the US and any recognized legal system.

Experts in international law criticized harshly this development and welcomed EU and Council of Europe legislation that attempted to strike a better balance between security interests, the rule of law and human rights guarantees. As Riedel writes: "legitimate security concerns cannot override elementary habeas corpus rights, which were won in a protracted struggle lasting for centuries."[5] Riedel also censured the UN Security Council, which was influenced strongly by the US after 9/11, for overstepping its mandate in the context of its sanctions regime related to anti-terrorism measures. Under this sanctions regime, persons charged with terrorism or aiding terrorists – who ended up on the list of the Council's Sanctions Committee – found themselves without any legal remedies to challenge the situation. The Security Council purposely did not set up a legal mechanism to control the actual listing procedures. As a later corrective measure, an Office of the Ombudsperson mechanism under the Sanctions Committee was established as a response to heavy criticism of this procedure, although it did not meet the strict requirements developed at the European level.

The discussion discharges into a debate about the role and mandate of the UN Security Council. Is this Council a law-making institution in its own right or does it have to adhere to overriding norms and values, including and perhaps especially with regard to the fight against terrorism? This reminds us of the debate described above between the 'political camp' and the 'legalistic camp' in discussions about origins and fluidity of international law. In 1950, then US Secretary of State, John Foster Dulles, still held the view that "[t]he Security Council is not a body that merely enforces agreed law. It is law unto itself."[6] Critics like Riedel hold this stance to be obsolete and conclude:

> [...] the UNSC that undoubtedly has the primary responsibility for maintaining peace and security, cannot have the discretionary power to disregard the rule of law, one of the foundational principles of a peaceful international order for which the UN was set up, including the UN Charter principles of arts 1-2. Thus, art 103 of the UN Charter cannot be read solely in conjunction with arts 24(1), 25, but is itself subject to art 24(2).[7]

Riedel thus refers in particular to the principle (Art. 24(2)) that reads: "In discharging these duties the Security Council shall act in accordance with the Purposes and Principles of the United Nations. The specific powers granted to the Security Council for the discharge of these duties are laid down in Chapters VI,

VII, VIII, and XII." In other words, the Security Council does not stand above principles of international law derived from various sources, from elementary habeas corpus acts to the UN Charter itself, even in perceived exceptional situations such as terrorist threats.

While these issues were discussed extensively inside the world body, the US went ahead with its national legal interpretation and controversial practices. And it did find allies – for some of its practices, at least – among other Western states, in particular in their intelligence and security communities. Thus it set the splits in favour of more lenient interpretations of IHRL, also and in particular by authoritarian governments that had a range of agendas, of which the fight against terrorism was just one. By systematically ignoring international law during the 'war on terror', by legalizing some forms of torture through internal memos (written by President Bush's Attorney General, Alberto Gonzales, which made torture an approved tool with the blessing of the Pentagon, the US Justice Department and the White House), the United States, in the perception of many Arabs and westerners alike, had allied itself with the crude methods of authoritarian regimes in the Middle East. Incidents of prisoner abuse in the Abu Ghraib prison in Iraq or Guantanamo Bay on Cuba added to the gruesome picture. The United States had even outsourced torture, as suspects had been sent to countries where mistreatment was notoriously used as an interrogation practice. For this purpose, the CIA executed clandestine missions that transported detainees to remote interrogation facilities, in Afghanistan, Egypt and Jordan amongst others. Until 2002, US officials even sent Al-Qaeda suspects to Syrian dungeons.[8]

These developments set the tone for authoritarian regimes in the Middle East that, from 2010 onwards, swiftly branded large parts of their discontented populations as terrorists during the Arab Spring. They also granted the regimes more leeway in dealing with their own people and citizens beyond international legal boundaries. In Syria, these actions evolved into one of the cruellest intra-state conflicts of the century to date.

The Myth of the Unlawful Combatant

The notion that something like an 'unlawful combatant' existed in the 'war on terror' extracts the individual from any IHL and IHRL context and protection. Thus it challenges the traditional regulations of *ius in bello*. Moreover, *total and asymmetric wars* of modern times, like the one in Syria, easily blur the distinction between military and civilian personnel in practice.[9] The scholarly opinion in modern IHL literature that even if the emerging rebels were unlawful combatants, they would be covered by the protection of IHL,[10] proved to be little more than a footnote.

By nurturing the one-size-fits-all narrative of terrorism, the Syrian government attempted to escape legal obligations that would have taken effect if it had recognized that a non-international armed conflict was taking place on its territory at all. In this case, it would have had to recognize the emerging rebel groups as a party to the conflict from the very beginning. The non-state groups would then have been accorded legal status and legitimacy.[11] In such cases, customary and treaty IHL demands that a clear distinction be made between combatants and civilians in non-international armed conflicts (NIAC). Indeed, protection must be granted to the same categories of persons as in international armed conflicts, such as civilians, medical and religious personnel and generally all persons *hors de combat.*[12] "The banner of terrorism has often been used by states," Bianchi and Naqvi write, "to denounce the legitimacy of non-state groups fighting in internal armed conflicts and thereby to deny the applicability of the Protocol or Common Article 3 [of the Geneva Conventions] in such situations" regarding the humane treatment of prisoners and other obligations.[13]

The global inflationary use of the term and notion of 'terrorism' after 9/11 has made it easier to dilute these international norms and obligations, and to stretch the notion of self-defence and proportionality.[14] In this context, the government of Syria deliberately chose to apply the narrative of terrorism (plus 'sectarianism' and 'foreign conspiracy') very swiftly in 2011 when the domestic situation was still one of popular unrest without any prevalent militant or sectarian colouring and without even the goal of regime change (at least during the early months). But this harsh rhetoric helped create a space of a somehow accepted grey area in which the government could hit back, a government that was not even equipped with trained tear-gas units or other de-escalating instruments used in democracies to disperse protests.

Indiscriminate killing, the use of heavy weapons in urban areas, torture, sieges and the deliberate starvation of parts of the population can be more easily sold to the domestic audience as well as to international allies when everyone on the other side has been sufficiently de-humanized or bastardized. This was one of the most successful war narratives of the Syrian regime. Adherence to IHL and to international conventions that Syria had signed – in particular the International Anti-Torture Convention of July 2004 – became subordinate to the headline fight against terrorism and to the regime's survival while struggling against the pressure for political reforms that may have endangered its very existence.

Poisonous Rhetoric

Despite rejecting the other side as a legal or even moral subject, the Syrian government had its arm twisted by its Russian ally to participate in the Geneva peace talks – at least from time to time. Unsurprisingly, instead of displaying a willingness to negotiate, the government used the public arena to brand the opposition as foreign-controlled terrorists in an allusion to their funding by Arab Gulf States and Turkey. The government chose the narrative that it was unacceptable to sit down with 'non-patriotic terrorists'. Therefore, they needed to test them as 'real patriots' by asking them to sign up to government-formulated 'essential principles' as an implicit precondition for further engagement. This tactic was applied in order to stall the peace process during the direct talks led by the UN/

LAS Joint Special Representative Lakhdar Brahimi in February 2014 and in the second round of the Syrian-Syrian Constitutional Committee in November 2019 under UN Special Envoy Geir Pedersen.

During several years of unsuccessful talks under UN auspices in Geneva, Bashar Jaafari – head of the Syrian government delegation and also his country's ambassador to the UN – , frequently used expressions such as 'terrorists', 'scum' and 'monsters' to address the Syrians on the other side who were sitting in the same meeting room at the Palais des Nations (under Brahimi's aegis) or who were present at the same time for proximity talks (with De Mistura). The strategy of de-humanizing the enemy was also applied in cases such as Colombia and Sri Lanka, and had long been an obstacle to embark on peace talks with armed groups. The argument went that the government cannot negotiate with 'terrorists'.

A powerful contrast in rhetoric was adopted by Colombian president Juan Manuel Santos, who successfully negotiated a peace agreement with the FARC guerrilla group between 2012 and 2016 after half a century of civil war. In his speech at the occasion of the Nobel Peace Prize ceremony in Oslo on 10 December 2016 he stated:

> Seeking victory through force alone, pursuing the utter destruction of the enemy, waging war to the last breath, means failing to recognize your opponent as a human being like yourself, someone with whom you can hold a dialogue with [. . .] Humanizing war does not just mean limiting its cruelty but also recognizing your opponent as an equal, as a human being.[15]

The use of rhetoric cannot be underestimated during peace talks. It is a very sensitive indicator of the political will present at the table and thus of the potential success of a mediation.

A Self-fulfilling Prophecy

The conflict in Syria undoubtedly evolved with growing levels of violence on both sides, as well as interference from regional proxy states. Increasingly radicalized rebel groups did commit crimes of all kinds against combatants and civilians alike, and was also responsible for war crimes in the later years of the conflict. Thus, they have also violated IHL. In this regard, the regime's war narrative has become a self-fulfilling prophecy in parallel to the uncompromising brutality of the regime's use of force from the very beginning of the upheaval, which in turn helped foster radicalization, religious extremism and escalating acts of aggression.

Interestingly, in 2011 and 2012 some western diplomats were already using the argument that Syria suffered from Islamic radicalism and terrorism. Often their main indirect point was that they were seeking a plausible justification for not getting involved in the fighting that was either looming or already in place. Again, this was linked to the political macro-climate described above in which no appetite existed for further humanitarian interventions. Such arguments provided a reason for not delivering even defensive weapons to the Free Syrian Army (FSA). At that early time, the FSA had emerged as a new structure of mostly defected army personnel who refused to shoot at unarmed civilians and indeed attempted to shield them from the regime's escalating use of violence.

Not only the FSA but also Syrians who took to the streets in daily despair begged the international community, especially the US and European countries, to supply armed opposition with TOW anti-aircraft missiles, known as 'man pads', to prevent civilian deaths from government air raids. They did not receive them, however, because the argument ran that they might fall into the wrong hands – that is, of 'terrorists' or 'Islamists'. Now, after several years of unfolding worst-case scenarios – and many thousand civilian deaths later – weapons have ended up in almost everybody's hands on the ground anyway.

While after 9/11 the concern was that an overstretched notion of pre-emptive war and interventionism on the pretext of self-defence would undermine the progress recently made during the 'third age of human rights', in which basic humanitarian norms would achieve some level of enforcement, the concern after the Syrian war has become to witness a relapse into notions of Westphalian international law of hard and unconditional state sovereignty. The victim of both developments are individual and collective human rights, especially in weaker states and within states whose governments kill its own people.

Chapter 6

DE-NEUTRALIZING AID: ALL ROADS
LEAD TO DAMASCUS

The growing international frustration with the Syrian government and the consequential support of cross-border deliveries against Damascus' consent was a threat to the regime's unlimited exercise of what I would call *integrative warfare*. This is a strategy of warfare that systematically and unscrupulously takes advantage of all international resources available from different sectors, including the humanitarian one, in order to use or abuse them on the ground by channelling or absorbing humanitarian deliveries in its favour or profiting from the international presence in other forms. The purpose is to alleviate (in this case) the the warring state's economic burden and to reduce state responsibilities vis-à-vis its population by integrating remaining resources into its wider war economy and military actions. The same applies to possible developmental support, including post-war reconstruction. Cross-border deliveries, by contrast, are beyond the grasp of the central government and thus in this scheme represents a lost resource in the integrative warfare of a predatory state.

The Government's Grip on Humanitarian Work

The systematic way in which the Syrian government has interfered with humanitarian work in its territory was elaborate and effective. A former Syrian humanitarian worker for the UN on the ground describes the reluctant attitude of the government and the dilemma of humanitarian work under these conditions as follows:

> It's like you are the owner of the house and you lock up your son in a room. And I as a humanitarian worker come to your house, knock at your door and ask you that I would like to enter to help your son. Since you are forced by the police to let me enter, you will not say 'no' directly. But the owner tries to manipulate my work, make my life difficult. In the end of the day, I live in his house. As a humanitarian worker I know that if the owner decides to kick me out of the house, the police will not force him to accept me again. The international organization needs to find a way to stay in the house and spend as much time as

possible in the house to somehow help the son. This means they have to abide to the owner's requests.[1]

As the owner of the house, the Syrian government reacted to the crisis in 2011 by gradually tightening its grip on the work of humanitarian and other NGO efforts. Initially, international cooperation required approval from the Ministry of Foreign Affairs and Expatriates, which created a list of approved institutions that were allowed to work with international NGOs and UN agencies on humanitarian support efforts without any additional requirements.

As the regime's struggle for survival intensified, this practice was tightened once again. Humanitarian NGO work became subjected to a heavily controlled system under which all international NGOs were supposed to operate under one of two main umbrellas: the Syrian Arab Red Crescent (SARC) or the Syria Trust for Development. The Trust is a government institution founded in 2007 and run by Bashar al-Assad's wife, Asma, with the aim of controlling 'civil society' activities in the country. Cooperating NGOs were given access to shared resources, research and administrative services, but had to stay within the regime's red lines since no legal activity was permitted outside this realm. In times of war, the Trust played a key role in controlling the flow of funding and activities in the government's interest.

The government also established the Higher Commission for Relief, affiliated to the Ministry of Local Administration and Environment, and composed of representatives from the Ministry of Foreign Affairs and Expatriates, the Syria Trust for Development, the Red Cross, the Red Crescent and UNDP. Here, humanitarian and development activity is organized as one hub. Development cooperation projects involving local NGOs and UN agencies were put under a very restrictive system under the auspices of the Ministry of Social Affairs and Labour through a committee in which municipalities also took part. As some representatives on the ground complained, this system in effect restricted international cooperation to a selected handful of tightly controlled NGOs that were also favoured by UNDP, which left little room for others.

The mandate of the Higher Commission for Relief covers: 1) the coordination of relief and humanitarian actions at the governmental level; 2) the adoption of a national strategic vision, the adoption of interim objectives and humanitarian projects in accordance with *national needs and priorities;* 3) the identification and supervision of partners in humanitarian and relief actions at all levels; 4) the monitoring of the implementation of plans set by ministries and provinces; 5) the evaluation of implemented plans; and 6) the coordination of the rehabilitation of affected areas to which "security and stability have been restored" with a view to returning the internally displaced to their homes, and providing logistical support to facilitate the return to normal life.

As much as this framework looks rational and in the sound interest of a state government in such a situation, the practice experienced by NGOs on the ground looked different. It was the powerful security apparatus that had the final say in any project or programme involving humanitarian aid. As has always been the case in Syria's modern history, the security services can reject or block any cooperation without the need to provide justification. Representatives on the ground reported that larger cooperation schemes from bigger donors such as the EU were given a particularly hard time due to an 'evolving state-centric conditionality', which was not really functioning.[2]

The system of humanitarian assistance in Syria was turned into a business model by the Assad regime. Each organization that accepted the conditions and was ready to work within the structure explained above, had to pay a licence fee to the state. In addition, the government obliged international organizations to buy from Syrian traders. Only 10 per cent of the goods distributed in government territory were allowed to be imported from outside. As a result, those businessmen who supported the regime and financed it (or who were forced to contribute with regular payments or revenue shares[3]), took care to obtain contracts for selling humanitarian and other goods. Often, these goods were overpriced. International organizations, if they wanted to be active at all, had a very limited choice of providers. And in order to secure a contract in the first place, the businessmen had to pay another fee to the regime. The system of humanitarian assistance thus also became a circular system of money-laundering. Bribes at checkpoints – 'security fees' – were a further routine charge applied by both regime and anti-regime forces alike.

Looking at the overall figures, it becomes clear how significant the influx of UN and other humanitarian services was for the struggling government. It eased the pressure on the authorities to deliver basic services to its people as a state, made an allocation of scarce resources possible to war-related expenses, and at the same time reduced the threshold on continued bombing of its own infrastructure if considered necessary, since external services would compensate for the loss anyway. Analysis by the *Syria Report*, an economic and business newsletter, shows that the UN provided US$1 billion in aid to government-controlled areas during 2018. In comparison, the actual budgeted spending of the government was about US$4 billion that year, according to Jihad Yazigi.[4] This roughly correlates with an unpublished report by the Syrian Center for Policy Research that contains the estimation that in 2017, the international community's total UN and non-UN humanitarian expenditure in Syria was equivalent to 35 per cent of the country's GDP.[5] This does not mean, of course, that all this money went into government pockets, but it gives a notion of the scope of what was at play financially.

Doing business with desperate and starving people in besieged areas was particularly lucrative. In the years of frequent and numerous sieges, the value of this kind of trade was estimated to be around US$7 million. The regime granted licences to selected businessmen who were allowed to trade a limited amount of goods with the armed opposition groups (or 'terrorist groups', as the regime called them) inside besieged areas. The resulting gains had to be transferred, to a large extent, back to the regime. The same was done with areas under IS or under other extremists' control. The highest-ranking regime member who oversaw these transactions was the president's brother, Maher al-Assad, who is said to have close links to Iran.

Inside the besieged areas, Islamist armed groups often used their newly acquired supplies to turn a profit themselves by pocketing the gains from selling those goods at a huge mark-up to the starving population or they stock-piled these supplies rather than distributing them to the needy. Tunnels or other routes into besieged areas were accepted by the Assad regime because some of its businessmen controlled or bribed the checkpoints, pocketed the profits and shared them with the regime as well as with the rebel leaders in charge. This clandestine trade enriched all warring parties at the expense of the civilian population.[6]

Regarding the Syria Trust, its significance as a tool of control and income generation increased sharply after the conflict broke out. Like their foreign counterparts, Syrian aid organizations that wanted to become active had to join the Trust and contribute to finance the umbrella organization. The Trust also played a significant role in 'advising' international aid organizations to finance projects in regime-controlled territories rather than elsewhere. Moreover, the Trust offered its services in facilitating visas against a 'handling fee'.[7]

After analyzing this corrupt system through dozens of interviews with aid workers and decision-makers, Human Rights Watch (HRW) came to this sobering conclusion in a 2019 report:

> The Syrian government has rigged the system for provision of humanitarian aid, to ensure that the benefit to the state supersedes the needs of the population. In doing so, it has compromised each humanitarian organization or agency's ability to program and re-oriented priorities towards obtaining greater access and resources, instead of serving beneficiaries impartially. [. . .]

> Moreover, in some areas, where government rights abuses are systematic or widespread, financing government activities without an attempt to reform the system in which they are operating, risks a humanitarian response that is effectively financing a machinery of repression. The result is that rights of Syrians are subordinated to the demands of the authorities, leading to increased risk of discrimination in distribution of humanitarian aid based on political opinions and perceived loyalties, a failure to assess and act upon the key human rights violations facing the population, and in some cases, active contribution to and financing of human rights violators and ongoing human rights abuses."[8]

Haid Haid, in a *Chatham House* report, reached a similar conclusion:

> The Syria case shows the importance of reassessing the way that IHOs deal with a sovereign state. The government has been able to dictate the terms of cooperation to IHOs, despite it being a party to the Syrian conflict. It has systematically committed mass human rights violations including using chemical weapons and starvation as a weapon to force hundreds of thousands of civilians to submit. This led to extensive international condemnation of the government but did not change the international humanitarian approach, which has been to deal with it as a sovereign actor rather than as a warring party.[9]

HRW quotes several staff of local partner organizations who said that their employer had to maintain very close and regular communication with branches of Syrian intelligence in order to conduct their work. This interfered with their ability to meet humanitarian objectives. According to them, "intelligence branches could at any point request access to beneficiary data, provide approvals for aid distribution and oversight of delivery of aid to populations in need," and security services were also responsible for inspecting aid deliveries, accompanying convoys on their distribution routes, or being involved in approving humanitarian projects or rejecting them. "Instead of protecting or facilitating the operations, though," the HRW report continues, "they used their access to actively interfere with the delivery of humanitarian aid, confiscate supplies for personal use or resale, and remove life-saving supplies from aid convoys."[10]

In fact, the government had all the information necessary to demand changes or exert a veto on decisions about distribution of humanitarian assistance. Even UN decision-makers have conceded this, such as Ben Parker, OCHA's Syria country chief until February 2013, who stated: "In government-controlled parts of Syria, what, where and to whom to distribute aid, and even staff recruitment, have to be negotiated and are sometimes dictated."[11]

For example, in 2015 nearly 75 per cent of all UN aid delivery requests were ignored by the government, while only half of the rest reached their destination successfully, which equates to just over one-tenth of all submissions.[12] The fact that UN convoys drove on several occasions through areas deemed insecure by the government in order to deliver aid elsewhere clearly shows that security risks were used, at least in part, as a pretext to manipulate aid distribution.

In an advocacy report, the opposition-supported human rights organization The Syria Campaign summarized in 2016 that: "the UN has allowed the Syrian government to direct aid from Damascus almost exclusively into its territories.

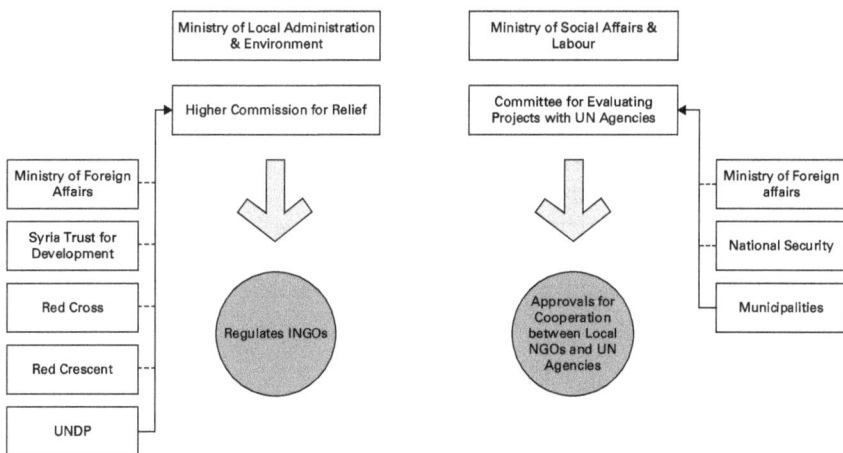

Figure 6.1 The Syrian government's organization of humanitarian assistance – in theory. In practice, the national intelligence and security branches (*mukhabarat*) called the shots.

In April 2016, 88 percent of food aid delivered from inside Syria went into government-controlled territory. 12 percent went into territories outside the government's control. In 2015, less than 1 percent of people in besieged areas received UN food assistance each month."[13] Reflecting on these figures, Syria expert Aron Lund points out:

> To be sure, many Syrian insurgent groups act in similar ways by routinely targeting civilians, seizing hostages, and preventing food and medicine from reaching besieged areas. Like the government, the rebels are known to block humanitarian convoys, steal deliveries, and impose political conditions on aid operations. But there is one major difference. Non-state actors may block roads, but they do not have the legal authority to stop an undesirable UN project by simply refusing to sign a paper, whereas the Syrian government has that power and exercises it liberally.[14]

Accordingly, the list of complaints against government authorities has grown over the years. Stalling in the authorization of convoys, last-minute withdrawal of given authorization, spontaneous blocking of convoys at the final checkpoint despite a government permit, removing highly needed items from humanitarian shipments such as surgical equipment, agricultural seeds etc.[15] Sometimes, such harassment of humanitarian work and IHL violations have been made public in an outcry of protest, while at other points the organizations on the ground have kept quiet in order not to jeopardize their relationship with the government.

Leenders and Mansour cite examples of how the government exerted pressure on UN agencies by influencing the overall narrative. According to their research, when OCHA drafted its initial needs assessment in 2012, the UN assessors hardly crossed lines and set their foot into opposition areas. Also, "state officials pruned the report that the assessors prepared and changed the draft's use of the word 'conflict' to 'events', insisted on the use of the term 'moving people' instead of 'internal displacement', and, most importantly, toned down both the scope and urgency of registered needs." The authors also hold that OCHA, under regime influence, underreported the number of besieged areas and of the affected population inside them.[16] Apart from direct government influence on even the operative internal processes of UN agencies, the lack of data and monitoring opportunities may have distorted reported results.

In 2016, OCHA itself conceded in a report that the majority of aid work inside Syria was delivered "with very light independent monitoring based on incomplete or non-existent assessment analysis," and that there was little data on the impact of aid operations. The report concluded:

> One area where the system (and OCHA) did not deliver was in assessing needs. Over five years into the conflict, there is still not an accurate picture of needs. Since 2012, the Syrian Government has effectively blocked attempts to do proper needs assessments, and access and security constraints have been huge. At various times, OCHA tried to get inter-agency needs assessments under way.

Nevertheless, the fact that the first unified assessment was only produced in 2014 indicates that more commitment and resources were required.[17]

In turn, the government manipulated its own data in order to increase the need factor for its own territories. The defected Syrian diplomat Bassam Barabandi in a conversation with this author referred to surveys conducted about internally displaced persons (IDPs) in Alawite areas. The result was: "When someone goes from Qardaha to a neighbouring village to work, the regime lists him as an IDP, sends the info to the UN and receives food baskets for him," Barabandi explains, "or when somebody from Lathakia does his military service in Damascus, the regime equally sends his name to the UN as an IDP for this purpose."[18] It should be added that opposition groups also inflated the number of inhabitants in besieged areas as they knew that they would get only a fraction of aid that they asked for. Even the UN itself sometimes inflated population figures because they knew that donors would give only a tiny proportion of what was really needed.[19]

Another of the regime's strategies for watering down the purely humanitarian need-based approach was to condition aid agencies' access to besieged civilians in the way that they had to deliver simultaneously to regime supporters into areas that the government could not access. This tit-for-tat approach often existed below the radar. Sometimes, however, it became more visible, as was the case in a UN-brokered deal during January 2016: UN agencies were given temporary access to the regime-besieged town of Madaya only if they provided aid to the predominantly Shia towns of Fuaa and Kafraya, which were under siege by Sunni rebels.[20] A less well known example comes from the battle of al-Qusayr in 2013, when MSF provided field clinics to the fighters of the Lebanese Shia militia Hezbollah, who fought on the Syrian regime's side, in order to maintain MSF's humanitarian access to civilians in the besieged city.[21]

A Syrian staff member at a humanitarian UN agency on the ground remembers a typical example of obstruction when opposition groups were still controlling rural Damascus. The ICRC had been working on a convoy for a month or two and had received approval from all necessary authorities. Finally, the convoy moved towards a village along the airport road. When it reached the last checkpoint, officials blocked the way and said "we don't care what Damascus said, even if you bring Bashar al-Assad!"[22]

Different levels of authorities would give different pieces of information to stop a convoy or the personnel (soldiers, *mukhabarat* or militias) manning a checkpoint would want to remove such a number of goods so that UN convoys decided to return to base – a tough decision when people were starving inside an enclave. Contradictory information may have been part of a stalling strategy or, just as plausibly given the country's increased fragmentation, a loosening of command chains. Journalists had similar experiences. A German TV reporter once told me that when his team showed a permit from Damascus to the armed guards at a checkpoint somewhere at the outskirts of Aleppo, they ridiculed them and said: "Documents from Damascus do not count here."

In other cases, UN convoys were harassed and came under fire. When the ICRC tried to send a convoy into the old town of Homs in September 2013, they were stopped several times. Security forces wanted to check the convoy again and again. When sunset finally arrived, they said that it was too dangerous now to enter, and that they should come back in the morning. The next day, when the ICRC attempted entry once more, government forces started firing at opposition positions inside Homs; the opposition forces replied, and the convoy got stuck in the crossfire.

In February 2014 a joint SARC/UNHCR convoy entered the old city of Homs. The government forces fired mortars on the area. When the humanitarian staff started offloading the convoy, the shelling killed some twenty-five local inhabitants. As one humanitarian worker recalls, the local people tried to protect the aid workers with their bodies and were injured or killed. After this incident, the local people started asking the UN not to come again, since every time they came, the bombing started.[23] The UN Resident and Humanitarian Coordinator Ali Al-Zaatari was part of the convoy and barely escaped himself. This was even more surprising since Zaatari had been criticized by many Western officials as being too regime friendly. The pictures of UN-marked SUVs delivering humanitarian aid, stuck amidst crossfire in narrow lanes, again symbolized the helplessness of the UN.[24]

Given the plethora of obstacles, and ongoing paralysis at the Security Council that could have enforced changes on the ground, diplomats looked to any available forum to address these issues. The Geneva-based Humanitarian Task Force (HTF), which is run by the Office of the UN Special Envoy for Syria, was an important platform for such debates. It remains a unique format where all countries involved – including (quite remarkably) the US and Iran in the same room – discuss humanitarian problems in Syria. Diplomats remember in particular former Senior Adviser to the UN Special Envoy, Jan Egeland, trying persistently – and often desperately – to create awareness through advocacy in his press conferences. Eventually, several small successes were achieved but as the military situation became ever more asymmetric, the government's appetite for cooperation waned. Without the advocacy of the HTF, the situation would have been even worse, as a German diplomat recalls.

Otherwise, the UN agencies on the ground have received criticism from diplomats and NGOs alike for choosing the easier path of least resistance in order to deploy their resources in areas where access was government approved. The UN was criticized that it did not negotiate tenaciously enough to enter hard-to-reach areas.

Omar Abdulaziz Hallaj, a Syrian scholar of architecture and urban planning, former CEO of Syria Trust (pre-2011), facilitator of dialogue processes and member of the UN-facilitated Constitutional Committee, elaborates on the criticism against UN agencies on the ground: "There has never been a comprehensive negotiation strategy on access. The government is happy to negotiate access with each and every actor separately. This diminishes negotiation power." Those agencies working from Turkey did this with equally poor coordination. "There is a health cluster, education, protection cluster etc. and these clusters don't talk to each other," Hallaj explains. "This created a gatekeeper economy on the ground; some people who work for the regime on the ground have taken up this role."[25]

Lack of coordination and internal turf wars are frequent reproaches made against UN agencies in Syria and more generally. In a 2016 Syria evaluation report, OCHA bluntly and self-critically admitted a lack of coordination and a great challenge for humanitarian leadership. However, the underlying reasons for this were the political divisions in the UN Security Council, which left the humanitarians to shoulder the symptoms:

> The Syria conflict has been characterized by deep divisions within the Security Council, leading to paralysis in attempts to resolve or contain the fighting. The split has constrained the UN's ability to act and meant that, at times, *humanitarian aid has substituted political action.*
>
> Against this highly challenging backdrop, the Emergency Relief Coordinator (ERC), supported by OCHA, has sought to exercise global leadership. As the crisis progressed, the quality of this leadership improved, with bold advocacy on behalf of people trapped by the fighting.
>
> The ERC sought to mobilize the humanitarian system to respond in Syria, with partial success. At times, the system has been slow and overly cautious. Its fault lines and fragmented nature have been sharply exposed by the highly contested nature of the geopolitics. The fact that the ERC struggled at times to bring the agencies with her should cause serious reflection within the global humanitarian leadership body, most notably the Inter-Agency Standing Committee (IASC).[26]

OCHA also conceded in this report that deploying "the best humanitarian leadership" to Syria and the region was hampered by the Syrian government and because of "differences of opinion with UNDP", the developmental branch of the UN family that has been accused of being far too lenient with the government in Damascus (UNDP receives both humanitarian and non-humanitarian funds).

This lack of coordination and lack of political support has additionally contributed to an asymmetry of power vis-à-vis a highly determined and well-organized government. The EU at some point attempted to encourage various UN agencies on the development side into coordinating with each other in the form of a consortium (UNDP, UN Habitat, FAO, WHO, WFP, UNICEF). Since 2016, the EU has conditioned development funding on that coordination. Reacting to this requirement, the UN created the position of consortium coordinator in Damascus. "At the same time, however," an EU project manager complains, "the humanitarian colleagues of UNHCR, UNDP, WFP etc. get hundreds of millions from humanitarian funds and channel them through Damascus without any critical analysis. The leverage that was supposed to be created by our consortium idea in the development aid is diluted by huge sums flowing into humanitarian aid, partly to the same UN agencies, without any conditions at all."[27]

The lead for the consortium's analyses lies with UN Habitat and not with the larger UNDP. Former UN Habitat chief, the Canadian Szilard Fricska, pursued this task with a great deal of energy, sources report, and exerted his influence on the government to whom he was regarded as uncomfortable and critical. Fricska's death in a plane crash in Kenya in early 2019 weakened UN Habitat and the consortium's position, however.

Another point of leverage that the Syrian government applied in order to exert its claim of sovereignty and control was granting or withholding visas for humanitarian or development personnel. This practice only intensified when the government regained the upper hand in the conflict, which created further project implementation problems. "Due to visa problems, we can no longer travel to Damascus as regularly as before," explains the EU project manager with the challenge of first-hand monitoring. "So we are losing contact with some Syrian channels and contacts."[28] In February 2015, the government expelled two foreign UN workers for negotiating humanitarian access with 'terrorist' rebel groups in Aleppo.[29]

The government's harsh line also affected other major actors who had experience in dealing with a difficult clientele. A former Syrian SARC employee remembers that when he and his colleagues faced difficulties in getting a permit for a convoy or any other problem, they would reach out to the colleagues from the International Committee of the Red Cross (ICRC). The employee told this author that, in his view, the main ICRC contact in Syria, Marianne Gasser, a Swiss national with an Egyptian family background, was a "nice old lady" but was "friends with the political leadership." This had an advantage, in that she was respected by the authorities and had regular access to them. The employee tries to describe the dilemma of her situation, however: "She was helpful in smaller, concrete cases. But in the long term, she spoke from a weak position and tried to be nice. She didn't have any impact on big decisions like a large convoy. Her goal was to serve her company, ICRC in Syria, as much as she could and not to be kicked out of the country."[30] In his opinion, in practice the national organization of SARC treated the ICRC like a "junior partner" although it received large parts of its funding from its mother organization.

When ICRC replaced Gasser with Magne Bath, who had the reputation of being tougher in defending humanitarian principles, the authorities let him run against a wall. He pushed hard for more humanitarian access. At some point, the government informed the ICRC – via SARC – that either he left the country or the entire ICRC had to leave.[31] The ICRC was faced with a tough choice. The employee recalls an ICRC staff meeting in which the organization told its employees that they had decided to take Bath out of the country in the organization's wider interest. "They wanted to stay inside Syria at any cost," the former employee says. After another replacement, Marianne Gasser returned to her old position. In March 2020, Gasser was appointed head of the UN Office of the Special Envoy for Syria (OSE) in Damascus. In this very different and political post, good access to the government can be helpful for mediation purposes. In addition, she had experience with the detainee file that – in the opinion of many Syrians – the UN mediation process had neglected over the years. And above all, she was granted a visa from the Syrian government when others were not. Again, the UN also in its political work was caught in a dilemma: submit to the conditions or to not work at all. The post of the head of OSE Damascus had been vacant for years because the Syrian government rejected visas for UN staff that were not acceptable to them.

Coming back to the ICRC's work in Syria, a Western diplomat who worked in Beirut for several years and took part in coordination meetings with the UN and other agencies, criticizes the ICRC and UN humanitarian agencies alike for having neglected protection issues during Gasser's term. It was widely known that the security apparatus of the Assad regime continued to persecute citizens, even after their return as refugees from neighbouring countries. In addition, many thousands of detainees were still kept in regime prisons under dismal conditions, were tortured or killed in regular mass executions.[32] Others were expropriated in their absence through Housing Land and Property (HLP) legislation.[33] When Western diplomats raised the concern with UNHCR that people disappeared upon their return to their homeland, its country director Sajed Malek answered: "We have Community Centres where people can go to and report their problems."[34]

The Western diplomat also complained to this author that ICRC did not pursue protection issues as insistently as its mission would have obliged them to. In 1990, the ICRC defined protection in a humanitarian context rather broadly and unspecifically as "all activities, aimed at obtaining full respect for the rights of the individual, in accordance with international humanitarian, human rights, and refugee law."[35] Niland argues from other contexts that "there is a long and sorry record of decision making by humanitarian actors who ignored and marginalized the critical need for protective measures when effective humanitarian action was their objective."[36]

In Syria, the ICRC has not even had the same access to prisons it has secured in other parts of the world. It is only able to visit some major facilities if it applies to do so well in advance. When OHCR, the UN Human Rights office, at one point attempted to initiate humanitarian food deliveries by the WFP to prisons in return for enhanced access for ICRC, the ICRC declined to take part, and the initiative died.[37]

Due to severe government restrictions and lack of initiative of some individuals or organizations, Human Rights Watch also concluded in its study that international humanitarians have lowered their bar of engagement. For example, "protection agencies have redirected sources to focus on 'soft' protection, such as raising awareness regarding sexual violence and developing community centres, rather than monitoring and reporting on detentions, mistreatment, violations of property rights, and restrictions on movement." According to HRW research, these policies translate into a series of gaps, such as "an inability to promote human rights of the population, or to protect them from abuses; inability to effectively consider the human rights implications of humanitarian, development, and reconstruction programming; an inability to mitigate or prevent human rights abuses directly related to their mandates; and an inability to establish independent and trusted protection and security guarantees that would fulfil one of the required factors to facilitate the return of displaced Syrians."[38]

On the other side of the spectrum, a highly assertive Syrian government strongly reminded ICRC and other humanitarian organizations on every possible occasion that they should not be influenced by the other side but remain 'neutral'. For example, when ICRC president Peter Maurer visited Damascus in March

2020, the government-backed media, echoed by Chinese and other outlets, ran a story with a barely veiled hint of displeasure: Then Syrian foreign minister Walid al-Moallem underlined "the need for the International Committee of the Red Cross (ICRC) to avoid politicization of its humanitarian work." It went on to emphasize that the Syrian government was keen to "maintain constant coordination and communication to overcome challenges and obstacles regarding the humanitarian work in the country." And Moallem "urged the committee to abide by principles of humanitarian work and prevent any attempts to influence or politicize its projects."[39] Once again, the international humanitarian organizations were taking fire from all sides. This hit also and in particular the humanitarian flagship ICRC and its Syrian member organization, SARC.

The Plight of the Syrian Arab Red Crescent in a Totalitarian System

According to the government regulations explained above, all international support activity in Syria was obliged to work under the aegis of the Syrian Arab Red Crescent or the Syria Trust for Development. SARC is the national partner organization of the International Red Cross with strict humanitarian principles derived from the Geneva Conventions. It came under particular scrutiny because of its self-imposed impartiality and neutrality, and because of the specific traits of the Syrian regime as well as the conflict itself: it was a highly polarized, immensely brutal, asymmetric scenario with an authoritarian regime of totalitarian nature as one party of war and, at the same time, as the High Contracting Party for humanitarian assistance.

The Ba'ath regime in Syria has been a totalitarian system since 1963 in which all organs of the state, including the shadow state, were under strict political control by the ruling dynasty and its security apparatus (*mukhabarat*).[40] This also applied to any national organization and to the slowly developing civil society and NGO landscape that emerged after Bashar al-Assad's ascent to power in 2000.

Therefore, by default, SARC too was a state controlled institution despite its humanitarian mission and nature, a potential mismatch that is mirrored in other countries as well. Until the crisis, SARC was even integrated into the Syrian government with a ministry of its own that was later abolished. During the war in which the ruling power demanded absolute and unconditional loyalty, SARC had to fight for its reputation as a credible humanitarian actor.

During the revolt, the entire healthcare and emergency system of the state turned into a frightening setting for many Syrian citizens. Reports circulated that wounded demonstrators were questioned, mistreated or abducted in state hospitals or ambulances that mostly carried SARC emblems. People feared the state services and sometimes preferred to suffer from a lack of medical treatment rather than risk torture in *mukhabarat* dungeons. Medical staff at the Tishreen Hospital in Damascus became particularly notorious for being accomplices to systematic torture. For example, mass executions at Sednaya Prison took place in presence of Tishreen medical staff. The corpses were brought to Tishreen Hospital where fake causes of death were established before the bodies were transported to mass graves near Damascus, as Amnesty International reported.[41] Early in 2011, Amnesty published a bleak report based on interviews with patients and medical staff that sheds light on abuses in Syrian state health facilities. Some of the conclusions were:

> The Syrian authorities have turned hospitals and medical staff into instruments of repression in the course of their efforts to crush the unprecedented mass protests and demonstrations that have wracked the country since March 2011. People wounded in protests or other incidents related to the uprising have been verbally abused and physically assaulted in state-run hospitals, including by medical staff, and in some cases denied medical care, in gross breach of medical ethics, and many of those taken to hospital have been detained.

In some instances, government security forces obstructed ambulances on their way to pick up wounded people. When the medical staff ferried the wounded to hospital, state security officials threatened SARC workers with violence or detention, and they interrogated wounded patients while the latter were being transported in ambulances. "They have ordered all those with firearm or other injuries related to the unrest to be directed to the military hospital, which is controlled by the Ministry of Defence, and such patients have been treated effectively as detainees while in hospital and held incommunicado." Furthermore, Amnesty reports:

> Hospitals have increasingly come to be seen as dangerous places for people whom the authorities suspect of opposing the government, and both private and public hospitals have been instructed to report to the authorities any patients who have sustained firearm or other unrest-related injuries. The security forces have regularly entered state hospitals in search of people injured during the protests, who are liable to be arrested, detained incommunicado and subjected to torture or other ill-treatment.

> [...] Doctors, nurses and other health workers who encounter people wounded in the unrest are now being confronted with a daunting dilemma – whether to obey the government's instructions and report patients to the authorities, knowing that this may very well lead to the patients' arrest, detention and possible torture, or to ignore or disobey those instructions, put their patients welfare first and thereby expose themselves to the risk of government reprisals.[42]

These findings don't lay blame on the entire organization of SARC, and SARC staff themselves were put under heavy pressure, as Amnesty describes. It was they who had to take the wounded to government hospitals. But direct criticism has been levelled at SARC as an organization by the Washington-based Syria Justice and Accountability Center in a 2019 report based on interviews with former SARC personnel.[43] It shows the pressure under which SARC had to work and the dilemmas in which its staff was caught. According to these findings, SARC teams received instructions from the government to limit their operations in opposition-held and contested areas. The SARC leadership passed on the message to its personnel, explaining that if they didn't do what the government said, they would not be able to operate at all. It was a tough dilemma. The report continues:

> By mid-2013, SARC teams in Damascus needed permission to enter all opposition-held areas. Approvals were rarely granted by the government, and even when they were, SARC volunteers were not guaranteed safety.
>
> [...] Syrian government memos obtained by SJAC show how intelligence agencies were giving explicit orders for its branches to work in close coordination with SARC to 'regulate the distribution of medical aid to these areas [under opposition control] and select the types of aid that will be allowed.

From 2013 onwards, dissenting staff members were increasingly forced out of SARC or even detained. The most visible case was that of Mohamed Raed al-Tawil, a SARC board member and coordinator of first aid teams, who was arrested by security forces inside SARC headquarters, and subsequently tortured during his four-month detention. Al-Tawil had been one of the leading figures pushing for humanitarian assistance to opposition areas. This incident changed SARC, as staff members report, and aid to opposition areas was further reduced. It created an atmosphere of fear among the workers because such thing could always happen again to anyone of them. Moreover, a system of mutual spying increased the intimidation.

A former SARC employee also told this author that direct cooperation existed between SARC personnel and intelligence officers who stole humanitarian supplies. He states pointedly: "We have thirteen security branches in Syria, and some call SARC the fourteenth."[44] In the end, the regime insisted on seeing and approving the CVs of potential new employees of SARC and other organizations active in Syria. HRW also reports testimonies of former SARC staff who witnessed incidents where intelligence officers collaborated with SARC in order to steal and resell humanitarian supplies. Another human rights activist shared images of aid supplies stored in what he said was an Air Force Intelligence branch office.[45] Local partners were much more vulnerable to such approaches and pressure. Intelligence operatives did not need to contact international personnel; locals were the lower-hanging fruit who would pass on the message.

In the later phase of the war, when the government became even more confident, SARC attempted to introduce tighter procedures for its international partners. In June 2018, SARC tried to exert an even firmer grip on those partners' internal processes, such as taking active part in recruitment processes and wanting to evaluate project plans. These attempts, however, were pushed back by international NGOs. Still, it shows the direction in which things were developing. The more the regime has consolidated itself, the bolder its attempts to interfere in the implementation of humanitarian principles have become.[46]

The war in Syria opened up primordial cleavages, too. For example, some Sunni SARC employees felt that their Christian colleagues were cooperating with the *mukhabarat*. The Human Resources officer was Christian, too, and employed predominantly people of the same faith, according to the former staff member. But he concedes that this is true for many other international organizations. And in Syria, far from all Christians supported the government. Not all of them were government informants, the source says, but some took open pro-government positions in social media, which should not be the case when working for a humanitarian organization.

Again, other SARC staff members were in personal danger because the government regarded them suspiciously – almost as opposition themselves – because they operated in rebel-held areas. For example, those SARC staff who had worked in the besieged neighbourhood of Eastern Ghouta took the evacuation buses to Idlib alongisde civilians and fighters in April 2018 because the government could not guarantee their safety.[47]

A former local UN humanitarian staff member told this author that SARC could do nothing without the consent of the government. In turn, the government trusted SARC much more than the UN or any other international organization, and therefore granted them more access in certain places. The former UN staffer defends the work of SARC personnel on the ground. He doesn't believe that SARC members did hand over patients to the *mukhabarat* for torture; or at least he is not aware of such a case. By contrast, he says, the vast majority of them were neutral: "I know colleagues who had great relations with all actors, from the government of Syria to radical Islamic groups. They are trusted by everyone."[48]

While even critics attest to the majority of local staff on the ground showing tremendous engagement and goodwill to do their best to deliver aid to the needy, judging the leadership of SARC was and remains difficult. The businessman Abdul Rahman Attar was SARC's head for several years during the crisis and had to balance regime demands against his organization's humanitarian mission. His links to the ruling regime were obvious, and part of the natural environment he worked in. A former representative of a Western non-humanitarian aid organization reported to this author his experience of 2012 and 2013 when SARC bought medical material from al-Attar's own companies. No proper procurement procedures were in place.[49]

Judgements on al-Attar as a person are split. Some criticize him as having been in line with the regime, while others argue that he was too reluctant to go as far as the regime wanted, so that he had to resign in 2016. I personally remember that Attar visited UN Special Envoy Lakhdar Brahimi in Geneva in 2014, and during the conversation, when Attar described the situation in Syria, the head of SARC began to cry. Working under such tough dilemmas had torn apart him, too. A European member of the Red Cross described Attar from personal encounters as a "real humanitarian" who "did his best under those circumstances."[50] In a 2015 interview with *Euronews*, Attar commented on the political events and tried to appear balanced, although there was a whiff of the regime's conspiracy narrative around the Arab Spring: "Unfortunately, calls for freedom, democracy and reform have been drowned out by the parties that have turned it into an armed conflict," he said. "We had hoped for a peaceful transition that would create a modern Syria. Unfortunately, the actions of regional and international forces forced the Arab Spring into another direction. The people of Syria didn't know what was going on."[51]

The Red Cross and its associates normally do not speak much about themselves and rarely deliver a counter-narrative even when they are attacked. But the intensive criticism against SARC made some PR adjustments necessary. In 2012, the IFRC published a defence of its member organization:

> The Syrian Arab Red Crescent (SARC) is saddened by allegations repeated in various media over the last week that the organisation is 'not to be trusted'. We are gravely concerned, and stress that these allegations are not only untrue, but are an affront to the sacrifices our staff and volunteers continue to make to gain access and provide humanitarian aid to all Syrian people in need, regardless of their nationality, religion, or political affiliation.
>
> [...] The repetition of unfounded allegations questioning the neutrality and trustworthiness of the SARC is not only undermining trust in the organisation and putting the lives of our staff and volunteers at risk, it is also hampering our efforts to deliver lifesaving aid on the ground, to all people in need.[52]

On the SARC website, Attar is still present – although he died in 2018 – with the following defence of SARC's work on the ground: "I stress here to mention SARC volunteers who face all kinds of danger, take the responsibility and give hope and calmness to vulnerable in compliance with neutrality and humanitarian principles irrespective of any other consideration."[53] As of 2020, sixty-five SARC staff members in Syria had been killed in the course of their work. Attar's successor, Khaled Hboubati, is another businessman. He owns Syrian casinos and shopping malls licensed by the government.[54]

Western Diplomats' Dilemma

Over time, the Syrian conflict scenario became increasingly complex and violent. Humanitarian actors, especially the staff on the ground, were in a predicament on many fronts. With limited resources, highly restricted access, and a High Contracting Party that was a strongly determined, smart and difficult negotiation partner, they had to weigh painful options. Often, they amounted to policy dilemmas of the worst kind. "Every humanitarian decision under such circumstances is also a political one," a German diplomat from the political side of the Syrian file phrased it, provocatively.[55] Humanitarians may not necessarily agree. But they can hardly deny that they were working in a highly politicized and polarized environment rather than in a political vacuum.

We also remember the comment of a diplomat from the humanitarian side who followed the Syrian crisis from 2013, and whose words probably resonate with many others involved in this diplomatic struggle: "I have been working for more than twenty years in the humanitarian sector, in NGOs and then in the government, but I have never seen such a politicized humanitarian situation and complex challenge like in Syria. Structures that exist to contain abuse of the system like the UN Security Council are blocked." Its permanent member, Russia, has become a party of the war with diplomatic support from China. In his earlier experiences, the same diplomat explains, conflicts were more clearly defined:

> You negotiated with two or three actors for access, and this was business as usual. In Syria, the humanitarian imperative counts less and less. Neither the government nor non-state actors give a damn about international law. I have no clue how one can resolve this. I'm clueless and shocked that we are turning in circles and that we discuss the same problems again that we had discussed five years ago.[56]

His feeling of helplessness reflected the overall *political* failure to find an answer to the brutal post-Arab Spring restauration. The humanitarian task was confined to curing the symptoms under worst conditions. The inhuman and cold-blooded approach of the Assad regime manifested itself both in its torture dungeons and on the battlefield alike, which is underlined by the following actions:

- so-called 'double-tap' attacks. When rescue teams and humanitarian personnel arrived to attend the aftermath of an aerial bombing raid, the site would be attacked again.
- targeting of civilian facilities like schools, bakeries etc. whether they were used as rebel shelters or not thus hitting pupils in class or civilians lining up for bread.
- targeting of humanitarian facilities like hospitals and nurseries and other medical equipment. In some cases, clearly marked humanitarian convoys were hit.
- applying mass starvation as a method of warfare.

In particular the final example points to the severe problem of access. The significant destruction inflicted on areas while obstructing access *cross-line* from regime-held areas to opposition-held areas has been an uphill battle that fuelled the debate about *cross-border* deliveries. Cross-border operations are deliveries entering Syria from neighbouring states that do not pass through government-controlled areas and thus provide relief to areas not controlled by the government. As we have seen in the above discussions on sovereignty, consent and obligations resulting from IHL and IHRL, cross-border activities remain controversial. The Syrian government for its part strongly insisted on single declarations from the UN context, in particular General Assembly Resolution 46/182 from 1991 that puts sovereignty and consent of the High Contracting Party into the focus.

Given the extraordinary violations of IHL and IHRL and the immense obstacles to access to the most vulnerable and needy, lively discussions took place in diplomatic circles around 2013–14 among several like-minded Western countries. The question was if they should stop funding humanitarian activities that were conducted in cooperation with the Syrian government and focus on cross-border deliveries only. The brainstorming among mostly Western diplomats about defying international practice hit several problems:

1. a relevant number of states would have to get on board to implement this policy effectively.
2. concerns existed that complete humanitarian disengagement may have represented a politicization of humanitarian work from their side.
3. good reasons existed for maintaining at least some cooperation with the government in order to reach more people on the ground in areas of government influence.
4. the UN is composed of basically all countries, therefore also of parties to a war. Those involved in Syria with their own stakes would have never cooperated in such a radical step.
5. the problem did not apply to Syria alone and was present in other conflict contexts too, if not always in scope but certainly in principle. What would have been the overall consequence of ending humanitarian activity?[57]

The other question was, however, whether the UN could have been more assertive within the constraints in which it needed to work. The rift between those who argued 'politically' and those who insisted on 'humanitarian impartiality and neutrality' was deep and ran through numerous foreign ministries. A leading German diplomat of the Middle East department of his country's Foreign Office at the outbreak of the Syrian crisis, remembers the discussions as follows: "There was a constant controversy with our colleagues of the UN department. They strongly defended the view that humanitarian aid had to follow the customary path. We from the political side, however, wanted to evaluate ways to find new options and adjust to Syrian realities. We didn't want to abandon the way the international system worked in general, but find new solutions in this specific case." For example, he suggested thinking about alternative partners to the SARC, which operated under heavy state control. But in the end, the more conservative interpretation of international law prevailed in the political leadership. "So, the problem was resolved according to a purely legalistic argumentation," the diplomat recalls in frustration.[58]

The counter-opinion to his view concentrates on the essential necessity of the UN Security Council and its stabilizing function for classical international law: without its approval, no decision can be taken that would violate a state's sovereignty. If the council is paralyzed, nothing can be done. Another high-ranking Western diplomat who supported this view and prevailed in his approach in his ministry justifies the stance that R2P was strongly conditioned on the Security Council's authorization and not on the scope of IHL violation: "It is unreasonable to hold that the magnitude of a humanitarian catastrophe overrides the vote of the Security Council," he argues, "since this would undermine international law." He adds: "It so happens that state governments do things that are not concordant with international law. You cannot make an exception each time." The diplomat adds that although it was obvious that SARC had to work under government control, Western Red Cross colleagues who cooperated with SARC had a high opinion of their colleagues' efforts. In order to prevent a humanitarian catastrophe in Syria, a military intervention would have been necessary, but it simply did not happen, the diplomat says: "If you want to be consistent, even humanitarian organizations would have had good reasons to call for a military intervention in Syria in order to stop the humanitarian catastrophe, but nobody of them would ever do that."[59] Indeed, there are enough humanitarians and academics who warn against humanitarians calling for intervention. This is simply not their job. Plenty of examples in history exist where humanitarians did so, or at least were embedded enough in a donor state's political and military agenda to make them favour intervention. This often turned out not to be in the best humanitarian interest either.[60] But politically and morally speaking, the diplomat's point is a strong one.

In the Syrian case, where an intervention may have suggested itself for humanitarian reasons, it is all too easy to criticize a lack of intervention, but the Security Council was against it, and Western countries had their respective domestic reasons for refraining from it. Therefore, the debates that condemned the actions of the Syrian government shifted from the paralyzed Security Council to the General Assembly or to the Human Rights Council. In these bodies, countries like Saudi Arabia – which themselves have a dismal human rights record – showed off as among the champions of the human rights discourse on Syria.[61]

Damascus or Cross Border: The Hard Choice

The gulf that existed between diplomats and political decision-makers within the same countries, and even within the same ministries, was mirrored in academic debates. A few progressive scholars of international law proposed diverging opinions to more conservative policy-makers. Michael Bothe, professor emeritus at Goethe University in Frankfurt/Main, for example, stated in a Legal Opinion in 2013: "[...] both the negotiating history of Art. 18 [AP II] and the practice of relief operations rather lead to the conclusion that the consent of the government in place is not necessary in this situation. *Thus, the consent of the Syrian government is not necessary for so-called cross border operations.*"[62] Bothe underlines his point by stressing that consent may not be refused for arbitrary reasons like national pride or "an intent to deprive a population of its means of sustenance in order to weaken its morale." It may be refused only for legitimate reasons such as a reasonable suspicion of abuse or the military necessity of combat operations on a temporary basis.[63] Bothe also pointed out that although a state may "abuse" its rights by withholding consent to relief operations, "in a practical perspective, however, it must be taken into account that undertaking a relief action without consent entails a high risk, regardless of the legal situation."[64]

Bothe focused his argumentation also on the right and duty of third states to facilitate relief actions under these circumstances. "In doing so, these third States also fulfil their responsibility to protect."[65] He argued that if relief actions are unlawfully refused, prevented or harassed, the affected organizations must be able to rely on other states for support against the state or other party acting unlawfully by refusing consent to the passage or delivery of relief. "Current international law thus provides a strong guarantee for humanitarian assistance."[66] This legal opinion that was tabled to decision-makers coincides broadly with the views of various other experts expressed at the beginning of Chapter 2 but in a more straightforward manner concerning Syria. It still constituted rather a minority opinion, and had no practical influence at that time.

Foreign ministries as well as the UN faced this policy dilemma. Giving up the conventional practice of humanitarian deliveries meant clearly taking a *political* stance against the position of strong UN member states. This again triggered the collective concerns of humanitarian functionaries that such a development might have collapsed the entire established system, tearing down the firewall between political and humanitarian work. In the end, the UN bit the bullet and reached an understanding with the Syrian government in August 2012 to accept the work under the strict conditions and limits imposed by Damascus rather than withdrawing from Syrian government areas in protest and as a last resort. This agreement allowed eight UN agencies (and initially the very limited number of nine international NGOs) to operate inside Syria within the framework of the UN Syria Humanitarian Assistance Response Plan (SHARP).

As a result, it has never been tested how the Syrian government would have reacted if the UN had seriously threatened or implemented its complete withdrawal. Damascus was very conscious of the value of UN presence, both in terms of international recognition and of practical benefits of international assistance, and could well have eased some of its conditions in tougher negotiations. The situation in Syria represented the opposite to other cases where a government simply blocked humanitarian assistance: in Syria, a government was in place that showed extreme interest in receiving humanitarian assistance through the classical channel, in strictly controlling this international support, and in benefiting from it.

Despite the legal controversy on the meta-level of events, cross-border operations had taken place on a regular basis since the beginning of the conflict. Several NGOs delivered assistance under dangerous conditions into opposition-held areas, mostly from Turkey to the north of Syria. Often, they were funded by the very Western states that, in their overall legal approach, were highly cautious and judiciously conservative but in their practical funding policy followed the consequent need-based argument. This frustrated the government in Damascus but since it had lost control over large parts of its territory, it was not able to prevent it. The consequence, however, was that those local humanitarian partners in opposition-held areas who received the funding and implemented the assistance were operating under highly dangerous conditions, often facing daily air raids by the regime.

Smaller NGOs that sneaked into opposition territory were in a difficult position. Very early on, they did deliver aid to the most needy when the large humanitarian apparatus was still working through the conventional channels in cooperation with the government. They established makeshift clinics, often underground, in areas where the bombs hit and did not operate in regime areas where the warplanes and helicopters loaded with bombs took off. But alongside the danger they faced on the ground, they had to confront a political problem, too. At the beginning of the crisis, the humanitarian camp in the foreign ministries tended to not recognize the smaller groups as humanitarian actors and denied them funding.

Those 'guerrilla NGOs', as one may call them due to their methods of operation, took great risks in going cross border in the early stages and in delivering aid and support right to the hotspots of fighting. Still, they were often considered as pro-opposition and thus as 'political actors'. Organizational and bureaucratic behaviour contributed to the fact that large sums were conveniently transferred as humanitarian assistance to the tried-and-tested UN organizations while funding a 'guerrilla NGO' entailed more argumentation and paperwork including the risk that the general auditing office may one day have inconvenient questions when checking on a ministry's accounting. Only over time were these smaller organizations able to establish themselves as serious humanitarian actors on the ground, too.

Examples of such NGOs are Mercy Corps, medico international or the Gaziantep-based Ihsan, which is registered in Turkey but run by Syrians. Although some of those small NGOs were able to deliver considerable assistance cross border, at times more than the UN,[67] obstacles to receiving funding and recognition remained. "In 2014 and 2015, potential donors were suspicious and checked our background very thoroughly," remembers a leading Ihsan staff member. Ammar Kahf from the Syrian think-tank OMRAN based in Istanbul, reiterates: "The non-UN actors, especially Syrian NGOs, were dealt with by applying a much higher bar. We did not cooperate with NGOs who got aid from the regime. UN agencies were bullying the Syrian NGOs on the opposition side to prove themselves to be 'neutral' by dealing with the regime and by avoiding Local Councils or other actors on the ground."[68]

Local Councils were civilian administrative structures that emerged in opposition areas during the upheaval, originally conceived by opposition-minded Syrians as a locally driven democratic alternative to the centralized Assad dictatorship.[69] They attempted to provide services for the population under opposition control. The UN did not consider them as neutral partners to work with on the ground. In their bilateral assistance, however, some Western governments did cooperate with Local Councils. However, only some councils were able to conduct truly democratic elections, and often they had little experience in handling deliveries and services. They were frequently hindered from functioning properly due to frequent air raids and destruction. Autonomous administrative structures that worked well ran counter to the government's narrative and were therefore particularly vulnerable to regime attacks. On the other hand, Local Councils had good access to information and to the needy, and their infrastructure was in place (as circumstances permitted). They represented the civil face of the revolution in contrast to the military offshoots, many of which radicalized over time.

Another complicating factor for humanitarian decision-makers was that local governance structures gradually slipped under the control of Turkey, an external party to the war. Others fell to radicals. In Idlib, where Local Councils had persisted the longest, given the government had lost the territory in 2012, they were gradually pushed aside by the so-called Salvation Government, a civilian off-shoot of the Al-Qaeda branch Al-Nusra or later HTS. But according to the principles of impartiality and neutrality, these were not insurmountable obstacles for cooperation, especially in the earlier years of the conflict.

Mazen Gharibeh, a senior programme manager at LACU (Local Administration Council's Unit based in Gaziantep), criticizes the UN for regarding Local Councils as unacceptable political players rather than as humanitarian interlocutors and partners: "The UN took a political decision not to engage with the local structures because they didn't want to jeopardize their presence in Damascus." With regard to the education cluster led by UNICEF and Save the Children, he recalls that working with local governance structures was seen as affecting the neutrality of their mandate and thus also their funding. In the health sector, as an exception, the local implementers on the ground had insisted that Local Councils be present at meetings of the health cluster, and OCHA accepted. In other cases, organizations engaged with Local Councils discreetly, for example, by hiring members of education directorates.

The problem was that with the principled rejection of cooperating with Local Councils, the UN agencies established makeshift alternatives and created parallel structures of service delivery, which weakened local governance structures. A competition emerged between these parallel structures and established local structures, Gharibeh says. As a side effect, the weakening of the bottom-up Local Councils in their function of service providers for the population played into the hands of the regime's war narrative of exclusive Assad state legitimacy and sovereignty as the better option for the people.[70] In this case again, humanitarian decision-making had also a political impact.

Criticism against the state-centred approach of UN agencies in Syria was reloaded in times of the coronavirus pandemic from March 2020 onwards. The WHO had delivered virus-testing kits to the Syrian government in February, but not to Idlib. "The northwest is not a country," a WHO spokesperson explained. Testing kits were distributed to government health facilities first, and only about one month later to cross-border areas. Given the obstacles to delivering supplies to a conflict zone, the WHO said, a month's delay was not bad.

The north-western province of more than three million inhabitants – one-third of whom trapped in overcrowded refugee camps – was under constant attack, and experienced one of the worst refugee dramas of this war during early 2020. The densely populated refugee hub was an ideal breeding ground for the virus. Turkey had closed its borders and the refugees were stuck in the remaining pieces of land of northern Idlib. For a long time, the regime denied that the COVID-19 was present in Syria at all. But soon, it became clear that the dismal conditions in prisons, improvised housing areas of IDPs and refugee camps were aggravating the disaster in a country where, according to the WHO, half of public hospitals and less than half of public primary healthcare centres were still fully functional,[71] predominantly in government areas, and where two-thirds of the medical staff had fled the country.

Many activists criticized the WHO approach: "You want us to wash our hands?" asked Fadi Mesaher, the Idlib director for the Maram Foundation for Relief and Development, referring to the recommended method of disinfection. "Some people can't wash their kids for a week. They are living outdoors." Syrian doctors reported that the international response to the coronavirus in Syria was slow to non-existent.[72] Others blasted the WHO for delivering testing kits to a government that had been bombing hospitals for nine years and which had caused the humanitarian disaster in the first place, which also led to the dire COVID-19 situation in Syria at a time when even entire medical systems of stable, developed countries had collapsed under the weight of the challenge. The opposition co-chair of the Syrian-Syrian Constitutional Committee in Geneva, Hadi Bahra, twittered: "It's a disgrace to know that WHO has allocated only 300 COVID-19 test kits to Northwestern Syria, [...] the lack of impartiality in the distribution of support must be corrected."[73]

The WHO justified its approach in a declaration: "Within the Whole-of-Syria approach, we are working from both inside the country and cross-border from Gaziantep in Turkey to accelerate preparedness and response for the first COVID-19 cases. We are working with partners to prepare the health system, the community and the leaders to respond quickly when the disease arrives." But the organization admitted that global shortages of testing kits and protective equipment was also hampering its work in crisis-hit countries such as Syria and Libya.[74]

The WHO's decision to cooperate primarily with Damascus on the coronavirus may have also resulted in the fact that it took almost two weeks to share crucial information with the Kurdish authorities in Syria's northeast: a man was taken to hospital in the Kurdish areas on 27 March 2020 and died on 2 April. His COVID-19 test was sent to Damascus. His test was certified as positive on 2 April. The Syrian government – hostile to the Kurdish administration – took three days to pass that information to the WHO in Damascus, which then took another eleven days to inform the Kurdish authorities. This is how a war environment helps spread a pandemic, since speedy interventions become impossible if crucial information is withheld for tactical reasons.[75] Some observers also speculated that allowing relatively free movement from Damascus to the Kurdish provinces was a deliberate move on the government's part to spread the virus in those areas.

The way in which the world's worst pandemic has manifested in Syria to date is only the most recent example of how important it is for international humanitarian actors to be able to act absolutely independently, impartially and in a neutral and professional manner (at best, the reporting of the COVID-19 case to the Kurdish authorities really did get lost in a bureaucratic black hole, but even that would be unprofessional).

On the other side of the spectrum, a number of smaller organizations decided not to cooperate with Damascus at all. In turn, they accepted obstacles and restrictions in their operations in Syria. Those were mostly the same ones that mainly – but not exclusively – operated cross border like Ihsan, medico international, SAMS (Syrian American Medical Society), UOSSM (Union of Medical Care and Relief Organizations), SEMA (Syrian Medical Association for Syrian Expatriates) as the main NGOs providing health services in the north, and also the Brussels based Jesuit organization Relief & Reconciliation International.

The rift between those who accepted working with the government side or avoided it went through the Church and religious relief organizations too. According to a senior humanitarian functionary, Pope Francis has been very critical towards the Syrian government's human rights violations. He deposed the Greek Catholic Patriarch Gregory Laham III, who had toured European capitals drumming up support for President Assad and warning against the potential doom of Christianity in Syria without him. Since the pope didn't trust his own administration when it came to Syria, he maintained some direct lines of contact to some Catholic functionaries who were engaged in humanitarian work, some of whom decided not to return back to Syria for the time being. By contrast, most Syrian church-based organizations have cooperated exclusively with the regime; one exception was the Jesuit Refugee Service (JRS), which worked on both sides of the frontline. Jesuit Pater Paolo, who disappeared in 2013 while intending to negotiate with IS extremists, was known internationally as a staunch regime critic. But the regime mounted its pressure on the JRS in 2016 and brought it back in line, which caused some members of the order to quit. "Within the church, there has been a very political controversy about the right way to act in Syria," a humanitarian functionary of a faith-based organization says.[76]

Those NGOs who kept their critical distance towards the government even when the conflict turned in its favour, faced increasing obstacles. While Ihsan concentrated on cross-border delivery to avoid regime cooperation altogether, medico was present in the North-East but also in the areas around southern Damascus where Palestinian neighbourhoods like Yarmouk were under siege (the district was pro-opposition initially and became IS controlled later on, another complication of the humanitarian work in place). When the government retook the areas, medico let the project fade out, although it would have been able to receive continued funding in this case from the German government. Medico's clear policy also derived from the bitter experience that their local partners became exposed to personal danger when the regime took the areas in which it operated. Three of them were arrested and disappeared in southern Damascus.[77] Nevertheless, medico continued to operate several small and rather clandestine projects inside regime-held areas with high security measures concerning communication in parallel to open projects in the North-East and Idlib.

What medico experienced is a pattern in Syria. As has been often the case in re-taken territory, the humanitarian situation became worse since many NGOs could no longer operate under regime control, and the government itself moved in with military force – but without state services. Apart from a lack of government engagement and governance in those areas, the regime did engage in the diversion of deliveries. Interviewees told Human Rights Watch that government restrictions translated into redirecting aid and funding away from areas previously held by anti-government groups toward areas where beneficiaries were considered loyal to the government without any consideration for the humanitarian needs of the beneficiaries.[78]

Nevertheless, the largest and continuous funding flow remained through the conventional route via the UN and Damascus. Also, almost all UNHCR warehouses were located in government-held territories; there was only one in initially pro-regime Kurdish areas, and none in opposition strongholds.[79] Therefore, humanitarian organizations that worked cross border kept criticizing the perceived lop-sidedness of UN humanitarian need assessments and deliveries. A leading staff member of a humanitarian NGO with a base in Gaziantep complained that with the increasing political and military asymmetry of the conflict, the 2019 UN needs assessment became equally asymmetric. The assessment took into account that access improved in the growing amount of territory over which the regime had regained control and as a consequence more people could be reached cross line. But at the same time, the humanitarian emergency situation in Idlib was worsening outside government control and as a result of government assaults. "The regime puts a lot of pressure on the UN to shift the needs from opposition area to regime areas," the NGO worker explained. "But the regime area is not bombed on a daily basis like in Idlib. We also have [the radical Islamist] al-Nusra present on the ground. There are a lot of high needs in the population."[80] While access in general improved inside regime areas, many people fled north, away from government areas, fearing persecution and the lack of humanitarian protection. "Need is increasing in the north," the humanitarian staff member says. "But the government of Syria plays its game and the UN goes along." He explains the difficulty of working with limited resources under these conditions. "So we have to go to Qatari charities or to other Gulf donors. This is a vicious circle because the money from the Gulf is even less 'neutral' than UN money but we have to do something for these people."[81]

Another Syrian former UN humanitarian worker disagrees and justifies the unequal share of distribution between government and non-government territory, especially in times of the regime's territorial expansion: "There is a massive need inside Syria too. You can't just ignore the people there."[82] Reports state that hundreds of thousands of people in areas recaptured by government forces in 2018 remain starved of basic aid, while international humanitarian organizations face increased pressure from Damascus as the regime attempts to expand or reinforce its role in shaping aid operations.[83] International organizations agree that the humanitarian situation across the whole country is disastrous, and there is little hope of an improvement anytime soon, particularly since with Lebanon – Syria's economic window to the world – on the verge of collapse and the coronavirus spreading uncontrollably. But even the so-called Assad loyalists (although the boundaries within the population are often much more nuanced) have been hoping in vain for some kind of peace dividend at the end of the war. Humanitarian organizations that have worked on the ground, especially in the later years of the conflict, state that "securing humanitarian access within the areas that have come under government control in the past two years is particularly challenging." The Norwegian Refugee Council (NRC) and Oxfam have reported "significant delays" and restrictions in scaling up their programmes in Daraa, Eastern Ghouta, rural Homs, and Deir el-Zor and Raqqa (under SDF control) governorates. According to these organizations, the approval process could take around four weeks but in some instances goes on for up to sixteen months.[84]

At the same time, the situation in cramped non-regime areas may get even worse if Russia and China maintain their strategy of terminating once and for all the already weakened UN cross-border mechanism. Even before the challenge of COVID-19 the humanitarian situation in regime and non-regime areas was disastrous. It would be all different if Syria had indeed become a 'normal' country that cared about its population, as Russian rhetoric suggested. But the regime has not shown any inclination to change its attitude vis-à-vis cross-line access. Even worse, after having destroyed large parts of the country's medical infrastructure, after numerous doctors and nurses were killed, persecuted or fled the country because they treated injured civilian protesters, the regime has proven unwilling and unable to handle coronavirus challenges. COVID-19 got out of control in Syria's regime and non-regime areas alike. Hundreds of thousands of deaths through violence are likely to be followed by thousands of deaths as a result of the virus thriving in conditions of catastrophic hygiene.

With a regime in place that focused solely on its grip on power, ignoring the needs of its population, and with cross-border options running out, the UN faced the continued humanitarian dilemma as from the outset of the conflict: should it operate in and from government-held areas only or not operate at all? While single states were able to act bilaterally against the regime's interpretation of unconditional sovereignty, the UN was not. The world body was bound to the decisions of an increasingly polarized Security Council.

Cross-border Controversies in the Security Council

It took three years of violence and destruction, and a high civilian toll predominantly in opposition-held areas, before the Security Council in a rare glimpse of unanimity adopted the so-called Cross-Border Resolution, Resolution 2165 of 2014.[85] This paved the way for the UN to officially fund and implement cross-border deliveries. Those P-5 countries critical of the perceived imbalanced UN humanitarian practice in government areas, such as the US and the UK in particular, now had a reason to spend money once more on UN lead operations with fewer concerns.

The cross-border resolution was a breakthrough after several declaratory attempts to soften Damascus' policy. One of those attempts was made by the General Assembly in May 2013 to the effect that *"demands* that the Syrian authorities facilitate the access of humanitarian organizations to all people in need through the most effective routes, *including by providing authorization for cross-border humanitarian operations* [. . .].".[86] In the same sense, the Security Council, in a presidential statement on Syria in 2013, enjoined the Syrian authorities to remove impediments for humanitarian action through "promptly facilitating safe and unhindered access to people in need [. . .], where appropriate, *across borders from neighbouring countries* [. . .].".[87]

The cross-border Resolution 2165 went further, with a more solid and practical approach. It allowed UN agencies to bring assistance across four border crossings from Turkey, Iraq, and Jordan in order "to ensure that assistance, including medical and surgical supplies, reached people in need throughout Syria through the most direct routes." Politically, and in an international law perspective, this resolution added value insofar as the UN plays a political and agenda-setting role beyond the actual aid it delivers. One has to bear in mind, however, that nothing much changed for NGOs *not* funded by the UN, since they used various other border crossings, too, and continued to do so.

The new cross-border mechanism was placed under the authority of the Secretary-General designed to monitor, *with the consent of neighbouring countries and notification by the United Nations to the Syrian authorities*, the loading of all humanitarian relief consignments. The resolution also affirmed that it would "take further measures" in the event of non-compliance by any Syrian party. It noted that the number of people in need of assistance, by 2014, had grown to over 10 million, including 6.4 million internally displaced persons and more than 4.5 million living in hard-to-reach areas, and that over 240,000 were trapped in besieged areas, according to the Secretary-General.

The Russian Federation emphasized, however, that there was *no trigger* in the text *for the use of force* in the event of non-compliance and said that the text reflected his country's concerns for the *respect of Syrian sovereignty*, as well as recognized Syrian efforts to cooperate with humanitarian aid delivery. In other words, with such a politically polarized Security Council, the threat of "further measures" against Damascus in the case of non-compliance was nothing but a symbolic diplomatic achievement.

The rest of the resolution's language also had to be diplomatic enough to bring together the diverging interests of the divided Council. Obviously, the government in Damascus, which had been under immense military pressure in 2014 before the Russian intervention, criticized this resolution and kept trying to work against its extension in regular intervals. It was rising international pressure and outrage at the deteriorating humanitarian situation in Syria, sieges and other blatant violations of IHL and IHRL that led to the point that also Russia and China were no longer able to ignore them entirely.

For UN-OCHA the cross-border Resolution was an important step that paved the way for expanding the UN agencies' reach and the one of their contractors. It represented also a creative piece of diplomacy that included a very practical manual. The conditions of Resolution 2165 entailed a so-called UN Monitoring Mechanism (UNMM) coordinated from the Turkish city of Gaziantep.[88] Trucks that came from the Turkish, Jordanian or Iraqi sides were checked by UN agencies or their contractors in order to confirm that the loaded goods were indeed of humanitarian nature only. Subsequently, the Syrian government was *notified* of an upcoming shipment, since the resolution overruled the necessity of formal consent by the government.

This certainly constituted a humiliation of the sovereignty-centred Syrian government, and all these checks and precautions had to be put in place to bridge the wide divide in the Security Council. UN-OCHA reacted swiftly. Only a few days after the resolution was adopted on 14 July 2014, OCHA conducted the first checks at the respective border crossings in order to facilitate the delivery of aid as quickly as possible. It created facts on the ground before any political manoeuvres from either side could have diluted the practical consequences of Resolution 2165.[89] However, some on-site humanitarian implementers pointed out that the monitoring mechanism absorbed many resources, and that similarly strict controls were not applied for trucks moving in government-held areas.

A former UN humanitarian staff member on the ground points to the unusual difficulties that the cross-border situation entailed. The work became very complex with three hubs of humanitarian work: Damascus, Gaziantep and Amman. "This is unique and not similar to any other international contexts," the humanitarian worker says. "It's very difficult to work like this. But it's not the UN's job to speak openly about their difficulties with the government. They would be kicked out immediately."[90] The former UN staffer emphasizes another dilemma inherent in this work: Turkey has become a major hub for cross-border humanitarian aid but, at the same time, this neighbouring country has become party to the war itself, occupying Syrian territory. Therefore, he says, it was an incomprehensible move for the UN to establish an OCHA regional headquarters in Istanbul in 2019. According to this interlocutor, he left the UN because it had lost its credibility in terms of impartiality and neutrality by delivering such a prestigious gift to Turkey under an erratic President Erdoğan. This decision was controversial within OCHA too, but regarded as a political balancing act that was also linked to the UN Secretary-General's re-election bid.[91] This shows again how quickly the UN can get under attack from both sides.

With regard to the UN's cross-border struggle with the Syrian government, the more asymmetric the conflict constellation became in its favour, the more Damascus tried to push away perceived infringements on its sovereignty. In parallel, on the macro level, relations between Russia and the US, and indeed the West in general, became increasingly sour. In 2019, Russia – meanwhile being the main political and military player in Syria in a division of labour with Iran – pushed for a termination of cross-border deliveries altogether. In a fierce tug-of-war in the Security Council, arguments pro and contra such deliveries were exchanged once more. But much more than that, the mutual attacks on the Council's decision-making displayed the deep rift far beyond Syria that was separating the opposed international camps.

The temporary compromise found in January 2020 was Resolution 2504,[92] which reduced the officially permitted border crossings from four to two, and even this lasted only for six months. Russia's strategy was to suggest normalization in Syria with the government fully in charge. However, the reality looked different. Despite massive Russian and Iranian support, the government in Damascus controlled merely about 70 per cent of its pre-war territory. The frontlines have increasingly stagnated, with Turkey controlling large areas in the north, and cross-border operations have become a normal routine for many non-UN-funded NGOs. So the effect of ending the legal status of cross-border delivery might be limited, as some diplomats conceded. But the *symbolism* of reducing UN cross-border options in the midst of an ongoing humanitarian crisis was huge. Humanitarians insisted nevertheless that channelling the massive UN aid flow through two border crossings only, instead of through four, did have an impact.

In the debate in January 2020, UN-OCHA chief Mark Lowcock criticized the continued "inadequate humanitarian response" of the Syrian government despite the de facto re-conquest of several of its territories. Western states criticized cutting the lifeline for millions of Syrians, especially with the war in Idlib escalating. The UN said 2.7 million people in north-western Syria and 1.3 million in the north-east relied on aid from their cross-border operations. According to OCHA, around

30,000 UN aid trucks had gone into Syria through the border crossings since the operation began in 2014. Altogether, some four million people in northern Syria were supported by UN cross-border aid. Western diplomats said the closure of the Iraq crossing would cut off 40 per cent of medical aid to north-eastern Syria. "There is no plan B. There is this operation, which helps hundreds of thousands of people and has done so for a very long time," said an OCHA spokesman. "It is the only viable, sustainable method that we have for reaching these people in need so it is critical that we get renewal of the provisions."[93]

The US described the reduced resolution as "grossly inadequate." "We gave the Russians an inch and they took a million," US Ambassador Kelly Craft said of efforts to reach a compromise. Britain's UN Ambassador Karen Pierce accused Russia of politicizing the issue: "Syrians will suffer needlessly as a result of this resolution. Syrians will die as a result of this resolution. [...] Syrian people have seen many sad days since 2011, but this day is potentially one of the saddest because it is the first time that a Security Council member has chosen to play politics with humanitarian assistance."

China and Russia, by contrast, warned not to politicize humanitarian aid. Russian Ambassador Vassily Nebenzya said the situation had changed dramatically and that the Security Council action should reflect that. "All these cries about imminent catastrophe, disaster, which the North-East faces if we close one cross-border point is totally irrelevant because humanitarian assistance to that region is coming from within Syria," he told reporters. Chinese Ambassador Zhang Jun called the Western claims a "totally groundless and unwarranted" display of "power politics." "Do you think we are still in a period of colonialism and the whole world has to side with the US and the UK?" he asked. "The time has long gone."[94]

Syrian UN Ambassador Bashar Ja'afari suggested that champions of the cross-border aid system wanted to "continue to interfere in our domestic affairs."[95] He elaborated in Syrian state media that Syria, since it had been fighting the "terrorist war" imposed on it, had exerted "its best efforts to guarantee the continuation of providing the basic services and offer humanitarian aid and support to all its citizens without any discrimination." He affirmed that improving the humanitarian situation in Syria required supporting the state's efforts and lifting the international sanctions imposed on the Syrian people. He added that his government and its main partners, like the Syrian Red Crescent and many civil associations, "have engaged in the humanitarian work in a serious cooperation with UN related agencies and many others." Ja'afari emphasized the core elements that his government was focused on also and in particular with regard to the government's interpretation of international law and standards: "Syria has facilitated and offered support to all international organizations with adhering to Syria's sovereignty, independence and territorial integrity as well as the principles regulating the humanitarian file included in General Assembly Resolution 46/182." He went on to say that there were many humanitarian, moral and legal impetuses behind Syria's stance in rejection of extending the authority of the cross-border resolution.[96]

Different political and legal interpretations were at loggerheads in the Council once again. The Syrian government's side insisted on the strict application of hard state sovereignty and the need for consent of the host government to any humanitarian activity coming from outside. The opposing side, including UN-OCHA, pointed at the Syrian government's ineffective performance in granting humanitarian access to its population without discrimination. This was an important and, at the same time, devastating conclusion that shed light on the Syrian regime's attitude vis-à-vis its own population: violations of humanitarian standards within areas of regime control continued and cross-line access to the needy remained heavily restricted. In other words, the gradual expansion of Syrian regime control on Syrian territory did not necessarily improve the humanitarian situation, especially in those areas of strongest need.

Aron Lund writes that UN assistance amounted to only about one-fifth of the total cross-border aid volume. The rest came from NGOs. In addition, trade played a role in sustaining millions of people in the north of Syria outside government control. But aid officials insist that Resolution 2165 had been a key to the Syria relief operation, in large part because of the leadership, logistics and political cover the UN's role offered.[97]

In July 2020, the cross-border stand-off in the Security Council repeated itself when UNSC Resolution 2504 expired. The world body once again became the a battleground as the international political climate deteriorated and splits in the Council widened. The fate of millions of people in Syria turned into a punchbag for geopolitical and ideological controversies.

Russia and China wanted to link a condemnation of sanctions on Syria imposed by the US and the EU to the approval of cross-border humanitarian access. In their view, it was primarily the sanctions that were responsible for the current humanitarian crisis and not the Syrian regime and its warfare. Amidst the coronavirus pandemic, a stagnant political process in Geneva and growing East–West tensions, the debate became even more heated than usual. In a rare outburst of personal frustration, the German ambassador to the UN, Christoph Heusgen, who happened to preside over the Council that July, told his Chinese and Russian counterparts to report back to their capitals that he had asked: "How those people who gave the instructions to cut off the aid of 500,000 children . . . are ready to look into the mirror tomorrow."[98] The Chinese counterpart rejected the "lecturing" of their German colleague. China and Russia condemned the German negotiation strategy that, in their view, intended to stigmatize both countries publicly instead of finding a solution.[99] This also shows that public perception continued to matter. The cross-border debate returned the Syrian crisis to worldwide headlines. People watched the humanitarian crisis in Syria with dismay and condemned the political bickering.

In the end, the compromise found by penholders Germany and Belgium, cast in UNSC Resolution 2533, reduced the number of border crossings to one bottleneck but extended their validity to one more year. Russia and China, which abstained, probably intended to avoid public stigmatization on this issue all too frequently. The successful vote came only after two failed votes on Russian proposals and two vetoes by Russia and China of resolutions drafted by Germany and Belgium. This increased Russian UNSC vetoes on Syria to sixteen since 2011. There was another interesting twist to this outcome: while Russia and China continued to blame the situation in Syria on terrorism, claiming that it was 'international terrorists' that benefitted from cross-border operations, they precisely chose Bab al-Hawa as the only border crossing through which the UN was still allowed to deliver humanitarian assistance. This 'windy gate' (in its Arab translation) between Turkey and Syria is controlled by the radical Islamist group Hayat Tahrir al-Sham (formerly Al-Nusra). While undoubtedly such groups did also profit from humanitarian movements inside their territories as the regime did, this decision made it easier for Russia and China to take up their familiar refrain of international support to terrorists whenever necessary.

Chapter 7

IN THE PILLORY: THE UN'S SYRIA DILEMMA

The UN-led humanitarian response in Syria has been coordinated from multiple locations inside and outside the country, partly in reaction to the difficult working conditions under the Syrian regime. Complementary cross-border assistance was set up from Turkey, Jordan and Iraq, as long as it was possible with the consent of the UN Security Council. The humanitarian hub in Damascus was established to serve people in need in government-held areas and was responsible for cross-line assistance, too. This was the toughest aspect, especially when it came to besieged and so-called 'hard-to-reach areas' (actually often a euphemism for places under siege). The UN called their efforts the 'Whole of Syria Approach', which is co-led by the Resident Coordinator/Humanitarian Coordinator (RC/HC) in Damascus as well as the Regional Humanitarian Coordinator (RHC) based in Amman. In this constellation the UN has overseen relief operations since 2014.

The regime in Damascus was obviously displeased with this dual arrangement since it was an effort to bring to the table both the cross-border humanitarian actors and those from within Syria so that they could coordinate, agree on priorities, strategic vision and so forth. Such an arrangement had become a way out of the dilemma that UN representatives in Damascus could not visit cross-border operations in Gaziantep (Turkey) or those coming from Iraq or Jordan. A senior former UN official told this author that this structure helped bring teams "closer" and agree on common vision and strategy, as part of a US$3.5 billion annual humanitarian plan for Syria. According to his assessment, the post of the Regional Humanitarian Coordinator was crucial in advocating for protection and in voicing issues that were challenging to deal with from Damascus due to the politicization of the crisis.

The parameters of the humanitarian response in Syria were set by the Humanitarian Response Plan (HRP). In Damascus, the Resident Coordinator/Humanitarian Coordinator (RC/HC) has been leading the Humanitarian Country Team that convenes senior representatives from across the humanitarian community – including from the UN, international NGOs and local organizations in order to develop common policies and advocate with the government on behalf of the response plans. The RC/HC plays a crucial role inside Syria and has been in the main line of political fire. He is the key advocate with senior members of the Syrian government on strategic access issues. In addition, there are Area

Humanitarian Country Teams chaired by the UN on provincial levels, including in Aleppo, Homs, Qamishli and Tartous (which is responsible for government-held parts of Idlib), as well as one covering the southern governorates.

Complicity with Evil?

After early skirmishes with humanitarian organizations like SARC, mounting criticism of the UN's work in Syria has been aired publicly in articles in the press and academic studies since 2016. This clearly added to the more general crisis of credibility that the UN has been facing in Syria, not only with regard to professionalism and humanitarian principles but also in a series of failed attempts to mediate this crisis politically. In both fields of action it has been perceived as toothless and helpless. Its main organ of enforcement, the Security Council, has been paralyzed in this conflict, and there have been no sufficiently committed and coordinated international efforts to support the UN in shaping a political solution to this war. The UN's position in this highly polarized and complex scenario has been definitely a very difficult one, although part of a larger bleak picture with regard to the stalled UN efforts in Libya, Yemen or Westsahara, for example. The big question regarding flaws in humanitarian assistance is to what extent UN decisions were taken by individuals or in a larger context that were still avoidable if basic rules of professionalism, humanitarian principles and general UN norms had been adhered to. Was the humanitarian Neutrality Trap really inevitable?

Criticism of the UN's conduct at key moments of recent history has been aired several times, even from within the UN itself. One such occasion was the report on lessons learned from UN peacekeeping operations produced for the millennium summit in September 2000. The Report of the Panel on United Nations Peace Operations is also known as the Brahimi Report, named after Lakhdar Brahimi, the former Algerian foreign minister, who was the successful UN mediator in ending the civil war in Lebanon in 1989, and not-so-successful UN/LAS Special Representative for Syria from 2012 to 2014. Brahimi has become known for his sharp analysis and frankness, and he was also harsh in his disappointment at the UN's performance after the political and humanitarian disasters in Bosnia-Herzegovina and Rwanda in the 1990s.

The panel of experts who scrutinized the UN's peacekeeping performance came to the devastating conclusion that "no failure did more to damage the standing and credibility of United Nations peacekeeping in the 1990s than its *reluctance to distinguish victim from aggressor.*" And: "Impartiality for such operations must therefore mean adherence to the principles of the Charter and to the objectives of a mandate that is rooted in those Charter principles."[1] Adherence to the traditional principles of impartiality, respect for national sovereignty and use of force only in self-defence may result in the UN's *"complicity with evil."*[2] This happened in Srebrenica and Rwanda, and – one can now add after more information has come to light – may also apply in different ways in Syria where the UN was delivering services perhaps too uncritically to a regime that killed its own people.

The Millennium Summit's Peacekeeping Report contained remarkable passages that called for very solid UN post-conflict engagement to avoid the Neutrality Trap. Brahimi recommended that the UN stay on as a kind of *Ordnungsmacht* or even occupying power delivering services, establishing a functioning and attractive investment environment, creating a banking system, collecting taxes, running schools and even imposing a "common UN justice package." This is a far cry from today's returning notion of hard state sovereignty. When the state leaders, some of them heading predatory and oppressive regimes, endorsed the Brahimi report, knowingly or unknowingly, they "made more vulnerable their own tin-pot sovereignty," as Robertson observes.[3] Twenty years later, things look quite different. While looking at failures in Syria, it makes sense to look at the Brahimi Report again more closely who put the fingers into the organization's wounds:

> Put simply, the United Nations is far from being a meritocracy today, and unless it takes steps to become one it will not be able to reverse the alarming trend of qualified personnel, the young among them in particular, leaving the Organization. If the hiring, promotion and delegation of responsibility rely heavily on seniority or personal or political connections, qualified people will have no incentive to join the Organization or stay with it.[4]

Political sensitivity and judgement is crucial also for humanitarian personnel, especially when operating in such dilemmatic situations as in Syria. The UN work culture pointed at by Brahimi and his panel has been subject to frequent criticism by other former high UN officials, too. Charles Petrie, who resigned from the UN in Burundi as Assistant Secretary-General in 2010, emphasized several structural problems to this author: UN officials generally shy away from conflicts with governments not only because they may share the incumbents' claim of statehood and sovereignty but also because "there exists an unwritten rule in the UN that if you become *persona non grata* in a country, it's not good for your career." Conflicting opinions and "incredible tensions" between UN staff who are based in a government's capital and those in the field in rebel-held territory also hamper a common approach. Those in the capital often "suffer from Stockholm Syndrome: They start to parrot the regime's line. They lose their sense of balance," says Petrie, speaking from his experience in the Democratic Republic of Congo. Similar to Brahimi's criticism of a lack of a meritocracy inside the UN system, Petrie says there is a problem with the senior UN leadership: "People are 'recycled' so much without assessment of their previous performance. Therefore, people keep repeating their mistakes." Concerning the humanitarian work, he adds: "The UN has not sufficiently participated in the reflection of impartiality and neutrality."[5]

In the discussion about state sovereignty, we saw the importance of narratives that strengthen or weaken political practice and, in the long run, international customary law. In a harsh account of the UN's role in this regard, Leenders and Mansour argue that the UN has unnecessarily and artificially reinforced the Syrian government's claim for unconditional state sovereignty through the behaviour and declarations of high-ranking UN humanitarian functionaries. They did this at a time when the government's legitimacy was arguably at stake, first, due to a large popular upheaval, and, second, when it lost large parts of its territory. "The Syrian case suggests that effective state sovereignty claims at times of armed conflict have been catapulted back into the international realm because of the regime's projection of its categorical state sovereignty assertions onto and through the largest UN-led humanitarian assistance effort in decades," Leenders and Mansour write. They also detail "how the Syrian regime's injection of its state sovereignty claims into the humanitarian aid effort gave it access to critical benefits and resources produced by the 'humanitarian space' built by UN agencies and international nongovernmental organizations (INGOs). At times of steep challenges against it, these benefits and resources were critical to the regime's resilience."[6]

As an example, Leenders and Mansour quote former UN RC/HC coordinator Yacoub Al-Hillo, who emphasized on Syrian state television that the UN was providing aid in Syria at the invitation of the Syrian government, according to international law, and following government approval. Hillo continued: "We recognize and respect Syria's state sovereignty despite the difficult situation and the extraordinary circumstances." He also described UN agencies' headquartering in Damascus as "something natural and self-evident."[7] Thus Hillo strengthened the narrative of a party to the conflict, not just of a host government in line with *one* interpretation of international law. Obviously, he needed to establish a good working relationship with this government, given that the UN had decided to cooperate with it. Undoubtedly, the Sudanese national had to walk a tightrope like many of his colleagues. Others describe Hillo as a strong advocate against sieges and the denial of access, who was engaged in daily struggles with government officials over access. He and his colleagues entered besieged areas in person, sometimes against the will of the regime and sometimes under fire.[8]

Those who had criticized Hillo soon became even more disappointed with his successor, Ali Al-Zaatari (in post 2015–19), a Jordanian national of Palestinian origin. A Western diplomat, who regularly participated in the UN coordination meetings in Beirut and Amman, recalls that Zaatari considered any criticism of the way in which the UN handled humanitarian assistance in Syria as "politicizing humanitarian aid." He was reluctant to brief Western diplomats in Beirut and evaded more detailed questions. "Zaatari said that the Western diplomats should come to Damascus if they wanted to be briefed by him, knowing full well that they didn't have diplomatic relationships with Syria and wouldn't even get visas," the diplomat says and underlines that this fed into the insistent sovereignty claims of the Syrian government. Damascus strived to achieve diplomatic normalization and money for early recovery and reconstruction without changing any of its political practices. Some UN representatives, like Zaatari, encouraged donors to consider reconstruction unconditionally, while others – such as the Geneva-based UN Special Envoy for Syria – were struggling in vain to keep the government engaged and to mobilize the last remaining incentives for it to take part in a peace process that aimed for political reforms. The Western diplomat says that Zaatari talked in derogatory terms about his UN colleagues who worked cross-border from Gaziantep "probably because he didn't consider their work to be legitimate."

According to his personal experiences, the diplomat recalled that Zaatari tried to marginalize the UN-colleagues from OCHA who "were more consistent in insisting on humanitarian principles." And he pushed back against a stronger role for human rights colleagues from OHCHR in the information-gathering activities of the Syria country team. Reflecting on the UN's personnel decisions, the Western diplomat wonders: "For some reason, the UN leadership in Syria were often still attached to old socialist Pan-Arabism and thus saw the authoritarian regimes of [Egypt's President] Sisi and [Syria's President] Assad as the best model."[9] Bassam Barabandi, a defected Syrian diplomat based in Washington DC, focuses in on this issue, pointing to staff from Egypt and Sudan in the UN's Syria teams. Both countries are known for their oppressive intelligence systems. In Barabandi's view, they don't work for the UN but in their own national security services: "For example, there's been a deal between Sudanese and Syrian intelligence from mid-last decade that Sudanese report all NGO activities to Syrian intelligence."[10]

Other critics have attested the Stockholm Syndrome to UN functionaries in the Damascus 'bubble' of state-controlled narratives. Such symptoms include an unnecessary identification with the regime that they actually have to confront as an interlocutor in difficult negotiations. As a German humanitarian diplomat recalls, within the UN system differing behaviours vis-à-vis the regime existed. Echoing the assessment of other diplomats, according to his experience, OCHA tended to push more strongly towards the adherence of humanitarian principles. As a consequence, they only very rarely received visas for Syria. The humanitarian diplomat says that UNHCR worked more closely with the government, and UNDP as a development actor anyway. This was also true for the WHO, he said. Diplomats well remember the incident when a WHO functionary thanked the donors "in the name of the Syrian government." The diplomats present at this meeting shook their heads in disbelief.[11]

Faced with increasingly critical questions, some UN functionaries made statements that did not really improve the situation. In an interview with *The National* in 2017, Amin Awad, UNHCR Bureau Director for the Middle East and North Africa, said: "I reject the argument that the UN is working with cronies of one regime or another." He continued: "For us, it is secondary who is who. I do not have a mechanism where we comb every single contract to see do you have one, 10 or 90 per cent connection with the regime or UNHCR on aid to Syria. [. . .] You are in a country and you have to deliver."[12] According to the interviewer, Khaled Yacoub Oweis, the UN exerted a great deal of pressure on the Abu Dhabi-based newspaper to withdraw this interview but *The National* refused.[13]

The same Western diplomat who was based in Beirut also recalls that Awad openly voiced encouragement for more refugees to return to Syria, knowing that the proper UN protection thresholds were not nearly fulfilled. Numerous incidents were reported of Syrian refugees from Lebanon or Jordan being killed or disappeared upon their return. "It was because the regime entertained this narrative of normalization and refugee return," the diplomat says, so Awad's policy "was an unconcealed UN contribution to regime legitimation." It was major donor countries, in particular the US, the EU, UK, France and Germany, who pushed back against the discussion about unconditional normalization. Some decided to re-direct a proportion of their funding towards host communities in neighbouring countries instead of UN projects operating in Syria itself.

Contracting Dangerous Bedfellows

The diplomatic – or undiplomatic – activities of some leading UN personnel also seemed to reflect priorities on the ground. Protection issues were neglected by UN agencies, as the above-mentioned Western diplomat criticizes from his own experience of numerous meetings with UN agencies: "I found it untenable that, in the Syrian context, we were channelling 90 percent of our humanitarian funding to the UN without a guarantee that the assistance is strictly distributed according to the criteria of humanitarian need or impartiality."[14] Similarly, HRW quotes a humanitarian worker who conceded: "The donors try to make protection programming the first line of every budget. What they don't understand is that in an operating environment like this, we cannot work on real protection."[15]

Ibrahim Olabi, founder of the Syrian Legal Development Programme (SLDP), met with UNHCR's Amin Awad at the Palais des Nations in Geneva to speak about the problems of contracting local partners. But in the meeting it was mainly Awad's lawyer who spoke, as Olabi recalls. Olabi's organization looked at 950 contracts and 420 suppliers financed by UN agencies in Syria in 2018. "We found a lot of sanctioned individuals on the suppliers list," he says and concedes that the UN was not bound by European or US sanctions. But this meant that the regime in effect uses UN money to circumvent EU and US sanctions. Even worse:, this UN money to a large extent comes from the very Western countries who have imposed these sanctions.[16] UNICEF, for example, has procured from security services with board members of sanctioned army generals who are responsible for IHL violations, Olabi says. He also criticizes an overall lack of transparency.

In his advocacy, Olabi tries to create awareness with donor governments about what he perceives as an infringement of the UN's neutrality and impartiality in humanitarian operations, and about the breaches of internal UN principles. In foreign ministries, things get "lost in the system" or he receives answers along the lines of "we have systems in place, we are trying our best." Olabi considers it a success that his organization managed to explicitly get Amin Awad's name mentioned in the US Congress' 'Act to Stop UN Support to Asad' (2019). "We have to go behind the people. People are hiding behind the institution. In this context they avoid accountability," Olabi argues. "These people have worked in many difficult countries such as Afghanistan, Iraq etc. They have negotiated with Saddam Hussein, and then they say they can't remove a supplier from the supply list in Syria? They are lying!"[17]

At the very least, UN agencies have been charged with a lack of sensitivity or poor diligence or scrutiny with regard to cooperation partners. At the end of 2019, it became public that a highly controversial nun had received funding from several UN agencies for sensitive protection projects. Mother Agnes Mariam de la Croix, a nun of Lebanese origin who is the mother superior at the Monastery of St James the Mutilated in Syria, has become known due to several political statements in favour of the Syrian government and rebuffed claims of atrocities committed by it, including major massacres and chemical attacks. Nevertheless, the UN tasked her to deliver shelters and community centres in formerly opposition-held territories where people were highly vulnerable and in danger of being detained as rebel collaborators. From previous negotiations about besieged areas in which Mother Agnes was involved, participants reported that several people who were evacuated with the nun's help were later arrested. Therefore, they suspect her of working closely with the intelligence services. The authors of the newsletter *Syria in Context*, who published this information, conclude: "Our findings raise renewed questions about the lack of neutrality – or judgement – that has plagued the United Nations aid effort in Syria for years."[18]

In a series of articles in 2016, the *Guardian* newspaper kicked off denunciations of the UN's work in Syria. This triggered an avalanche of public criticism, advocacy from the opposition and human rights side, and sent shockwaves through the diplomatic community and the UN itself. Among other things, the *Guardian* quoted a UN spokesman who focused on the difficult dilemma of the UN's work:

> Of paramount importance is reaching as many vulnerable civilians as possible. Our choices in Syria are limited by a highly insecure context where finding companies and partners who operate in besieged and hard to reach areas is extremely challenging. [...] When faced with having to decide whether to procure goods or services from businesses that may be affiliated with the government or let civilians go without life-saving assistance, the choice is clear: our duty is to the civilians in need.[19]

The UN spent large amounts of money with organizations belonging to government cronies or even pro-regime war militias without proper procurement screening. Among the recipients of UN money were businessmen whose companies were under US and EU sanctions.

The Syrian regime has established a "hybrid commercial-charity structure"[20] with the aim of channelling international money back into regime-controlled entities and often to particular members of the Assad dynasty. The organization Ramak for Humanitarian and Development Projects, for example, was owned by Rami Makhlouf, the maternal cousin of President Assad and, until he fell out with Assad in 2020, the most powerful businessman in Syria. He had profited additionally from the war economy. The 'charity' Al-Bustan, which financed loyalist militias operated under the Ramak hub. According to the *Guardian*, in 2015 the Al-Bustan Association received US$268,000 from UNICEF to provide education and basic services in regime-held areas.[21] Al-Bustan is also a partner of the International Organization of Migration (IOM).

HRW found out that at least three NGOs in the local partner database of the UN are publicly affiliated with members of the Syrian army or affiliated militias, the Syrian government, or individuals and/or entities who are under international sanctions, including for involvement in abuses of human rights and IHL. One of them is the Al-Shaheed Foundation, owned by the founder of the National Defence Forces (NDF) in Homs. Some UN agencies also partnered with ministries implicated in human rights violations.[22]

Further examples mentioned by the *Guardian* include the Food and Agriculture Organization (FAO) contracting with state-owned fuel supplier Mahrukat, and the WHO subsidizing Syria's national blood bank, which is controlled by the Defence Ministry. Moreover, so the more general criticism goes, UN agencies and government-approved international NGOs in Damascus transferred significant amounts to SARC and Syrian government institutions to pay for salaries, services and the use of warehouses. These transactions took often place at inflated prices to the benefit of state institutions. Another criticism is that the UN accepted the condition to operate under the aegis of the Syria Trust, run by Asma al-Assad, in the first place.[23]

While many of the accusations are plausible and have not been refuted by the UN or anyone else, other elements of the *Guardian's* research do appear to have overshot the mark. For example, criticizing the UN for using the Syrian mobile phone network (owned by Rami Makhlouf) while operating in the country is far-fetched in comparison to the more serious problems described. The use of dozens or hundreds of satellite phones would have been even more expensive and would have provoked claims of waste.

By contrast, the enormous bills that the UN has paid for accommodation in the Four Seasons Hotel in Damascus – owned by the loyal businessman Samer Foz who has passed on the money to the government – amount to US$26,000 per day, i.e. some US$10 million per year. This has been flagged up not only by the *Guardian* but also by Western governments.[24] On the one hand, arranging this type of accommodation may be part of an overall compromise in a work environment of precarious security, but critics argue that security had improved and other lodging could have been sought. The restrictions imposed by the government in this case are also sad examples of how any international operation can easily feed into a conflict's war economy. It displays the painful trade-off and the political dilemma that the humanitarian side of the UN has to cope with in a conflict that the political side has failed to resolve.

The *Guardian* also quoted a senior member of the humanitarian community in favour of UN efforts of transparency: "[…] at least the UN publishes the names of their suppliers. Many of the international NGOs won't even do that. Very limited transparency is a problem that affects the whole aid effort in Syria. Given that the aid industry has been talking [about] the need for more transparency for decades, it's high time we had proper independent scrutiny of where this money is going and how it is being spent."[25] However, criticism has emerged that UN organizations like the WHO have precisely stopped publishing their data after the *Guardian* revelations.

The London-based scholar Reinoud Leenders upheld his criticism of UN practices in Syria after these reports, despite UN attempts to draw attention to the extremely difficult situation and decision-making dilemmas in the Syrian context:

The Syrian regime drew up a list of some 120 local NGOs accredited to work with the UN – but UN agencies can still choose from this list, or indeed decide that none of them qualify and distribute aid themselves. Some of these local charities are largely apolitical and do a fair job in providing humanitarian aid. From this perspective, there is no reason to partner with an 'NGO' like the Bustan Association that is run by President Bashar al-Assad's notorious cousin let alone one that finances the regime's death squads. Neither would Assad's wife have to be elevated to the status of benign benefactor by teaming up with her 'Syria Trust' charity, not to speak of several other NGOs that publicly glorify the regime or present themselves as patrons of 'the martyrs of the Syrian Arab army.'[26]

Leenders also considers the UN's contracting policy with regime individuals who were put under EU and US sanctions as something that cannot be done innocently, since the names were publicly listed. However, he dismisses allegations that the *Guardian's* and his own research was a call for the UN to withdraw from Syria entirely. The UN should stop being 'submissive', as he puts it. And he suggests an investigatory panel to scrutinize the UN's conduct and performance in Syria.[27]

In the face of these allegations, the question arises why such practices could occur in such frequency and consequence. The UN staff consists of a selection of UN member states, obviously, and some of those support the Syrian regime that is killing its own people. Others sympathize with Islamist groups who also kill people under their control. This is a matter of fact and policy-makers have to deal with it. Sympathies and ideological polarizations are frequent in UN missions, from humanitarian work on the ground to the UN headquarters in New York or to the office of the Special Envoy for Syria in Geneva. The determination of the government in Damascus to extract a high price from international engagement on its territory, and the UN principle decision to pay that price and stay in the country only exacerbated the dilemmas with which they had to operate.

Another problem is that local UN staff members in developing countries and beyond often stem from the educated upper or middle class who speak English and who understand how to apply for such well-paid and prestigious positions. Often, they also profit from 'connections' somewhere in the system. This is a circumstance that applies to several countries and that cannot be changed easily. It's another dilemma that one has to live and work with. However, a *deliberate* employment of close confidants or even relatives of high-ranking political decision-makers *during* such a conflict, is a different matter. Here, another line of public criticism against the UN sets in.

Again, it was the *Guardian* who took the lead in these denunciations but one can find plenty of additional information while talking to former or still-active UN staff. For example, UNHCR hired Saleh Mekdad, brother of then Syrian deputy foreign minister Faisal Mekdad, in the field of communications as the interlocutor between UNHCR and the Ministry of Foreign Affairs *during* the conflict under the tenure of UNHCR representative Tarek Kurdi. A former UN staff member on the ground who left the UN's humanitarian work in frustration, said that on the one hand, it was a good thing because Saleh Mekdad was able to obtain helpful access in difficult situations "but at the same time, you have an element of government inside your office. This is not very professional. This guy abused his position."[28]

In 2016, the WHO employed Shukria Mekdad, the deputy foreign minister's wife. Faisal Mekdad, who is known to be a government hardliner, became foreign minister in November 2020. He played a decisive role in shaping and implementing precisely the policies of conditionality and obstruction under which the UN humanitarian effort suffered in Syria for many years. Having his wife present in UN meetings reportedly created "a climate of fear and self-censorship." In addition, her recruitment had negative implications for the perception of the organization's independence and impartiality.[29] A high-ranking humanitarian UN official remembered one of these awkward situations taking to this author: "We were sitting in a meeting of UN agencies and discussed our strategies of humanitarian delivery in Syria. A colleague passed a handwritten note over to me, warning that Mrs. Mekdad was sitting at the large table as a senior adviser. I should be careful of what I said." He was appalled: "This is almost mocking the system!"[30] While family members of the regime listened to the internal strategic debates of the UN, the UN official said in frustration, "we were negotiating in vain for weeks and weeks to get people out of besieged areas who needed urgent medical treatment. You feel that you have tried everything and yet you are not succeeding to help civilians who are caught up in politics and pay the ultimate price, including children. Where do you draw the line and say: enough is enough?"

Similarly, former UNHCR staff on the ground reported to this author the dominating influence of regime relatives in the UN offices on the ground. "Whenever we had a dissenting opinion, they barred it as being 'political' and not fit for a humanitarian office, while their own pro-government views became the mainstream of the office," they said in a conversation with the author in Beirut in 2014. In the end, they had to quit their jobs, flee Syria and settle abroad without the UN being able or willing to protect them.

One former UN manager told the *Guardian*, which had obtained UN staff lists, that every UN agency had at least "one person who is a direct relative of a Syrian official."[31] Among the senior local staff employed by UN agencies were individuals known for their ties to the Syrian secret police and relatives of senior regime incumbents. The *Guardian* quotes a UN spokesman saying that "family connections are not taken into consideration nor investigated" when hiring staff, and that the UN did not question prospective workers about their political affiliations. The spokesperson also denied that the presence of people close to the government was a threat to the UN's work and said staff needed to reflect "the fabric of Syrian society."[32]

To what such UN personnel policy can amount to is well illustrated by a striking example from some 20 years earlier. During the 1994 Rwanda genocide, a UN employee from the Hutu tribe allegedly oversaw the killing of thirty-two Tutsis. Callixte Mbarushimana had declared himself UNDP's officer in chief in Rwanda after the other staff had left the country. He took over control over the organization's technical equipment and vehicles that were then used to hunt down Tutsi victims.

The UN employee later eluded prosecution by the UN war crimes tribunal for Rwanda and by courts in Germany in France. Despite these weighty allegations, the UN continued to employ him in Kosovo. Charles Petrie, who brought up this case after his work in Rwanda, resigned from his position as UN Assistant Secretary-General in Burundi in protest at the UN's inability to draw consequences from this case. Mbarushimana is currently being prosecuted again in France.[33]

This example shows once again the UN's inability to learn lessons from past mistakes. Throughout the years of an ever-escalating Syrian conflict, one in which no red lines have been left intact to prevent the systematic killing of civilians and wounded, to halt the use of chemical weapons, or to end systematic torture or mass executions in regime prisons, the UN's credibility as an impartial and neutral actor has become increasingly tainted. The incidents listed above have certainly contributed to this quagmire as part of an overall feeling of helplessness due to a paralyzed Security Council and stalled peace efforts in Geneva.

Between All Fronts

These exposures also culminated in a rare collective action against the UN by dozens of NGOs in protest at the looming humanitarian disaster in the city of Aleppo at the end of 2016. After a long vacuum in the UN peace process since March of that year, a last-minute fall-out between the outgoing US administration and their Russian counterparts on a comprehensive deal on Syria (which would have included a joint fight against Islamist radicals), and stasis in the US political system due to its intensive and polarized election process, the opportunity was more than inviting for President Assad and his allies to shape facts on the battlefield. At the end of the year, one of the cruellest battles loomed on the horizon: the re-conquest of Eastern Aleppo from opposition forces and Islamist pockets that hid among them. Many thousands of civilians were affected by heavy bombardments. Healthcare facilities were once again among the main targets, while a helpless and toothless world watched. Once again, the UN's credibility as a neutral and impartial actor crumbled.

On 8 September 2016, a 73-member alliance of aid groups and NGOs working in rebel-held areas announced their withdrawal from a joint monitoring mechanism directed by the UN office in Damascus in protest at what they described as the Assad government's "significant and substantial" influence over the UN relief effort. In their letter to UN-OCHA, the groups said that they would no longer tolerate "manipulation of humanitarian relief efforts by the political interests of the Syrian government that deprives other Syrians in besieged areas from the services of those programmes." The letter continued:

> The Syrian government has interfered with the delivery of humanitarian assistance in multiple instances, including the blocking of aid to besieged areas, the removal of medical aid from inter-agency convoys, the disregard for needs assessments and information coming from humanitarian actors in Syria, and the marginalisation

of other humanitarian actors in the critical planning phases of crisis response. [...] The Whole of Syria information-sharing mechanism was created in order to prevent gaps in the response by including all humanitarian actors providing cross-border relief. Yet, UN agencies based in Damascus and their main partner, SARC, have been making the final decisions, shaped by the political influence of the Syrian government. [...] This deliberate manipulation by the Syrian government and the complacency of the UN have played hand in hand.[34]

Most of these groups were linked to opposition groups or pro-opposition governments, and their letter of withdrawal was clearly a political signal. But they were important partners of the UN relief effort in Syria nonetheless and provided assistance to more than 7 million people there and in neighbouring countries. Moreover, the NGOs' withdrawal from the common information-sharing programme left the UN with much less oversight over developments on the ground.[35]

Opposition-minded Syrians criticized various UN interlocutors, saying that their information flow and decision-making processes were influenced by regime manipulation. Defected diplomat Bassam Barabandi recalls the example whereby the UN insisted on the claim that only one road into Aleppo (the Castello Road) was safe to deliver humanitarian assistance. "We told them that this is fake info by the regime. We showed them another road, since the Castello Road was Russian and regime controlled. UN-OCHA suggested this road to [UN Special Envoy] De Mistura but he insisted that this was the only road."[36] One UN agency shifted the decision to another until it ended up with the OCHA office in Damascus. In the end, this one road remained the official route for humanitarian access only.

The credibility of the UN system suffered further damage when it became increasingly obvious that medical facilities were being bombed, even though their coordinates were shared with the UN for their protection. The purpose of the 'de-confliction mechanism' – providing warring parties with precise locations of humanitarian sites that are exempt from attack under IHL – was turned on its head. NGOs feared for the security of their humanitarian and medical facilities *precisely because* they had shared the geographic coordinates with the UN. NGOs and human rights activists suspected that coordinates that they had shared with the UN ended up on the target list of Russian-supported Syrian fighter jets.

The de-confliction mechanism works by sharing the location of humanitarian sites with Russian, Turkish and United States-led coalition forces operating in Syria, on the understanding that they would not target those sites. The system is voluntary, but relief groups said they felt intense pressure from donors and UN officials alike to participate. The *New York Times* compiled a list of 182 no-strike sites by using data provided by five relief groups and by compiling public statements from others: "Of those facilities, 27 were damaged by Russian or Syrian attacks in 2019. All were hospitals or clinics. Such a list is likely to represent only a small portion of the exempt sites struck during the Syrian war [...]." Local journalists and relief groups recorded at least sixty-nine attacks on no-strike sites since the Russian military intervention in favour of the Syrian regime began in October 2015, all but a few of them most likely committed by Russian or Syrian forces.[37]

This became a dilemma for NGOs: should they continue to share data with the UN or not? They had to weigh risks and benefits. A leading humanitarian employee of Ihsan says: "We have support centres for women and children and shared the coordinates with OCHA to avoid our facilities being bombarded. But unfortunately, our offices and hospitals have been hit several times. We don't know how our data is being used. There is no security, we are highly disappointed. The other side uses the humanitarian facilities as obvious targets." But in the end Ihsan decided to keep delivering its data to OCHA due to donor pressure. Other NGOs also continued to add their sites to the de-confliction list despite the high risk involved, since hitting those targets would at least leave Russia and the Syrian government with no deniability, which may become important for possible war crimes trials in the future. The Ihsan staffer welcomes the fact that OCHA has started to investigate the incidents and is considering its practice. "They also came to us and asked us at what time we shared the coordination, who exactly is the owner of the respective building etc."[38] In its investigation, the UN found out that some locations had indeed been submitted incorrectly by a few NGOs. This strengthened Russia's argument that had always questioned the credibility of the system as being vulnerable to misuse such as hiding rebel positions.

Jan Egeland, a Norwegian humanitarian diplomat, who was senior adviser to the UN Special Envoy for Syria from 2015 to 2018, said the UN had failed to impose sufficient repercussions on those responsible for targeting civilian and medical infrastructure. "In general, de-confliction can work if there is a very loud, very noisy, very reliable investigation follow-up, accountability-oriented mechanism around it," Egeland said, "so that the men who sit with their finger on the trigger understand there will be consequences if they don't check the list or if they even deliberately target de-conflicted places."[39]

The board of inquiry to investigate a few of the strikes on de-conflicted sites that UN Secretary-General António Guterres established in August 2019 was not equipped with a mission to name or shame the perpetrators but to establish facts only. Accordingly cautious, in April 2020 the Board reported that it was "highly probable" that the Syrian government or its allies had carried out attacks on three healthcare facilities, a school and a refuge for children in north-west Syria the previous year. Notably, this conclusion referred to a small area and to a very limited period of time only.

Subsequently, Russia withdrew from this voluntary arrangement in June 2020 on the grounds that the UN investigation had shown that the mechanism was flawed and abused by "terrorist groups." Some of the de-confliction facilities were actually used as terrorists' headquarters, Russia said. Such a practice is possible. But the Russian side never mentioned the overwhelming majority of real and working medical facilities that were deliberately hit by the Syrian air force or even by Russian pilots all over Syria throughout the conflict. Instead, Russia's Permanent UN Representative, Vasily Nebenzya, insisted: "We have repeatedly stressed that Russia's aerospace forces use an efficient target verification system, which excludes any possibility of attacks on civilian facilities."[40] Hence, the solution in Russian eyes should be from now on that OCHA pass on the sensitive data directly to the Syrian government. In this case, at least, it would not be Russia that would be blamed for passing on data to the perpetrator – but the UN itself.

Chapter 8

CREDIBILITY CRISIS

The UN Reacts

The withdrawal of numerous NGOs from cooperation with the UN in Syria, and the accompanying series of critical articles in the media as well as in NGO and academic publications, sent shockwaves through the UN system. Having been incapable of resolving key conflicts of our times in Syria, Libya and Yemen through mediation, the UN's remaining task of curing the conflicts' symptoms was attacked as flawed in addition. This affected the organization's overall credibility, although different UN agencies and personnel were doing different things in different contexts, sometimes even pulling into opposite directions. Syria –with its extraordinarily challenging operating environment – became a litmus test for the UN at a time when key member states were retreating from multilateral ideas and engagement. "There is no work in Syria that would be fully compatible with human rights," concedes lawyer Ibrahim Olabi of the Syrian Legal Development Programme (SLDP), while adding, "but there are worse and less bad actors. The UN is a worse actor."[1]

It was only in 2013 that UN Secretary-General Ban Ki-moon had pledged, also with reference to Syria, that his organization would not repeat mistakes made elsewhere when he reacted to the devastating report on UN systematic failure in Sri Lanka. His call for UN integrity, titled 'Renewing Our Commitment to the Peoples and Purposes of the United Nations', contained, among other things:

> On behalf of the senior leadership and all staff, I solemnly renew the commitment of the UN Secretariat, funds and programmes to uphold the responsibilities assigned to us by the Charter, the Security Council and the General Assembly whenever there is a threat of serious and large-scale violations of international human rights and humanitarian law.
>
> We will be vigilant in identifying emerging risks and will ensure that our actions are guided by more effective use of the information that is available to us from UN human rights and humanitarian mechanisms and other entities.
>
> [. . .] We will speak out publicly where violations are ongoing.
>
> We will exercise due diligence in implementing all our mandates.
>
> [. . .] Above all, we renew our commitment to 'We the peoples' of the UN Charter.

As we look at Syria and other difficult situations going forward, this commitment will be fulfilled promptly and systematically, with compassion, integrity, impartiality and with courage by us all.[2]

These words ring hollow when checked against facts and actual behaviour on the ground in Syria, even at the very moment Ban Ki-moon uttered them two years into the Syrian conflict. Actors on the ground in Syria told this author that the UN should do more in practice to implement lessons learned. "The regulations themselves are there. It's a matter of implementing them," one NGO staffer said. Others report that after the criticism in the media, some UN agencies have withdrawn from the public eye. One conversation partner said that from 2016 onwards, several UN agencies refrained from publishing data from Syria on partner organizations and procurements altogether. So the public stigmatization of UN's work might have led to *less* transparency rather than more. As mentioned above, most interlocutors who have experience with humanitarian work on the ground say that within the UN humanitarian family, OCHA was the one that most consequently insisted on humanitarian standards and, as a consequence, was granted fewer and fewer visas for their personnel from the government. But other UN agencies who are in regular contact with diplomats in Beirut have pointed to the need for bottom-up reforms within their systems to avoid mistakes of the past. WFP and UNHCR, for example, have initiated structural reforms in their risk management. This means that when a new project is suggested, screening processes shall be critically reviewed and applied.

As a political reaction to the mounting and bitter criticism against the United Nations, the UN Department of Political Affairs (DPA) and UNDP developed the 'Parameters and Principles of UN Assistance in Syria' in October 2017. Under the lead management of UN Under-Secretary-General for Political Affairs, Jeffrey Feltman (in post 2012–18), the following fundamentals were formulated that, strictly speaking, would not have been necessary if the existing body of principles of international law, especially IHL and IHRL, had been adhered to by all UN member states and by the UN and other agencies alike. Among the formulated parameters are the following:

> [. . .] *Humanitarian principles of neutrality, impartiality and independence* apply to life-saving humanitarian assistance as well as early recovery and resilience activities with humanitarian objectives. The UN, with the active engagement of the Secretary-General, will endeavour to secure the *maximum possible flow of humanitarian assistance* into Syria, including through the *most direct route*, ensuring *non-interference* with its operations, to sustain operations envisaged in the Humanitarian Response Plan (HRP) [. . .]

At the same time, the document distinguishes between urgently required humanitarian and longer-term recovery efforts that would be necessary in Syria's future. The reconstruction aspect was part of a lengthy negotiation process that would be dealt with independently. However, the following conditions were set:

"Only once there is a *genuine and inclusive political transition* negotiated by the parties, would the UN be ready to facilitate reconstruction." Moreover, the above-mentioned principles of neutrality and impartiality had to be deployed in conjunction with a human-rights-based approach, as emphasized in the UN document. Given experiences gained in Syria, the Parameters and Principles (P&Ps) explicitly state:

- Assistance must be *prioritized based on the needs of the population (rather than government driven)* with a particular focus on the needs of vulnerable groups and individuals, in a manner that protects human rights as an outcome.
- It must be delivered in a *fair, equitable, non-discriminatory and non-politicized manner.*
- The UN shall work directly with communities and households, such that United Nations assistance is delivered with uniformity throughout Syria, *regardless of zones of influence.*
- The UN shall consider carefully *human rights and protection implications,* especially with regard to where and how assistance is provided. UN assistance must *not assist parties* who have allegedly committed *war crimes or crimes against humanity.*
- UN assistance shall be determined consciously and explicitly without prejudice to the *goals of accountability* for serious human rights violations, and the goals of legitimate, equitable, and sustainable political settlement. [...][3]

These P&Ps were approved by the Secretary-General. A multi-disciplinary working group under the auspices of the UN Syria Inter-Agency Task Force was assigned to monitor adherence to these guidelines. Member states who had been pushing for the strict adherence to humanitarian principles and the priorization of assistance now had a concrete, up-to-date and operative reference point that they could come back to, and they did so repeatedly.

Meanwhile, however, inside the UN, opposing camps fought their own battles about the P&Ps. Under-Secretary-General Feltman, the very initiator of the P&Ps, did not conceal his disappointment when talking to this author in 2020:

Given that it derives entirely from the UN Charter and the UN's well established normative agenda, the 'Parameters and Principles' guidance should not have been as difficult to negotiate as turned out to be the case. And almost immediately after it was adopted by consensus in an interagency and interdepartmental process, the UN Country Team in Damascus [headed by Ali Al-Zaatari] tried to re-litigate, water down, and ignore it, consistent with the regime's desire to refocus UN activities away from humanitarian relief and life-saving emergency aid to reconstruction in regime-held areas.[4]

According to senior UN sources, Zaatari must have been under heavy pressure from Damascus as he tried to camouflage reconstruction under early recovery, "but he came across as completely untrustworthy." Moreover, the Russians obtained a copy of the P&P paper and immediately contacted Secretary-General Guterres in protest. They publicly criticized the initiative and accused its authors in the UN political department of acting on behalf of the Trump administration. "Guterres, never a profile in courage in the face of powerful state bullying, quickly lost interest in the P&P paper," a former high official laments. When the topic came up in the Executive Committee meetings, usually raised by UNDP and encouraged by Zaatari, Guterres would inch toward more early recovery work decoupled from the UN's own mediation process in Geneva and independent of any political deliveries from the Assad government in return. Consensus on the Parameters and Principles among the UN family remained fragile: the Office of the High Commissioner for Human Rights (OHCHR), the Office of the Special Envoy for Syria (OSE) and the Department for Political Affairs in New York (DPA) were strongly in favour; the Development Program (UNDP) first ambivalent and then, prompted by Zaatari, hostile to the P&Ps; UNICEF and others somewhere in between. It was this tenuous understanding between the different UN actors that made practical progress so difficult. Donor countries repeatedly criticized the fact that the promised UN Inter-Agency Taskforce, which was supposed to monitor the P&Ps, had not even met or begun work by the time this book went to print.

Donors React

Frustrated by their observations of bickering inside the UN, some donor countries demanded further steps and a more visible, sustainable and thorough overhaul of the system. For this purpose, in 2019 a number of Western states (mainly Germany, the US, the UK, France, Denmark and the Netherlands) started to compile a list of critical cases of violations of the UN Parameters and Principles, mainly based on open sources. The original goal of this diplomatic initiative led by Germany was to formally hand over a letter of concern to the UN Secretary-General. This discussion coincided with rising political polarization and heated debates in the Security Council about the fading out of cross-border Resolution 2165 (2014) under Russian and Chinese vetoes.

The internal list compiled by like-minded donor countries included criticism of UN decisions under regime interference, such as personnel decisions in Syria, the prioritization of sectors and geographic areas for programming of humanitarian and development programmes, procurement practice, the selection and assessment of implementing partners, and the inhibition of programming in the field of protection like the monitoring of human rights abuses, detention and legal proceedings that returning IDPs and refugees face as a daily reality. The conclusion to this document was: "Alongside this constant, structural form of interference, individual UN interventions periodically appear more in sync with Damascus' political agenda than any conventional humanitarian or development logic."[5]

However, even the like-minded donor countries had no unified view about how to use this initiative. One side argued in favour of enhancing public awareness and advocated for rubbing it in in New York due to the severity of the allegations. They held that the Parameters and Principles, i.e. rules that the UN gave to itself, must not be watered down in any UN humanitarian and development activities in Syria. This group within the like-minded donor countries was determined to step up the pressure for sweeping consequences within the UN system. Others, by contrast, argued that a more lenient interpretation of the P&Ps would allow the UN to exert more leverage and deliver more assistance in Syria. Rehashing past mistakes and making harsh denunciations would only provoke a defensive attitude from the UN. Discreet follow-ups in meetings in Beirut with the UN country team at lower levels might be more helpful, according to this view. In the end, the document was sent to the Deputy UN Secretary General in January 2021.

"We are dealing with a systemic problem inside the UN," a Western diplomat explained to the author. "Therefore we just cannot do business as usual." On the other hand, the right balance had to be found in terms of reactions. "The UN should not be pilloried either. We have to solve this problem in cooperation, since we – as donors – are in the same boat as the UN. We are also criticized, rightly so, for our funds being misused if the UN system doesn't function according to humanitarian standards." It was unacceptable that the internal UN monitoring of the Parameters and Principles by the Inter-Agency Task Force was not functioning. "The Task Force has not even met once, which would have been the least and easiest thing to do," the diplomat complained. If the UN continues to ignore its own 2017 Parameters and Principles, "this is a real dilemma," the Western diplomat concedes, "since we can't stop humanitarian support to the UN altogether. What we *can* do is to resort to funding other forms of assistance such as resilience measures in a development context."[6]

Within individual UN member states, other forms of repercussions emerged. Domestic debates inside the United States about UN neutrality and impartiality in Syria have produced controversial debates among lawmakers. In 2019, the Foreign Relations Committee in Congress introduced the 'Stop UN Support for Assad Act'.[7] This bill aimed to stop all US funding that was channelled, directly or indirectly, to the Assad regime, including through UN organs. It would require the Secretary of State to certify that UN programming in Syria did not materially support Assad and that it adhered to the UN's own Parameters and Principles. The Act reads, among other things, as follows:

- [...] During the past eight years of conflict, the Assad regime has repeatedly weaponized access to United Nations aid in prolonged and unlawful sieges of civilians as part of a widespread "starve or surrender" campaign, with the United Nations estimating 975,000 Syrians under siege at the peak of this strategy.
- The United Nations Office for the Coordination of Humanitarian Affairs (OCHA) has reported repeated failures to deliver aid to the hardest-hit areas due to such obstructions by the Assad regime.[...]

- The United Nations continues to procure goods and services from several entities that have close ties to the Assad regime, despite their role in supporting the Assad regime's gross human rights violations and international crimes— including torture, sexual violence, the targeting of medical facilities, weaponized mass starvation, enforced disappearance, and forced displacement—for which the United Nations itself has found the Assad regime culpable.
- A 2016 study of the UN Report of Procurement showed that UN operations in Syria delivered $4 million to Syria's state-owned fuel industry, $5 million to blood banks operated by the Syrian Arab Army for the benefit of its troops, and $8.5 million to charities co-opted by members of the Assad family.
- International NGOs working with the United Nations are forced to select local partners, many of which are controlled by the Assad family and inner circle, from a government-approved list, therefore allowing these actors to profit from humanitarian relief efforts and perpetuate the conflict, international crimes, and human rights violations.[...]
- The Assad regime has regularly siphoned humanitarian funds for the war effort and bypassed international sanctions through exploiting humanitarian exemptions.

In conclusion, the US policy should be as follows:

- [...] programming provided through the United Nations based on United States funding should be determined according to greatest need, not only greatest access;
- United States assistance to Syria should not be manipulated for political or financial gain of any party to the conflict, especially those most responsible for compounding the suffering of Syrian civilians, including the Assad regime, the Russian Federation, the Islamic Republic of Iran, any entities owned or controlled thereof, or non-state actors involved in international crimes and human rights abuses; [...]
- the United Nations procurement operations throughout Syria should abide by its own United Nations Supplier Code of Conduct, which states that suppliers to the United Nations must "ensure that they are not complicit in human rights abuses"; and
- the United States will continue providing humanitarian assistance to Syria while also continuing its efforts to facilitate a negotiated political transition from the Assad regime, in accordance with its commitment in United Nations Security Council Resolution 2254.[...]

The last item was a clearly political point that articulated the US' overarching goal of regime change in Syria. This mix of humanitarian and political goals is problematic from a purely humanitarian perspective. The originally humanitarian intervention in Libya in 2011 also ended up in helping implement a regime change via the death of Libya's leader, Gaddafi. Even if the quoted US Act referred to a UN-brokered political solution, the other side surely regarded this as a unconcealed threat to its existence, and therefore might also consider all humanitarian projects funded by the US or the West as a danger that must be contained. In the Syrian government's view, Western humanitarian aid would strengthen the resilience of rebel fighters in opposition areas.

One of the persons who had lobbied for the Act in Washington DC was former Syrian diplomat Bassam Barabandi. He explains the genesis of the Act: The Trump administration had general problems with the UN, "therefore it was easy to convince them that such an Act was necessary to correct UN actions." Similarly, Russia and like-minded countries have in turn often claimed that the UN was influenced by the West, both during the negotiations in Geneva and in other contexts. This general mistrust turned into outright alienation when UN findings on the use of chemical weapons in Syria by the Assad regime were flatly rejected or other grave human rights violations denied. The UN has thus become an easy target, a low-hanging fruit, for critics on both sides of the ideological gulf that divides power politics today.

There was another angle to the fact that made the 'Stop UN Support for Assad Act' timely and interesting for US lawmakers in 2019. It was less the humanitarian situation of the Syrian population as such, who since 2011 had suffered significantly from violations of IHL and IHRL and as a result of UN ineffectiveness. It was, instead, the problem of growing Iranian influence in Syria. "When things overlap with Israeli interests in the US, you can use them to frame your issue from this angle," explains Barabandi. "So we framed it through the anti-Iranian angle and the threat to Israeli security. Syria itself was not of interest."[8] So the driving force for an Act that called for adherence to humanitarian principles was primarily a political one, at least for those who voted for the Act in the US. Syrians like Barabandi may have had humanitarian motivations but they had to disguise them in order to get an ear at all. It was a disillusioning experience to realize that the Syrian people's suffering was not the key driver for US lawmakers. This went beyond the US, of course, and applied to large parts of public opinion and political actors involved in the Syrian crisis from faraway capitals in Europe and around the world.

Chapter 9

DIVERSIFYING AID: ROADS TO CIRCUMVENT DAMASCUS

Difficulties with humanitarian assistance in Syria triggered yet another major consequence: the creative use of different – non-humanitarian – tools for similar purposes. At the time when the upheaval unfolded, diplomats in various capitals debated the best way of curing the symptoms in the absence of decisive political engagement that could have enforced adherence to IHL and IHRL. The gulf between humanitarians and political diplomats persisted, and new approaches regarding humanitarian practices or progressive interpretations of IHL remained weak. The traditionally extensive funds earmarked for humanitarian emergencies were readily available and channelled through the UN into government-controlled Syria to a large extent.

'Humanitarian Plus'

Other means had to be found to get funds to those areas where bombs were raining down without changing the entire system of humanitarian assistance. But developing new ideas and tools takes time, and time was running out for many Syrians. The options discussed were cross-line or cross-border deliveries, both of which were restricted or sometimes impossible under the conditions imposed by a regime that was struggling for its own survival. Another option for donors was tapping into different funds and putting different 'labels' on assistance packages. Some measures were hard to distinguish from standard humanitarian deliveries, while others went beyond and followed a more developmental approach. The decoupling of aid from humanitarian principles, of course, entailed the danger of implementers becoming part and parcel of the donor states' political agendas and more dependent on their cultural and ideological biases and approaches. Donini criticized this with reference to experiences in Afghanistan: "Neutrality is not an end in itself; it is a means of fulfilling the humanitarian imperative. The abuse of the term *humanitarian* for stabilization activities that are not based on need but on a political-military agenda dangerously muddies the waters."[1] On the other hand, in Syria, the waters were already muddied to an unbearable extent with the humanitarian space having been severely corrupted. Humanitarian needs could neither be addressed in negotiations nor with the application of core humanitarian principles. Therefore, other ways to alleviate suffering were found but, naturally, this approach entailed a large set of other risks.

Alternative ways of spending donors' money reflect varying degrees on the scale of engagement. They have different names, such as 'resilience measures'[2], 'rehabilitation', 'early recovery measures', 'stabilization measures' or 'development-oriented transitional aid' – often lumped together simply as 'humanitarian plus'. This term was an emergency invention of sorts. In fact, it means several things at the same time: donor countries can hide behind the positively connotations of the term 'humanitarian'; it suggests that activities remain very closely linked to merely humanitarian measures without veering too far into development aid, the latter being politically more controversial; at the same time, donors can use different, non-humanitarian funds and circumvent the strict rules for humanitarian delivery. So the added value of this term was twofold: with a collective nomenclature, it was possible to brush over manifold project measures without providing further explanation. And it provided the political impression of measures being undertaken in good humanitarian faith, although they might also go beyond traditional humanitarian boundaries (without indicating how far beyond). One step further than 'humanitarian plus' would be 'reconstruction measures'. They have also entered the debate in more recent years. Still, the distinction remains fuzzy.

All such non-humanitarian measures can be conducted without state partners and through NGOs or the respective UN agencies in areas out of regime control or, of course, in regime-held areas with government cooperation. 'Humanitarian plus' can include reconstructing very basic infrastructure and services such as water and electricity networks, support for rebuilding agrarian capabilities in certain areas, de-mining, investing in schools and the education system, establishing protection programmes, etc. Funding and operations take place detached from the strict humanitarian principles and can be conditioned according to the donor's priorities, including political deliberations.

The term 'stabilization' has a political connotation and motivation, although it may lead to similar actions on the ground as humanitarian assistance. Examples ranged from the delivery of wheat to be milled for bakeries, which was conducted by stabilization and humanitarian actors alike, to the supply of ambulances or other technical equipment for medical purposes. Moreover, donors to development projects in Syria sometimes oriented their decisions according to the UN humanitarian response plans despite the fact that their decisions were taken independently of humanitarian principles. So the lines remain blurred but the funds from which the money flows on the donor's side are strictly separated in administrative terms. This complex scenario also leads to challenges within the ministerial bureaucracy of donor countries. Differing goals, interests and modes of procedures are at play. A Western diplomat from the humanitarian side explains the complicated nexus:

> When we sit together, political and humanitarian departments plus the development people, the discussion goes like this: The development ministry wants to do as much on the ground as possible because they merely think in

terms of development and not of war dynamics; the political department wants to do as little as possible because they have political problems with Assad and human rights violations in mind, so they prefer measures that are as humanitarian as possible only. We humanitarians say that the development people should do as little as possible that resembles humanitarian work and leave it to us for several reasons: A blurring of competencies and goals may endanger the work of humanitarian personnel on the ground and destroy the firewall between politically motivated and humanitarian work. It also has reasons related to budgetary clarity inside the government's bureaucracy.[3]

Apart from such internal challenges, there were other hurdles to surmount if the aim was to work effectively against the asymmetry of humanitarian assistance in government and non-government areas. The construction of a network of partners and funding flows through non-humanitarian actors took time, at least with Western operating procedures. New trusted partners had to be identified who could work cross border and bring assistance to the government-bombed areas in which both needs and dangers were high. Money had to be transferred mostly in cash due to the lack of infrastructure, which posed logistical and accountability problems. The highly monitored Western systems of funding are mostly project oriented, need a proper implementation framework and are thus slow by default (unless a fast-track mechanism is established through a political decision taken at higher levels). By contrast, support from other areas such as the Arab Gulf countries in the framework of 'Humanitarian Plus' meant that deliveries of dual-use goods or even military assistance were quick, cash based and entailed fewer monitoring procedures.

The time factor was particularly crucial in the first months and years of the Syrian crisis when large areas were under heavy government bombardment but out of government control; every day saw high civilian injury and death tolls and no proper access for humanitarian assistance. The instruments developed to counter this situation could not compete time wise with urgent and tried-and-tested injections of emergency aid, and only gradually established themselves via project-implementing actors in southern Turkey.

A Double-edged Sword

Discussions among Western donors about alternatives to purely humanitarian assistance gained momentum after the formation of the National Coalition of Revolutionary and Opposition Forces (SOC) and its recognition as "the legitimate representative of the Syrian people" in the final communiqué of the Fourth Ministerial Meeting of the Group of Friends of the Syrian People in Marrakech, which took place in December 2012. However, it remained unclear how many of the 114 participating countries really shared this definition, since some made slightly differing individual statements after the conference.[4] Above all, this was not a *legal* recognition but rather blurry and undefined *political* support. Western diplomats started to think about how to support this structure, which was also planned to operate in opposition areas. The goal was to improve its legitimacy on the ground as a political actor and as a deliverer of services to the population.

So the motivation to diversify funds away from the traditional humanitarian channels was double edged: it was both humanitarian due to the lack of access *and* political in form of support for opposition structures that were seen as a moderate and democratic alternative to the Assad regime. Like-minded countries came to the conclusion that new tools had to be developed due to the scope of the challenge.

One instrument that was established in 2013 under the leadership of Germany and the United Arab Emirates was the Syria Recovery Trust Fund (SRTF). A Western representative of a non-humanitarian agency who was part of the implementing partners told this author that the involvement of many countries and stakeholders as well as the project-based approach involved a lengthy bureaucratic process not comparable to the fast and established funding flows to UN and other humanitarian actors via Damascus – and often too slow to get help quickly to the population on the ground when destructions occurred. The interlocutor recalls a typical incident from summer 2013 when the north-eastern city of Raqqa fell to the radical armed group Ahrar al-Sham. Representatives of the moderate Local Council met with the German development agency GIZ and asked them for small amounts of cash so that the council could pay the street cleaners. US$50 per week would have been enough. "This was a huge challenge for our operating procedures," explains the representative. "Radical organizations like Ahrar al-Sham and the Islamic State came with suitcases full of money. We were not able to compete with them to support the moderate actors on the ground. They were always quicker and less bureaucratic. On the other side, we were also competing with a regime that tried to buy loyalties."[5]

Apart from bureaucratic hurdles, another challenge in getting funds to the right people were the assistance 'supra-structures' being formed by the opposition outside Syria. The Assistance Coordination Unit (ACU) founded by the SOC in Turkey did not work smoothly and effectively. At least at the beginning, its staff did not know how to properly define the difference between humanitarian and non-humanitarian assistance. The organization was accused of corruption and competed for international funds with the Local Administration Coordination Unit (LACU), a supra-structure of Local Councils based in the Turkish city of Gaziantep. Western donors initially faced an impasse because they could not release their funds to support these opposition structures as the political decision-makers in Western capitals desired. But over time, they did develop a more tested network of cooperation partners on the ground and delivered an increasing amount of cross-border humanitarian and non-humanitarian assistance to opposition areas.

Things changed when the Assad army – with Russian and Iranian military support – re-conquered the eastern part of Aleppo and established full control across the city in December 2016. This was a major blow to the opposition and its forces, and a watershed moment for Syrian revolutionary aspirations in general. From this point on, Western policy-makers began to think that their support of opposition actors on the ground with some small projects would no longer make a big difference. "You cannot win a war with mobile bakeries and corn mills," as a German diplomat put it.[6] The overall impression in Western and opposition-leaning Arab states was that the war was basically lost. So the second of the two motivations to find alternative ways of assistance gradually fell away – that is, enhancing the legitimacy of opposition actors in Syria through the funding of humanitarian and non-humanitarian assistance on the ground in a range of creative ways. The humanitarian motivation to relieve the suffering of Syrians in the ever-shrinking number of opposition-held areas, however, remained.

Another challenge was the increasing radicalization of armed actors on the ground and the obstacles to delivering assistance in their areas. Radical Islamist organizations appropriated the civilian infrastructure and administration, especially in the embattled region of Idlib in north-Western Syria. Western donors temporarily withdrew their stabilization measures where Al-Nusra and its camouflaged 'Salvation Government' had largely taken control. Yet again, civilians suffered as a result of this decision.

Sceptics of this approach describe the dilemma that Western donors were also facing in terms of a 'humanitarian vacuum' that opened up where political decisions guided the implementation of non-humanitarian aid. An EU diplomat in Beirut told me: "Small mobile clinics were financed in opposition areas or at the frontline, like in Idlib. When the regime conquered the area, the mobile clinics were quickly taken away northwards, so that the areas had no longer had medical services at all because the regime didn't deliver them." The diplomat went on to say that a similar situation unfurled in Wadi Barada, in rural Damascus, and led to an outbreak of cholera in 2017. Cholera was only barely prevented in other areas, too, for the same reasons. In another example from the North-West, a French-funded project paid the medical staff of hospitals and mobile clinics. When the regime took control, not only were the mobile clinics taken away, but the foreign donor also stopped paying the nurses, who then left the area. "In this way, the local population is being punished for their failure of not fighting hard enough against Assad," the EU diplomat criticizes. "This is how we have made development policy. We did health projects for political purposes."[7]

A similar (but reverse) scenario occurred when donors like Germany withdrew their non-humanitarian-funded health projects from Idlib when the radical Salvation Government took over. This also affected the ordinary population first and foremost. But as debates in the Netherlands have shown, even temporary support for opposition groups on the ground that later turn radical can result in a wave of criticism by political opponents, as happened in The Hague. Politicians and diplomatic decision-makers naturally aim to shield themselves against political vulnerabilities at home. Often, political decisions are less grounded in facts on the ground than in domestic deliberations. The concern of being attacked by the political opponent of supporting Islamist radicals or potential terrorists, who would later turn against societies in the West, is higher than the concern about repercussions from funding humanitarian assistance through conventional channels, even if vast amounts of this effort end up in hands of a government that kills its people – but its own people only.

The Reconstruction Gamble

The later phase of the conflict, in which the Syrian government consolidated its predominance in large parts of its territory, created a new momentum. In Damascus, the international money put aside for humanitarian-plus projects raised the appetite for more. This was also true for its allies. Russia did not intend to invest large sums in early recovery, rehabilitation or reconstruction, and Iran – which has been struggling economically – couldn't afford it in the first place.

In 2018 and 2019, Russia wanted to divert the discussion away from the battlefield towards a post-conflict paradigm that would focus on challenges ahead such as rehabilitation, early recovery, reconstruction and refugee return (from all these 'Rs', one was missing: reform). In short: the narrative of beginning normalization in Syria without any change in governance and political behaviour. To underline their narrative, in January 2018 Russia hosted a 1,600-member intra-Syrian 'Reconciliation Conference' in Sochi with Iran's and Turkey's support as part of the Astana Format. They tossed aside the detail that war was still raging in parts of Syria, especially in the north, and that about one-third of Syria's territory remained out of the government's reach. In addition, arbitrary arrests, torture and mass executions still characterized the Syrian system, most refugees did not feel safe enough to return, nor had any genuine process of reconciliation been launched inside the war-torn and polarized society.

Nevertheless, around that period of time several countries like the United Arab Emirates and even Saudi Arabia were about to pursue a more pragmatic approach towards Damascus, hedging their bets about normalization. Several Eastern European countries did the same. The US and other European states, however, pushed back, and the reconstruction and normalization debate faded out, at least for some time, also in the light of the heavy fighting and humanitarian disaster in Idlib. In particular, those Western states that had taken in large numbers of Syrian refugees – such as Germany and Sweden – refused to be blackmailed into such a discussion that they considered premature. In addition, the EU stuck by its political conditions: it continued to link reconstruction and other measures – including the potential reestablishment of diplomatic relations with Damascus – to the government's full engagement in the stalled political process in Geneva and a political transition (meanwhile be it with or without Assad) or at least genuine reforms in this regard. The EU still considered the sums of money that they were in principle ready to invest in post-conflict Syria as a tool to improve conditions in the country. This was regarded as impossible without political reforms.

Equally, the mission of the EU Regional Trust Fund stated that European money, hitherto reserved for Syria's neighbours and refugee host communities, could be used *inside* Syria one day, provided that the government were willing to implement sweeping reforms: "The Trust Fund could also be asked to address needs and provide support in a post-conflict Syria, subject to a credible political transition firmly underway, in line with UNSC Resolution 2254 (2015)."[8]

Meanwhile however, the EU's strategy of carrots and sticks – offering conditioned money while maintaining or tightening sanctions – proved to be a blunt sword since Assad has not moved an inch. Ultimately, he fears that Western conditions will still aim at regime change through other means. Facing a US 'maximum pressure' strategy with ever tightening sanctions these fears may look even more realistic in Damascus, although the US had declared they had changed focus from pursuing 'regime change' to seeking 'behaviour change' from the existing regime. On the European side, a step-by-step or more-for-more approach has been discussed for some time in the sense that more rehabilitation measures or even early recovery may be thinkable if the regime implements gradual reforms – but so far, it seems, Damascus and its allies, especially Moscow, have shown little interest in taking up this logic. The consequent stance of political conditioning has always been a difficult balance given the dire need of providing education for a 'lost generation' as well as delivering basic services, boosting societal resilience (for what is left from Syrian civil society) and promoting longer-term stability in the country. Syria has entered a stage where conflict and post-conflict scenarios exist in parallel.[9] Assad is still in conflict mode, and as long as the regime kills unwelcome returnees, early recovery or reconstruction measures are not really needed, as Western donors argue.

One question has been in whose favour time was playing out in the political sense: for Assad, who could still count on support from Russia and Iran but whose country's economic and security situation has remained disastrous without a change of governance and without any peace dividend in sight for the suffering and increasingly impatient population? Or for the EU, which would continue its carrot-and-stick approach on the surface while facing increasingly heterogeneous attitudes among European governments towards Syria, some of which were ruled or strongly influenced by right-wing populist parties that had no problem with human rights violations in Syria but with Syrian refugees at home? The centrifugal forces within the EU became so strong that in 2019, for the first time in years, the EU member states refrained from formulating updated Council Conclusions on Syria. They feared that they would no longer be able to find a common language.

In the end, a completely unexpected external factor might have closed the window of opportunity for Assad to receive easy reconstruction money. The coronavirus pandemic starting in 2020 absorbed the budgets of pretty much all relevant states, which were focused on trying to prevent the collapse of their own economies that fewer development resources might be dedicated to countries like Syria in the long run. Already under normal circumstances, the scope of the reconstruction effort is mindboggling: estimates range from US$250 to 400 billion or even up to US$1 trillion.[10] Figures aside, Syria has also accumulated huge structural problems like the braindrain of skilled labour, a collapse of state services, and a basically worthless currency.

In addition, since the regime has tried to corrupt the system of international humanitarian assistance, it will probably do the same with any further-reaching measures providing services and rebuilding infrastructure. In fact, this process has already begun with numerous actors active on the ground implementing their non-humanitarian projects – they are not so much responding to needs but to their own priorities, and they are depending on opportunities granted by the regime. The money continues to flow into the ongoing war and crony economy, cementing the forced resettlement of populations. Since 2011, the Syrian government has issued more than sixty laws and decrees that regulate housing, land and property rights (HLP) to provide a legal framework for post-war reconstruction.[11] These regulations enable the government to expropriate individuals more easily, especially those who are not able to return and (re-)claim their rights in time or who are denied civil documentation. The government has demolished entire neighbourhoods to keep the non-loyal population from returning to their homes but has established so-called development zones with the purpose of facilitating vast and rapid construction for loyal inhabitants and for the benefit of loyal businessmen.

To date, the government in Damascus has shown little inclination of being ready to cooperate with the international community and potential donors on reconstruction efforts. In fact, it seems to be doing anything but. It has been trying to tighten its grip and to formalize its control over international and national actors and related humanitarian and developmental programmes.[12] The likely scenario is that Syria will resemble Egypt, the population of which ended up under an even more oppressive regime under President Sisi than it had before the Arab Spring. If President Assad and his regime showed some goodwill in rhetoric and practice, several countries would certainly be eager to release funds for post-conflict stabilization purposes sooner rather than later.

But Assad's mindset is different: the president is convinced that he can navigate through the remaining turbulences long enough with external support of Russia and Iran avoiding accommodating humanitarian or other international principles. He is aware of the likelihood that his regime would collapse, or that street protests may resume, if he embarked on reforms that included more freedoms. He continues to feel besieged and considers international assistance efforts, and even the political process in Geneva, as attempts at regime change by other means, spurred by occasional comments from the US and some European diplomats – even though a political transition has basically been dropped from the daily agenda of the political process in Geneva as well as from the agendas of most Western countries. Assad himself, and his entourage in Damascus, live in a bubble of perception and may have over-estimated their strength and resilience in a country that will neither be territorially united nor socially, economically and politically stable in the foreseeable future. The Syrian regime has no ambitions to create an environment that is inviting for refugees to return, since it considers most of them as having been brainwashed by Turkish or Western narratives or simply spoiled by a democratic experience abroad. While rejecting any efforts of reconciliation, Assad knows that current and future dangers will linger in a new and vibrant diaspora civil society and their use of social media networks, and therefore he has attempted to tighten the NGO law and to increase the security services' control over contents in social media. He knows that Western actors are torn between stricter measures against the regime and its cronies, including a push for more consequent adherence to and robust enforcement of humanitarian principles, and the will to release funds for reconstruction and development without meaningful reforms in place.

Reconstruction is a highly political issue. In the Syrian government's reading, it serves the purpose of solidifying the rocky rule of the Assad dynasty, and it caters to Russia and Iran with lucrative investment projects as a compensation for their war efforts. In short, it will once again be a mechanism that would instil life into a predatory system that has favoured loyalist businessmen who share their profits with the regime that continues to keep refugees out and dissenters quiet.[13]

Nevertheless, concerns are mounting that the status quo is equally untenable in the long run. And Assad is playing for time. The current conflict will not transform into a peaceful, post-conflict scenario anytime soon, at least not against Assad's (or Russia's) will. Therefore, those voices argue that donor governments should at least try to decouple rehabilitation measures from the regime's political behaviour at home and in Geneva. Some suggest, like Muriel Asseburg, that attempts should be made to liaise rehabilitation projects predominantly with local authorities and cooperation partners in order to minimize exposure to the predatory centre.[14] Others, like Julien Barnes-Dacey, hold that stronger partnerships with civil society on the ground could help serve a similar purpose and create resilience.[15]

All of these approaches, however, are rather driven by the desperate need to effect some kind of change, mainly for humanitarian reasons, than by political optimism or a master plan. Nobody can spell out for sure if such approaches would actually work in practice and be tolerated by the regime's strong grip on activities in its reach. The NGO law and NGO control have been tightened, with the result that civil society activities have shrunk rather than expanded since the aborted Arab Spring. Concerning the argument about the municipal level, the local 2018 'elections' (as flawed as they were, given the government's limited territorial reach and record of manipulation) displayed a clear return of the Ba'ath Party.[16] Consequently, President Assad has made sure that NGOs remain under sufficient control at the local level, too. The Ba'ath Party had played an important role in social control in the old days under Hafez al-Assad. When his son Bashar took over in 2000 he, in a sense, de-ideologized power. This trend continued in the wake of the 2011 demonstrations. In February 2012, a constitutional amendment even abolished Article 8 of the Syrian constitution, which had enshrined the Party's rule and role in leading society. In parallel, several laws (Decree 107 of 2011, Decree 19 of 2015, and Law 10 of 2018) gave local administrative bodies more autonomy in the management of local development projects.[17] However, as of 2017, Assad re-discovered the Ba'ath Party as an important tool to forge loyalties and dependencies. He timely reorganized the party's leadership boards in preparation for the local 'elections' and has now even made sure that a decentralized approach of rehabilitation (and any form of reconstruction measures) would not bypass the regime's central coffers and control.

Such behaviour from the government makes working coherently with the different branches of UN difficult because it represents incentives for one silo of experts and a red line for others. As the Rosenthal Report on the UN's performance in Myanmar pointed out in form of a rough caricature, "those that work in the 'development pillar' prioritize support for the Government's development efforts, implicitly leaving human rights considerations to others, despite the mantra that development, peace and security and human rights are inexorably intertwined and mutually reinforcing." If these incremental activities are overstretched under an intractable and unscrupulous regime, this leads to a breaking point. "Conversely, those that work in the 'human rights pillar' and in the organization's humanitarian activities naturally prioritize the Government's complying with international law and norms in defense and protection of human rights, usually favoring more robust advocacy measures. Senior officials and staff that work in the 'peace and security pillar' come down somewhere in-between." These different approaches of UN officials and staff are "forged by narrow mandates (in contrast to the UN's wider over-all responsibilities), differing operating cultures, diverse background of the persons involved, and many other factors that shape the sometimes dysfunctional presence of the United Nations System at the country level," which appeared with special intensity in Myanmar and, one could add, in Syria as well. Such a parochial perspective within the three main pillars (or silos) in the UN system runs the risk of losing sight of the essential point: "that each of those pillars has the capacity to leverage the United Nations' activities in the others."[18] But as several cases have shown in the past, including the Syrian one, this potential is rarely exhausted.

Despite the disappointing clarity on how foreign money would be or is already (ab)used in Syria without any political or human rights impact, the debate around rehabilitation, early recovery and reconstruction is caught in a similar political and moral dilemma as the humanitarian quandary. Non-action punishes large parts of the population, no matter on which side they stand. It would perpetuate the Syrian disaster by creating a huge education gap among Syrians and by accepting a largely impoverished, unstable, quasi failed state in the middle of a strategically highly sensitive and essential region in Europe's neighbourhood. These are pressure points of which the regime in Damascus is well aware.

Chapter 10

IRRECONCILABLE POSITIONS: ROADS TO NOWHERE

"Somebody from the Danish Refugee Council once told me: 'Even if only 20 per cent of aid arrives with the needy, it's better than nothing.' The point is that the other 80 per cent are fuelling the conflict!"

This is how former Syrian diplomat Bassam Barabandi summarizes the Neutrality Trap from his experience. He points to the core of the dilemma in the face of a regime that applies integrative warfare: "If you stop the aid for six months, some more people will die, yes, but it may even end the conflict because it takes away the additional resources from the regime that is mainly responsible for the humanitarian crisis." But Barabandi concedes: "It's a hard choice. I have a point and they [those who adhere to a purely humanitarian argumentation] have a point, and both don't match."[1] In a similar vein, a high-ranking humanitarian UN diplomat remembers: "People in Aleppo told us that we were prolonging the suffering because humanitarian delivery, they said, is a business for us."[2]

In another interview with this author, a representative of a Western section of the Red Cross counters this view and defends the strict separation of humanitarian and political deliberations: "I can say that most humanitarian workers and decision-makers do their very best. We have powered through as much as we can in Syria and tried to deliver to the neediest as well as it was possible under those circumstances." She points out that the clear demarcation between humanitarian and political work has the advantage that "as a humanitarian actor, you have your guidelines that help you to function. You don't need to look right or left, since everything else is politics, and it's up to politicians to resolve."[3]

By contrast, Barabandi and other opposition-minded Syrian activists have tried to link humanitarian motives with a broader political concept that, in their view, would have reduced or even ended human rights violations. As an example, he points to the issue of releasing detainees, both a humanitarian and a confidence-building measure that the government in Damascus has declined to conduct in any relevant numbers. "If you stop humanitarian aid when Assad doesn't release prisoners, Assad will be put under pressure and he may lose leverage in the conflict. This is a humanitarian request," Barabandi says justifying this approach. "The issue is how much is legal and how much is moral in your demands."

Syrian activists and opposition repeatedly approached the UN Special Envoys in order to press the detainee issue. "We are not asking the regime to leave power but only to release women and kids," Barabandi says. But UN Envoy De Mistura told him that conflict mediation and detainees were "two different files." Indeed, if originally humanitarian issues make it onto the agenda for political talks, their purpose may not be served. If the parties are not sincerely ready to create confidence and to negotiate, such a move may even endanger lives. In the history of the Geneva talks since 2014, incorporating the file of detainees into the talks either as a humanitarian gesture or as a confidence-building measure has never been successful.

Still, Barabandi tried various possibilities to push these issues and also attempted to get the UN Human Rights Council involved in the Working Group on detainees, abductees and missing persons that comprised Russia, Iran, Turkey and the UN with the ICRC as an observer. This working group is loosely attached to the Astana Format. Barabandi said that the UN argued that involving the Human Rights Council was not possible because this would be a politicization of the humanitarian detainee issue. "But having the ICRC at the table of this working group is not enough," according to Barabandi. "We need other UN agencies at the table but all refused." He criticizes the UN member states for having been too passive to exert their influence. "It's not true that countries don't have a leverage on these developments. They pay millions to the UN and *can* influence developments."[4] Charles Thépaut agrees: "The United States and Europe account for 90 percent of funding of humanitarian assistance to the Syrian people. By dispatching their funding differently inside and outside the U.N. framework, they have leverage – and they must use that leverage to restore humanitarian neutrality and ensure aid helps people in need rather than the regime of Syrian President Bashar al-Assad."[5]

A Fig Leaf for Political Failure

On the other hand, the humanitarian camp might well argue that putting a regime under pressure that violates IHL and IHRL is up to political actors. It is *their* job to invest political and military capital in enforcing access, in sanctioning the regime or in applying military measures such as no-fly zones or even limited or fully fledged interventions. Since it was precisely the political system that failed to stop the cruelties in Syria through a hamstrung UN Security Council, all the subsequent problems of aid work in Syria were offloaded on the shoulders of humanitarians. They were left alone to cope with a regime that committed war crimes, used chemical weapons, and suppressed and manipulated humanitarian work as a tool in this conflict. The large sums of money that political decision-makers released for humanitarian assistance in Syria did not compensate for the lack of international will to enforce a minimum standard of human rights by emergency measures outside the Council (like the controversial decision to intervene in Kosovo 1999) while appealing to higher norms such as R2P. In the classic division of labour, humanitarians dealt with symptoms only. The causes of humanitarian disasters were never addressed. And even in dealing with the symptoms, grave mistakes have been made that exacerbated the problem under difficult and exceptional circumstances.

"As humanitarians in Syria we continued to operate in emergency mode, like a fire brigade, responding to fires for ten years in a row but without ever seeing a solution to the root cause of the fire," former humanitarian Regional Coordinator for Syria, Panos Moumtzis, said to this author. "Political problems require political solutions. We always did everything we could to respond to needs, probably saving thousands of lives with our timely life-saving assistance, but at the end of the day we were left with a feeling that this man-made madness could have been prevented and lives could have been saved if there was a strong political will that put the Syrian people first."[6]

Again, the Syrian case is not unique. As Donini writes: "Humanitarians have been used from that day [when the first Geneva Convention was signed in 1864] to this as fig leaves to veil government action or inaction in the face of war crimes and genocide."[7] And Dallaire concludes from his military perspective: "Humanitarian organizations also cannot – and should not – be expected to be the fig leaf for states' failure to intervene politically to prevent or solve crises. In fact, if donors and politicians did their job, there would be less need for the gigantic humanitarian enterprise of the twenty-first century [...]."[8] Rieff quotes a senior UN official who once called humanitarian assistance a "containment system for the rich world."[9] Some have described the problem as a "humanitarian trap" that humanitarian assistance can prolong wars or give great powers an excuse either for intervention or non-intervention – like in Syria.[10]

Double Deficiency

The Syrian case flagged up a *double deficiency* of the current international system: first, multilateral instruments were paralyzed and political will was lacking to effectively contain the conflict in a timely manner and address the humanitarian disaster as a political problem. Second, humanitarian actors were left alone with the symptoms and the policy dilemmas entailed in working under the shadow of a regime that was killing its own citizens. Some of these humanitarians showed structural or personal deficiencies in dealing with this situation on the ground or a lack of assessment, diligence, interest or sensitivity. In singular cases, political bias may have also played a role in why they deviated from the application of strictly humanitarian principles.

Progress at the Security Council was blocked mainly because of frequent Russian vetoes, supported by China. In this context, the question arises why Russia made itself an accomplice to the *methods* of an unscrupulous regime. Politically, there are many explainable reasons why Russia decided to get involved in the war, some of which have been mentioned above in relation to the discussion about preventing a further spread of the R2P-logic. Iran had its own reasons, mainly a regional power-play against Saudi Arabia and the creation of a land bridge of influence from Teheran to Hezbollah in Beirut, the so-called Shia Crescent. For Russia, several geopolitical reasons played a role, as did the more or less explicit intention to prevent Western-style democracy in the Middle East after the Arab

Spring, as a Russian diplomat in Geneva told me. But this still does not explain why Russia and Iran felt the need to be complicit in the gravest IHL and IHRL violations witnessed this century. In other words: was there a military necessity to go as far as to bombard, and help destroy, medical facilities in a targeted manner, or to kill and terrorize as many civilians as possible as a war strategy?

The double deficiency left ample room for greater powers to determine outcomes on the Syrian battlefield and in related political arenas, especially for Iran and Russia on the pro-government side. But both pursued completely different concepts of intervention in Syria. Iran entered Syria on the micro-level. This means with boots on the ground, mostly with proxies like Hezbollah and other Shia militias lumped together with mercenaries or former prisoners, including from Iraq, Afghanistan and Pakistan. Often, the government in Damascus readily granted them Syrian nationality, which goes hand in hand with Iran's aim to increase the percentage of the Shia population in Syria. Entering on the micro-level also implied that Iran intended to influence Syrian religious and societal life. It invested in real estate to create Shia neighbourhoods and tasked missionaries with leading Alawites back to their Shia roots. But most Alawites were not interested in converting at all, enjoying their religious freedom and secular customs, drinking arak and relative gender equality.

For many of those reasons, Syrians, even some of those in opposition, openly or silently preferred Russian to Iranian influence, for Russia had entered Syria on the macro-level with relatively few boots on the ground, while deploying air power and looming over societal life. Russians didn't care what Syrians believed in: many had been brought up in a secular environment, like Russians themselves. Syrians in government and opposition alike remembered with some degree of nostalgia a colourful student life in Moscow. Russians enjoyed sharing vodka and arak with their Syrian counterparts. Russia also tried to build institutions in Syria, for example by integrating former rebels and formerly defected soldiers back into the Syrian Arab Army in its Fifth Corps. It was a Russian idea to advance discussions about a Syrian constitution in the political process. Despite their destructive military approach, Russians had an interest in state-building and stability, partly in order to reduce their own operating costs. By contrast, Iran undermined the institutions weakening them by proxies and militias (and with some Revolutionary Guards on the ground), and thus further impaired an already complex and chaotic cross-cutting chain of command. Of course, both Iran and Russia have attempted to ensure lucrative economic paybacks for their military engagement in saving Assad's neck. Consequently, Assad has started a process of basically selling Syria's infrastructure and reconstruction projects to the invited foreign, and to some extent, occupying powers. Both Russia and Iran have been competing with each other but, at the same time, need each other in order to not having to deal with the Syrian mess alone.

But precisely because Russians had no interest in shaping Syrian society, because they were secular, powerful and strategic, they had an edge over Iran in terms of soft power. However, Moscow, despite its political investment in the conflict, has foregone the opportunity to take advantage and properly use this chance.

Russia's Soft Power Failure

In late 2015, Russia entered the Syrian war with decisiveness and full engagement on three levels in parallel – militarily, politically and diplomatically – at a time when Western countries were largely absent. Pursuing all three goals simultaneously, Russia urged for the start of the Geneva Talks at the beginning of 2016 while its military continued to support the bombardment of – or themselves bombed[11] – civilians or opposition and rebel positions, including hospitals, ambulances, markets, bakeries and other non-military targets. This was no contradiction in the Russian view. Russia fought a war as if there existed no negotiations and yet pushed for negotiations as if it were not actively engaged in the war. Russia wanted to enhance its power by contributing to a Syrian settlement mainly on its own terms. Therefore, it engaged on all playing fields in leading roles. Thanks in addition to a weakening political and diplomatic role of the United States under the Trump administration, the Syrian conflict(s) allowed Russia – after its stigmatization resulting from the Ukraine crisis – to get back on eye-level with the US. Although sanctions against Russia have not been lifted, the long-term gain in geopolitical leverage and in regaining national pride were essential outcomes for the Russian side.

However, it was precisely this blatant violation of international legal principles and the creation of immense human suffering that prevented the long-term success of Russia's global political aspirations beyond the Syrian conflict. Had Russia restrained itself and the Assad regime militarily, had it not vetoed IHL- and IHRL-related measures and questioned UN findings on the regime's use of chemical weapons, it would have still won the war with its military might and commitment despite the possibility of increased costs of warfare and a slightly delayed military victory. Moreover, Moscow would have gained the opportunity to smoothly mutate from a party to the war to a perceived peace-maker in the later phase of the conflict. Russia already saw itself as a pacifier in Syria, having created the Astana Format to catalyze the stalling Geneva process and forcefully established so-called reconciliation areas with Russian military advisers and police on the ground. Although all this was an obvious combat tactic and applied by force, many in the Syrian opposition preferred a Russian role in Syria to an Iranian one. But Russia missed its chance to consolidate its soft power in Syria and internationally through Syria.

Had it done so, in very practical terms Russia would have alleviated its own burden in Syria by gaining international stabilization and reconstruction support. It could have played a stabilizing role that would have been even appreciated by a paralyzed and reluctant West – if only it had broadly adhered to norms of IHL and IHRL by pursuing its military agenda in line with *ius in bello* principles, by *seriously* engaging in the Geneva process and by obliging the Syrian government to do so, too.

One reason behind Russia's behaviour may have been the gulf between the Russian military and diplomatic machineries and traditions. The rivalry between the Defence and the Foreign Ministries has been obvious throughout this and other conflicts. Since Syria was a war zone, it was in the hands of the military and its logic. The political colleagues at times took the helm away from the military, like in the last days before the Sochi 'Reconciliation Conference' in January 2018, when the propaganda event risked turning into a failure. But it was the military that decided the strategy on the ground and not the diplomats. President Putin covered both approaches simultaneously and, when push comes to shove, he himself tends to fall back on hard power than on soft power. His behaviour mirrors the general tendency that hard power is more enshrined in Russian political culture.

The victims of this approach were Syrian civilians and the hard-earned principles of IHL and IHRL. Paradoxically, in the attempt to prevent at any cost an international environment driven by all too progressive R2P ideas after the Libyan experience, Russian behaviour in Syria made protection an even more essential necessity of our times from both humanitarian and legal perspectives.

Contempt for Multilateralism

Lack of long-term visions of peace and stability, lack of multilateral approaches and, instead, unilateral power politics amounted to an uneasy mix. Not only did the notorious UN-bashing of US President Trump enter the scene but long before him pro-Assad allies showed an ever-dwindling respect for the UN, strategically and in particular towards those agencies that have been working on collecting evidence on potential war crimes, such as the Organisation for the Prohibition of Chemical Weapons (OPCW) work on the use of banned weapons, the Commission of Inquiry's (CoI) investigation of accountability issues, or the International, Impartial and Independent Mechanism's[12] (IIIM) assistance with the investigation and prosecution of persons responsible for the most serious crimes under international law committed in the Syrian Arab Republic since March 2011. Russia, in the Security Council and beyond, took a position of constant denial and shrugging shoulders: all the evidence collected by international UN experts against the Syrian regime were simply called fake. UN expert work – and thus the UN itself – was discredited as either sloppy or biased. The UN became the scapegoat in a constantly widening gulf between the major powers and their irreconcilable positions, and the victim of national disinformation campaigns portrayed as a tool in the hands of Western powers. However, all this has not kept Russia, China and even Syria from using the UN's platform for their own purposes wherever suitable. It must be mentioned again in this context that the CoI and IIIM have also accused Syrian rebel forces of war crimes, something that is indeed accepted and reported by Russian and Iranian media.

Respect for the UN has slipped to a dismal low. The world body has become a punchbag for powers and an arena for denial. President Assad himself openly conceded his contempt for the United Nations in an interview at the outset of the Syrian crisis in 2011 with ABC's Barbara Walters:

Walters   You do not think the United Nations is a credible organization?

Assad   No, for one reason, they haven't implemented, they never implemented any of the resolutions that related to the Arab world for example the Palestinians to the

Syrian land why don't they, if they talk about human rights what about the Palestinians suffering in the occupied territory, what about my land is my people that live their land because it's occupied by Israel, of course not.

Assad For every citizen it is not for me as president I am telling you about the perception in the whole region.

Walters You do, you do not think the United Nations is credible?

Assad No.

Assad Never it's not something before my generation it's something we inherited as a concept as a belief.

Walters You have an ambassador to the United Nations.

Assad Yeah, it's a game we play. It doesn't mean you believe in it.[13]

Against this background of eroding legitimacy and support, of ideological polarization and the unilateralism of great powers, it has become increasingly difficult for the UN to pass the test of being a guardian or even implementer of international law, and of IHL and IHRL in particular. The humanitarian branches of the world organization are regarded either as a disturbing element or a welcome low-hanging fruit that provides additional resources for warfare. Declarations of impartiality and neutrality may even sound nothing other than naïve to the ears of unscrupulous power elites.

Chapter 11

ARGUMENTS FOR CHANGE: HOW TO AVOID THE NEUTRALITY TRAP

Drawing lessons from the complex Syrian scenario is hard without sounding hypocritical or too academic, given that political and humanitarian decisions had to be taken on the hoof in muddy circumstances and amid the push-and-pull of international power constellations. Nevertheless, every dilemmatic situation offers lessons for the future, even – perhaps above all – the Syrian case, where the stakes, brutality and human toll were extremely high. 'Business as usual' looks like the worst option after what has happened, not only for Syrians but also for the sake of rescuing humanitarian innocence worldwide as well as for the sake of international law's resilience. Arguments in favour of change and against current international practice may be summarized as follows:

1. The *need-based argument*: Humanitarian assistance does precisely not arrive at the most needy and does not reach enough needy. Under such circumstances, the principles of impartiality and neutrality become a farce.

2. The *IHL-based argument*: Contemporary legal opinion strongly supports alternative forms of humanitarian cooperation like cross-border deliveries in extreme situations against the will of the respective state and, if necessary, even without the consent of the UN Security Council. But this may become an increasingly brittle position if the erosion of multilateralism continues and the pretension of hard state sovereignty gradually returns.

3. The *value-based argument*: Diverted and abused humanitarian assistance may strengthen unscrupulous regimes in an already asymmetric conflict. Those regimes commit large-scale violations of human rights that have become an integral part of our universal value system. Some, especially autocrats, may still argue, that such value systems are not universal but Western, European or else. This is a complex debate that spans continents and cultures. The Arab Spring and many popular uprisings in non-Western countries have proven and are still proving the contrary. At the very least, there is no way to deny that these values have entered the Charter and practice of the United Nations and its agencies where practically all countries are members, voluntarily so.

4. The *mediation-based argument*: A stronger party of the non-international armed conflict (mostly the state) has more opportunities to channel and abuse

humanitarian resources to its own advantage. The resulting increased asymmetry renders any form of third-party mediation, especially by the UN, more difficult – if not impossible, since it removes any incentive for the stronger party to come to the negotiating table. This may prolong the conflict and the humanitarian suffering.

5. The *credibility-based argument*: In practically all of today's ongoing conflicts, the UN has failed to achieve a mediated political solution; its personnel and agencies have been blasted for their handling of humanitarian aid and other assistance. We have seen the extent of discontent in the Syrian case and the UN's need to adjust and conduct internal investigations. This may leave a lasting mark on an organization that, at the same time, has to defend its added value in difficult times given sceptical bilateralist national leaders, budget cuts and a lack of concerted support for its peace initiatives, field missions and other activities. The uncoordinated efforts of different UN agencies that often cancel out each others' efforts (such as offering unconditional development assistance despite a stalled mediation process) adds to the picture.

6. The *economics-based argument*: Diverted and abused humanitarian resources may soak up millions of dollars and euros in a war economy, which prolongs the conflict. It may also strengthen the structures of a predatory state and allied regime cronies. During a conflict in which the state is a party that does not care about its people, it unburdens a state from delivering services without discrimination, enables it to use its remaining resources on its clientele, and to create further destruction and humanitarian suffering.

The economic argument also exists as a criticism against humanitarian assistance in general. Some types of aid destroy local economic structures and increase external dependence, a criticism that has also been expressed in the Syrian context.[1] When it comes to the post-conflict period and possible reconstruction, the same doubts hold true about fostering a predatory system that may even exclude parts of its population from the benefits of these efforts. In the long term, this will not create economic, social or political stability.

Let us recall what the humanitarian Neutrality Trap implies: well-intentioned decision-makers from donor countries tend to insist on remaining nominally strictly 'neutral' and 'impartial' when they take decisions about releasing humanitarian funds. For this purpose, they try to keep aloof from any political considerations and implications regarding a conflict. Consequently, they also dispel possible alternative delivering of assistance other than the one through the channel established by a tested 'international consensus', which is through the incumbent government (despite the fact that, as we have seen, strong IHL argumentation meanwhile exists against this perceived consensus). According to this approach, anything else would be 'politicized aid' because it goes directly to rebel territory, thus supporting rebels, and crosses borders without the host country's active consent. In such a case, by eclipsing the political reality on the ground, neutrality may turn into a form weakness vis-à-vis the stronger party (mostly the government). Hence, neutrality in spending becomes anything other than neutral in practice on the ground. Those decision-makers who assume (or in some cases pretend) to act in a strictly humanitarian – and thus neutral and impartial – manner, tend to provide little resistance against political manipulation and may fall prey to the very power relations that condition their work.

Obviously, there are two radical options for how to avoid this trap. One is to flatly admit that under such extremely adverse conditions, the delivered assistance is not (any longer) humanitarian, or perhaps remains so in motivation even though this is impossible in practice. The other radical option is to withdraw humanitarian work, either tactically and temporarily, in order to gain negotiation leverage, as happened in Bosnia during 1993 or Yemen in 2020. It will never be known how the Syrian government would have reacted in 2012 if the UN and other international agencies had collectively threatened to withdraw. Would the regime's threat to expel them have turned into a bluff?

To be realistic: if and when links to a host government are cut and strictly humanitarian assessments make large cross-border activities the central focus, humanitarian work on the ground may not be possible without political and/or military cover. It needs a commitment from the UN Security Council or at least of parts of the international community – in case they are ready to act without a UN mandate – to shield such assistance should it contravene the will of the host country and its possible allies. Obviously, no-fly zones come to mind. But they make sense only when they are effectively enforced by surface-to-air missiles, planes or drones. In more difficult cases humanitarian work may have to be covered on the ground, too, if overland attacks are launched. Whether one of these radical options is feasible, therefore, depends to a large extent on the individual constellations, circumstances and power relationships during the crisis.

We have also seen that there are solid and plausible humanitarian counter-arguments against any of these radical options. Among them is the firewall argument, which aims to protect humanitarian deliberations and actions from any potentially corrupting political influence. Another one is the legal stability argument, which holds that the international legal order is at risk if decisions are taken individually and differently each time a crisis occurs. One example is the question if the consent of a host country is deemed necessary for cross-border delivery or not. Promoters of the legal stability argument are also concerned about insecurities and dangers for staff operating on the ground because of conflicting legal interpretations. They argue that such a flexible approach may set a precedent and erode even more the acceptability of and adherence to international legal principles. Political abuse is always possible along the road of the decision-making process.

Apart from lofty humanitarian argumentation, very practical – and by nature political – aspects come to mind against a radical decision to disengage from humanitarian cooperation. Such a step may create new flows of refugees like in this case from Syria into neighbouring countries and Europe, something that Western donors are eager to prevent.

Since no humanitarian relief effort will ever take place in an ideal world and the threshold for radical measures is high, critics of the current practice of humanitarian assistance in Syria have come up with a laundry list of recommendations for improved practices *within* the current overall framework. They are designed to increase the resilience of humanitarian organizations vis-à-vis abusive state governments and to reduce the policy dilemma under which they are operating. In particular, Human Rights Watch, Chatham House, the Norwegian Refugee Council and Oxfam[2] have published several practical measures that could help relief efforts avoid the traps that are common in difficult real-life circumstances and enhance the possibility of delivering principled aid.

Although academic and legal debates may look pointless with a regime that is determined to fight for survival with all available means, one recommendation is that international humanitarian organizations (IHOs) should be more insistent about the reading of international humanitarian law, in particular Article 3 of the Geneva Convention, which states that "arbitrary or capricious" reasons given by a host country to deny humanitarian access are simply invalid. OCHA itself put forward the following "important recommendation" in the Syria Evaluation Report of 2016: "OCHA should do further work on codifying the concept of arbitrary denial and build on the access work it has achieved around Syria through a body of work. A permanent capacity at HQ to analyse access and undertake humanitarian access negotiations should be considered."[3]

One major lesson learned from Syria in comparison to other humanitarian scenarios is that a tougher stance by humanitarians may pay off as a negotiation tactic with the regime. Haid points out in his overview of humanitarian deficiencies in Syria that some international humanitarian organizations did actually negotiate successfully with the Syrian government. They achieved their goals through patience, persistence and by making clear from the beginning their non-negotiable principles and refused to compromise. During negotiations, they explained they would cancel or postpone projects if they were not permitted to implement them on their own terms. In many cases, the government withdrew the restrictions or conditions they imposed. On other occasions, the organizations simply cancelled their projects.[4] We saw that there are parallels in Bosnia or Yemen where at times the position of UN humanitarian agencies was more impactful and in line with humanitarian principles.

Another main recommendation, linked to the above, is that IHOs should join forces, coordinate better and thus create negotiation leverage to confront the regime's quite successful 'divide and rule' strategy. A joint approach would make it more difficult for the government to bully or expel individual organizations. Even UN agencies have not coordinated between themselves effectively, even though donors like the EU have urged them to do so. In a nutshell: assistance offers should be largely pooled, packaged and conditioned. They should be handed over as a take-it-or-leave-it option. Of course, the regime might reject it altogether, which leads us back to the above-mentioned radical options. But given the gravity of the situation, at least in Syria, it should have been tested. Haid points out that IHOs, particularly UN agencies, have enough leverage to increase their negotiating power without fearing reprisals from the government. An estimated 11.7 million people are in need across the country, 7.2 million of whom live in government-held areas.[5] "The government is trying to stabilize the areas under its control, but it does not have the resources to do this alone."[6] True, but above all, it strives to spend the money it has on other purposes or to transfer those funds to its cronies' bank accounts abroad.

Here we should also distinguish between the various phases of the conflict. Such a take-it-or-leave-it approach would have worked better in the early years of the conflict, when the regime was desperately struggling for survival. At that point, the regime needed the UN as a resource for its war chest and as a source of legitimacy more than the UN needed the regime. But this was the decisive period of the conflict when the rules of the game were set, and the UN agencies caved in. In the later years, when the government once again held coherent parts of territory, issues around access and manipulation still remained, but the most severe violations that should have provoked most severe reactions have become less such as sieges and large-scale bombings with huge humanitarian repercussions combined with cross-line blockages. The number of active frontlines has also diminished. Despite the dismal economic situation, the regime itself has collected its forces and – in its sense of self – has survived the most difficult times. Therefore, why should it give in either to political or humanitarian demands precisely now when the worst is apparently over? Bluffing with the threat to pull out humanitarian aid is much less likely to work now than it would have been between 2012 and say 2018.

"Given the UN's usual deference to power and respect for member state sovereignty," a former high-ranking UN official concluded to this author, "even principled and well-intentioned UN staff on the ground have few tools to push back against member state bullying."[7] This is why well-intentioned staff on the ground need the support of well-coordinated donors. Such collective action can exert the necessary political pressure. In practical terms, IHOs could establish a funding consortium and exchange information about government restrictions, and about successful and unsuccessful negotiations for access. Donors should establish a clearing-house mechanism for programming that would enhance transparency and streamline conditions and deliverables of planned projects. A common definition of red lines is necessary as a consistent stance from all IHOs if the government insists on unacceptable conditions. Again, this can only work if *all* the participating organizations show credible readiness to withdraw a project or even their presence in the country, if necessary.

Collective action is also enhanced by establishing detailed common operational guidelines that enable IHOs to freely choose local partners, to develop transparent mechanisms for procurement and to create independent monitoring and evaluation processes. An overarching common goal would be to reduce and limit the acceptable bureaucratic permissions required for operations on the ground. Another suggestion has been that IHOs should enhance their abilities to conduct systematic, comprehensive and impartial needs assessments, monitoring and evaluation processes through direct and reliable access to the field. For this purpose, they must insist on opening more field offices on the ground. If the government in charge denies this – as the case in Syrian-regime-held territories – then a more radical option might be considered.

The 2019 Rosenthal Report on the UN's performance in Myanmar distinguishes two approaches below the threshold of the radical option of humanitarian withdrawal (and apart from business as usual). One concept revolves around forceful collective action and robust diplomacy as described above but within the limits of existing political spaces. This strategy of "maximum influence" is referred to in the Report as "outspoken diplomacy" approach. The softer, more silent, approach is coined "principled engagement" or "quiet diplomacy". Both are tactical approaches, of course, and neither right nor wrong. They can occur in different shades of grey and operate in parallel.[8] Within the possibilities of the more silent tactics and intermediate steps towards more principled humanitarian access, various measures can be undertaken in everyday practice. For example, the Syrian case makes it obvious that IHOs must not accept any external interference in their internal recruitment processes. They should also refrain from employing local staff close to, or part of, a warring party even for tactical reasons, since this undermines the credibility of the organization and creates an atmosphere of mistrust and intimidation inside a supposedly humanitarian working environment.

Furthermore, IHOs should stop sharing procurement files with the government or entities affiliated with it, such as SARC or Syria Trust. Thus individuals affiliated with the regime should not get an unfair advantage in the tender process. IHOs should also create a thorough vetting process to exclude people involved in humanitarian violations or those who are on sanction lists for good reasons. Apart from ethical deliberations and questions of credibility of the humanitarian work, these sanctions are established by the biggest donors like the US and the EU that do not want to see people on the sanctions lists profit from their donor money, even if only indirectly. Donors should also engage more to support IHOs in those efforts, if not in direct contact with the government, then by negotiations with third parties. Some of the issues have already been repeatedly raised by donor countries in the Humanitarian Task Force of the Office of the Special Envoy for Syria in Geneva.

Given the deficiencies of negotiated access, IHOs should learn how to develop capacities in conflict sensitivity and humanitarian negotiation in order to improve access dialogue with Syrian counterparts. This includes in-depth training of field staff on humanitarian principles. Humanitarian negotiating at the frontline is still an underdeveloped field in the studies of the humanities.[9] Structural deficits within the UN account for a lack of accountability from senior staff and a very flat learning curve from previous mistakes. So it is by far not only the staff in the field but also senior officials that need better training, proper evaluations and a human resources department that draws the right conclusions.

As NRC and Oxfam point out, the UN leadership in Damascus should ensure that their many sector heads maintain a proactive, regular dialogue with relevant ministries, which would enable them to support advocacy linked to broader access issues. They should also relay issues back to sector meetings and represent IHOs' advocacy messaging to government ministries. Using more local spaces to enhance humanitarian deliveries is another recommendation brought forward by those international humanitarian organizations that have in principle accepted the government's ground rules. For example, the Roman Catholic organization Caritas Internationalis has readily cooperated with Syrian partners registered with the government. According to their reports, they enjoy a certain level of freedom to operate, even in some neighbourhoods that are regarded as anti-regime. More of those little spaces should be used, says Caritas.[10] Still, it remains a balancing act. It is probably easier to deliver assistance without major interference if an agency concentrates on some local areas in which they can help, without being preoccupied with the overall picture. In any case, such an approach does not avoid the Neutrality Trap altogether.

That said, leading practitioners on the ground in Syria stressed the significance of the variety of local actors. Former Regional Humanitarian Coordinator in Amman, Panos Moumtzis, recalled to this author: "It was amazing to see the setting up of national NGOs by Syrians from the diaspora who left their jobs and came to work, serving their people primarily though the cross-border operation. Having lived and worked in Syria for years, I came to respect and admire the compassion and drive of the Syrian community to help their own people. This also applies to the thousands of SARC volunteers. No other operation in the world is localized to the extend I saw in Syria."[11]

On the international donors' side, there is also room for improvement. One recommendation is that they should diversify flexible and multi-year funding for the response from the Damascus hub, enabling organizations to scale up programming when access does open up. Those few states that do maintain diplomatic representation in Syria or visit the country regularly, mostly from Beirut, should engage proactively, using the same talking-points with government ministries in support of increasing access in line with humanitarian principles, and donors without this representation should support these efforts indirectly.

Apart from more mutual cooperation and collective action to support those who have to negotiate on the ground, organizational behaviour and individual incentives in donor ministries should be reviewed, mostly in ministries of foreign affairs or/ and development. Political survival instincts and organizational behaviour alike tend to take the path of least resistance. Risk aversion and sometimes lack of engagement from individual diplomats may promote a spending scheme that caters for the big and well-known organizations but neglects the small ones that fly under the radar. Transferring humanitarian money to the UN is easy; few would question it. The auditing authority will happily tick off such funding. In addition, the donor government can quickly add these large sums to its public record of humanitarian assistance in the usual international competition of the selling of indulgences. In contrast, scrutinizing the evolving political situation on the ground may infringe on the firewall but is also a time consuming laborious effort. Finding out – and admitting to oneself and to the public – that traditional spending schemes may have led to distortions of humanitarian principles, will result in controversies and the need to adjust procedures. This again calls for the availability of alternatives. Finding these may be difficult, however. And even if there are any – for example, smaller organizations that dare to go cross border in difficult circumstances because of principled humanitarian assessments – they may have less experience in handling larger sums of money or in accounting in general. The auditing authority may pose questions. What is needed here is both increased individual and political courage to commit more strongly to trying out new ways and partnerships – in other words, adjusting to realities that have rendered conventional practice unbearable. To a certain extent, this has already happened, particularly in the gradual diversification of money towards 'humanitarian plus' efforts, as we have seen. But clearly this is a lengthy process of gradual learning from the insufficiencies of readily available humanitarian toolkits. In any case, foreign ministries should make sure that no firewall creeps in between humanitarian and human rights deliberations when it comes to their own decision-making and procedures.

Moreover, donors should make every effort to look deeper into the UN system, to question reports and procedures. As a high-ranking former UN official puts it: "Donors are going to have to be far more diligent in monitoring the end use and make it clear that the UN will not be the chosen means of delivery, if the neutrality trap means that those doing the killing are the primary beneficiaries of the assistance."[12] Diplomats from donor states should keep asking questions and digging for reasons like why particular partners on the ground were offered a contract. They should stay interested even in the often all too arduous work of reading between the lines in detailed updates from the ground. Diplomats from donor countries should actively engage their UN counterparts in coordination and strategy meetings. They should question wording that trivializes atrocities, plunging them in foggy semantics. As we have seen, some donors have come together and prepared a list of deviations from humanitarian principles, although they shy away from sharing it publicly in order to spare the UN's blushes in already difficult times. Indeed, this is a balancing act. But also and in particular diplomatic language behind the scenes has a potential of nuances and should not shy away from using its entire repertoire when necessary. Unacceptable incidents must be called what they are, for example when not the slightest progress is visible and a task force supposed to review the UN's adherence to the Parameters and Principles simply does not meet.

If taken seriously after the Syrian disaster, some of the above-mentioned lessons learned and recommendations may lead to concerted actions by operators and donors of humanitarian aid so that the radical option of complete withdrawal remains the last resort. But it needs to be a realistic option. In the end, it is a poker game with risks on both sides. And yes, there are situations in such conflicts when humanitarians do have to take part in a *political* gamble if they want to salvage their own principles. In the end, it is not about politicizing humanitarian aid from the donors' side but rather shifting the goalposts back to the centre that the Syrian regime had snatched and buried in the far corner.

Chapter 12

CONCLUSION

This book has attempted to shed light on the various policy dilemmas faced by political and humanitarian actors in a highly complex conflict environment. Lessons from the Syrian war on the handling of humanitarian and other assistance have been put into a wider perspective regarding the development – and creeping retrogression – of international law. One of my aims has also been to carve out arguments for change to current international practices, and to deliver possible recommendations and guidance for political and humanitarian decisions in similar hostile environments and conflicts to come.

The Syrian conflict has challenged the international community and international law in extraordinary ways. The scenario involved a highly complex set of actors and interests, extremely large regional and international repercussions from conflict and proxy involvements, a mutual paralysis in the Security Council, and tremendously high human displacement and toll on civilians. This has been accompanied by systematic torture, strategic starving and other massive violations of international humanitarian law (IHL) and international human rights law (IHRL), a strong asymmetry of resources, weapons and political alliances in gradual favour of the Syrian government – a government that, at the same time, was responsible for the vast majority of civilian deaths and the devastation of medical and civilian infrastructure. The conflict also displayed a fragmentation of actors, territory, civilian and military structures, the radicalization and Islamization of armed actors on the ground, passivity of Western countries towards the massive violation and disturbance of international human rights standards and values even after a vast refugee crisis spilled across their own borders and challenged their domestic political contexts.

This complexity represented a nightmare not only for Syrian civilians but also for any attempt to mediate this conflict and conduct negotiations for a political solution. On a macro level, various overarching political and legal tendencies contributed to a protracted disaster without a comprehensive political solution in sight: an unresolved power struggle in a multipolar world between the US, Russia and China on a global level, and between Saudi Arabia, Iran and Turkey regionally, a mounting assertiveness of authoritarianism and bilateralism in a post-modern world, a resulting crisis in multilateralism and international law, manifested by a gradually weakening binding force on international values and legal standards.

This included a lack of public outrage against violations or a lack of political commitment to sanction violations, and, finally, a creeping revival of the old concept of hard and unconditional state sovereignty.

Taken together, all of this has formed obstacles to a human-rights-oriented approach in Syria and to a principled humanitarian practice. The notion of an international responsibility to protect human life and human rights has faded. A large number of Syrian civilians paid the price. Their public demonstrations for human rights, dignity, better life opportunities and personal and political freedoms happened at the wrong time within broader global developments. In a longer-term perspective, an unstable, traumatized, deprived and radicalized region will continue to boomerang on Europe and its wider neighbourhood. In fact, the Arab Spring – and the Syrian crisis in particular – hit the international community in a fragmented world lacking strong political leadership.

The humanitarian community has paid a heavy price, too. Many of its staff have been injured or killed, its medical infrastructure on the ground largely destroyed and very often its morale has crumbled as well. In addition, humanitarians, especially decision-makers within UN agencies, have been put under extraordinary pressure from an unscrupulous regime and criticized extensively over their handling of the crisis in Syria. This has left dents in the world body's credibility in the eyes of many, not only of Syrians. Even if one takes into consideration the difficult circumstances and the dilemmatic decision-making environment, several humanitarian organizations and individuals took decisions that were not comprehensible in light of international humanitarian standards and, in particular, in light of their obligation to work according to principles of impartiality and neutrality.

Diplomats who were interviewed for this book said that in the past decades in which they worked on humanitarian files they have never experienced anything similar to the complexity of the Syrian situation, to the scope of humanitarian manipulation, and to such a politicized debate about humanitarian assistance. The Syrian case has shown that politicization of humanitarian assistance took place less from the international donors' side (which has been a frequent problem in humanitarian history) but that it was part of a constant struggle to rectify a discourse and practice instigated by a violent regime and its allies that had abandoned existing norms and humanitarian principles. In other words, it was about shifting the goalposts back to the centre after the regime had buried them far off in the corner.

The Syrian case flagged up a double deficiency of the current international system: first, multilateral instruments were paralyzed and the political will was lacking to use effective methods that could have contained the conflict in a timely manner and tackled the humanitarian disaster as a *political* problem. Second, *humanitarian* actors were left alone with the symptoms and the policy dilemmas entailed in working under a regime that kills its own people. Some of these humanitarians also showed structural or personal deficiencies in dealing with this situation. It is difficult to keep humanitarian and political decisions strictly separate when the overarching principles of IHL and IHRL are at stake to such an extent. As one Western diplomat put it: "Every humanitarian decision is also a political decision." And a humanitarian demand may be genuinely humanitarian or also politically motivated or both. The Syrian opposition's frequent demand of the release of detainees is such a case.

In a wider context, it is not just international law that has been challenged in the Syrian conflict(s) and which will probably be partially rewritten in the longer run; hitherto consensual international practices based on a (selective) reading of this law will also be affected. On the one hand, it is hard to imagine that business as usual will be acceptable to donors having witnessed the painful lessons of humanitarian practice in Syria that had to deal with the symptoms of a failed political approach to contain the conflict. On the other hand, these bitter experiences have also offered the authoritarian side of the global political spectrum a golden opportunity to alter international legal understandings and practices that may turn into principles according to their preferences. Great powers like Russia and China, but also the US on some other occasions, have used narratives of both the political and the legalistic camps selectively. On the one hand, they use political and military force to re-shape the development of international law, in the Syrian case in a regressive fashion towards the notion of hard state sovereignty and non-intervention with all its consequences. On the other hand, this very insistence on non-intervention has been part of a legalistic and stability-oriented argumentation from the same players. The latter can also be found in some parts of the Western donor camp.

Since international law is a moving target and constantly developing, the recent events in the Middle East will definitely leave their traces. One concrete example is that the concept of Responsibility to Protect (R2P) has largely lost plausibility as a guideline for concerted action. In fact, R2P has almost disappeared from discussions. The development of this notion has come to a temporary halt despite its permanent evolution following the end of the Cold War, the fall of the Berlin Wall, the intervention in Kosovo, the experiences of unhampered genocide in Bosnia-Herzegovina and Rwanda, and the beginnings of the Arab Spring. In the end, ultimately R2P has been buried under the Syrian rubble as a long-term result of the ill-advised and mismanaged US intervention in Iraq in 2003 and through the controversial international intervention in Libya in 2011.

Russia had several political reasons for intervening in the Syrian conflict. One of its goals was to prevent precedents of humanitarian-inspired state interference and thus to strengthen the notion of hard state sovereignty. This was a policy of prevention, so to speak, against a potential scenario in which Russia, China, Iran and other countries with a dismal human rights record may have been confronted with popular upheavals similar to the 2011 Arab Spring, the Green Movement in Iran, the Chechen war during the early 2000s or the 2019 Hong Kong protests. With these policies, authoritarian governments have been trying to prevent a situation in which they would someday sit at the receiving end of a potential humanitarian intervention.

In this context, the question arises if Russia in particular acted wisely in its long-term interest when it made itself an accomplice not to the Assad regime as such, but to the *methods* of such unscrupulous warfare. In all probability, applying and shielding these methods was not even a matter of military necessity or efficiency. Russia would have gained the upper hand anyway given its combined political, diplomatic and military investments. But Moscow risked – and probably lost – the diplomatic and political credibility to morph from a warring party into an internationally recognized peacemaker after its main strategic goals in Syria had been reached. At least, this is what Moscow aimed at with its various diplomatic initiatives such as the 2018 Sochi 'Reconciliation Conference' or the rash post-conflict debate about quick reconstruction. But in this context, such initiatives lacked credibility and Russia got stuck in Syria, as did an economically fragile and narrowly self-interested Iran, without any broader international support for post-conflict challenges. Indeed, largely apathetic Western countries would have been happy if just someone, even Russia, had been an acceptable *Ordnungsmacht* in Syria regardless of its national interests that it pursued in the Eastern Mediterranean – had it only not violated so massively IHL and IHRL during this war. Nobody could skate over that. Russia forewent the chance to gain valuable soft power through its role in Syria. Instead, the Kremlin chose to rely on hard power only, of the most unscrupulous kind. It is a bitter irony that, in the attempt to prevent at any cost an international environment driven by R2P ideas, the Russian and Iranian methods of warfare in Syria made protection even more vital in our times from both humanitarian and legal perspectives.

The decline of the R2P concept goes hand in hand with the revival and mounting defence of hard state sovereignty, typically derived from a modern understanding of classical international law of Westphalian logic. Foreign interference of any kind, even with humanitarian motives and consisting only of small-scale cross-border activities, tends to be rejected more assertively now than was the case in the two decades either side of the millennium. The notion of state sovereignty is drifting back into traditional concepts that detach the state from obligations vis-à-vis the population. Damascus, in our example, violated its governmental responsibility towards its citizens to the worst extent possible. However, legally speaking in modern IHL, the pretext of being at war does *not* diminish state actors' responsibilities regarding fundamental principles of human life. This is reinforced by the fact that IHL and IHRL have grown more closely linked.

One of the paradoxes in such conflicts is that political actors still tend to defend their actions with reference to international law, even if they violate it. Ultimately, however, international law can be read highly selectively and may become part of a political bargaining process. The Syrian government has made extensive use of legal argumentations on the few international stages that were still open to the widely shunned state, be it at UN headquarters in New York or at the Geneva peace talks. The key words in Syrian diplomats' international discourses oscillated around sovereignty and the government's legitimacy at times when both were most at stake.

Damascus also took up legal narratives in defending its war as a 'fight against terrorism', with all its legal implications. Like other governments in this situation, Damascus was reluctant to recognize the level of hostilities as a non-international armed conflict. This was also because the recognition of insurgents as a party to the conflict would result in the non-state group being accorded legal status and legitimacy. But in the end, the problem in Syria lay less in the difficulty of distinguishing civilians from combatants but in the deliberate annihilation of civilians, a characteristic of the total and asymmetric wars of modern times. Moreover, the global inflationary use of the term and notion of 'terrorism' after 9/11 has made it easier to dilute international norms and obligations by stretching the notion of self-defence and proportionality. It also represents a welcome strategy to de-humanize and bastardize the other so as to legitimize unscrupulous warfare vis-à-vis its loyal constituency at home. The scholarly opinion in modern IHL literature that even if emerging rebels were 'unlawful combatants', they would be covered by the protection of IHL, remained purely academic.

The Syrian case has also taught us that weakness on the part of humanitarian negotiators, decision-makers and leaders in countering suffocating restrictions of their work constitutes part of the problem on the operative side of the story. The crisis in Syria has pushed international practice to its moral and political limits. It also challenged diplomats worldwide and their patterns of thinking and decision-making. Inevitably, due to blatant violations, humanitarian activities became an increasingly political issue, and rightly so. For there was a government in place that was party to the way, the High Contracting Party *and* responsible for some 90 per cent of civilian deaths but also received huge chunks of humanitarian assistance that went, during some periods, almost 90 per cent into government territory only. The government rejected cross-line deliveries, tried to prevent cross-border activities, placed international humanitarian activity under strict state control, and used any form of international contribution as an additional resource for its war economy. Some calculations estimate that the international resources received by the Syrian government through all kinds of assistance constituted about one-third of the country's wartime GDP. The scope of barred or diverted aid and the influx of international money had a stabilizing effect for a regime that was struggling for survival by all means available.

This kind of practice may be called integrative warfare. This is a strategy that systematically and unscrupulously takes advantage of all international resources available from different sectors, including the humanitarian, in order to use or abuse them on the ground by channelling or absorbing humanitarian deliveries in its favour or to profit from the international presence in other forms. Cross-border deliveries, by contrast, are beyond the reach of the central government and thus cannot be used as a resource for the integrative warfare of a predatory state.

Under these circumstances, conventional humanitarian assistance was increasingly questioned and alternatives to current international practice were discussed. Diplomats and political decision-makers who had to decide about funding humanitarian assistance faced the danger of falling into the Neutrality Trap. In their intention to uphold the firewall between humanitarian and political realms, they tended to focus strictly on the humanitarian principles of impartiality and neutrality with the aim of shielding their decisions from the toxic impact of political contexts. Humanitarian assistance had to be delivered without discrimination to the neediest and to the highest possible number of people in need. For this purpose, political considerations are eclipsed, since they distract from humanitarian principles. This approach also tends to reject alternatives of delivering assistance other than through the incumbent government, since this is regarded an established international consensus (or 'soft law' created by UN practice). Thus, according to this approach, a neutral position does not seek to question such consensus but rather to preserve it. Anything else would be regarded as a politicized approach that might derail international givens or even benefit or encourage non-state actors in conflict with a government.

Of course, this state-centred humanitarian approach has been born out of and is based on the original presumption that a government has a particular responsibility and broadly follows its IHL and IHRL obligations vis-à-vis its population. There are also practical deliberations: delivering assistance with the help of a state actor is mostly more efficient and safer than eschewing it. Therefore, political interests or manipulation by the state government are conveniently overlooked, or if humanitarian decision-makers are aware of them, they may argue that it is not their task to make a political judgement on the government's behaviour but rather to act without delay. Humanitarians do not consider it as their job to enter into a political contest. Their mission is to deliver as well as they can under given circumstances

If, however, the government is party to the war that is killing its people on a large scale, the majority of whom being unarmed civilians and non-combatants, and if the government abuses humanitarian assistance and even turns it into a weapon of war, the banner of impartiality and neutrality becomes a farce; and the intention to uphold these principles runs into a difficult dilemma, if not a political trap. In the worst case, humanitarian assistance itself becomes political. The well-intentioned position of neutrality and impartiality turns into the opposite. The decisions taken may prolong the war and suffering. During controversies in a muddy reality such a position may even end up mutating into a hollow dogma after losing its impartial and neutral innocence.

Still, nobody has claimed that it is easy to escape or avoid the Neutrality Trap. Alternatives are difficult to implement and also entail high risks. This dilemma triggered controversial political debates between humanitarians and political decision-makers within and between ministries of donor countries who fought about their legal and political approaches. In parallel, a passionate debate between different camps of international legal experts unfolded.

Both camps, the political or pragmatic one and the legalistic and state-centered or conventionally humanitarian one, have strong arguments on their side. The political camp argued that politics and military actions have shaped international law, and politics adjusts these principles whenever political determination is forceful enough to set a precedent (making war means making law). By contrast, the legalistic camp is concerned with the stability of international law and links all possible changes and actions to a mandate of the Security Council. Concerning humanitarian assistance, the legalistic camp favoured the existing practice of delivering humanitarian aid through a state government in absence of any contrary decision by the Security Council. The political camp, by contrast, pointed to the manipulation and diversion of this aid and to the massive scale of IHL and IHRL violations, which, according to a progressive reading of contemporary IHL, would allow measures also *outside* a Security Council mandate when this body is once again paralyzed . In their view, such a situation would permit to actively ignore the host country's consent to humanitarian assistance also and in particular when it is delivered cross-border. Large-scale cross- border operations were important in the Syrian context since most of the devastation, especially that resulting from air raids, and humanitarian suffering occurred in northern Syria, close to the Turkish borders, and cross-line assistance from Damascus was mostly barred by the regime.

A somewhat intermediate approach can be found in the 2019 Rosenthal Report that shed a critical light on the UN's performance in Myanmar. If the UN Secretariat cannot find support in the Security Council to avert horrific outcomes or reverse the carrying out of human rights abuses already committed, then the options of the UN are indeed limited. "Limited, but not without alternatives," the report suggests, "since even above and beyond binding Security Council resolutions, the United Nations can expand its leverage by partnering with other multilateral institutions, influential bilateral actors, and sometimes even non-governmental entities."[1]

The regime in Damascus capitalized on the paralysis of a Security Council that barred itself from shaping solutions or progressively developing international law. The Syrian government tapped into the existing legalistic narrative and insisted on its absolute state sovereignty, underpinning its position with General Assembly Resolution 46/182 (1991), which focused on sovereignty and consent of the High Contracting Party. On the other side, IHL experts and the more pragmatic or political camp of the debate insist that current international law provides a strong guarantee for humanitarian assistance. They hold that both the negotiating history of the Geneva Convention (Art. 18 AP II) and the practice of relief operations lead to the conclusion that the consent of the government in place for cross-border operations is not necessary under certain circumstances. This is when the scope of humanitarian suffering is extensive and the host government refuses access for arbitrary or capricious reasons like national pride or an intentional deprivation of the population. In Syria, this was the case and even reached levels of besieging areas with the clear goal to weaken the morale of the dissenting population by starving them to death if they did not surrender or to punish them for tolerating the presence of armed groups in their neighbourhoods.

Nevertheless, within most Western governments the legalistic stability-oriented approach prevailed as an overarching principle of policy during the Syrian conflict. Certainly, it remained a highly *political* and risky decision to determine when the circumstances reached a critical threshold that made it almost a moral duty to ignore the resistance of the High Contracting Party. And inevitably, this turned into a large confrontation with other UN members that were allied with the Assad government. Humanitarians also feared that any attempted paradigm shift might collapse the entire established system, tearing down the firewall between political and humanitarian work that has been established over time. It would endanger humanitarian work in any future context. But at the same time, diplomatic efforts continued to push for legitimizing UN cross-border operations through the Security Council, and bilateral funding continued to be granted to NGOs that delivered cross-border independent of the Council's blessing. The Syrian regime had temporarily lost control of large parts of its territory and border crossings and was not able to prevent an erosion of the very sovereignty that it promoted so fiercely on the international stage.

The debate was not only about formalizing the legitimacy of cross-border deliveries for UN operations to the most affected areas of the war. This was finally achieved in 2014 with UNSC cross-border resolution 2165, three years into the conflict (although in 2020 Russia and China decided to let that resolution fade out). Other problems remained, such as the unequal distribution of assistance within government-controlled territory, the abuse of humanitarian presence and the high conditionality placed on humanitarian operations. The policy dilemma that international organizations faced was the question if they were ready to work under such conditions in order to reach at least some of the needy. The radical alternative was to challenge the government up to the point of a possible withdrawal of international humanitarian and non-humanitarian activities, either temporarily as a tactical means to gain negotiating power or as a broader scheme of action. It was a very risky option indeed.

By contrast, in 2012, the UN took the momentous decision to accept strangulating conditions and work under the Syrian government's tutelage. The determined attitude of Damascus to extract a high price from international engagement on its territory only exacerbated the dilemmatic conditions in which the UN had to operate. We will never know how the government would have reacted in the face of the radical option of UN withdrawal, since it was never tested. Unlike in other cases, such as the conflicts in Bosnia or Yemen, UN agencies in Syria held back from the ultimate sanction, partly due to the fact that in Syria a state and its original government with all its privileges still existed. In the end, it remained unclear whether the government's ostensibly tough position was mere posturing or if Damascus was really ready to give up any access to international resources and to let the last remaining international presence leave the country – a presence that served the government well in its narrative of being a cooperative member of the international community. As examples from other NGOs in Syria have shown, a harder and more coherent negotiation strategy might have resulted in concessions from the government and may have opened some more doors via which to operate according to the humanitarian principles of impartiality and neutrality.

The situation in Syria was the exact opposite to some other conflicts, like that in western Sudan's Darfur province, where the government blocked humanitarian assistance or expelled aid workers completely. In Syria, the government was indeed cynical about international assistance but, at the same time, highly interested in receiving it through established channels since it had a well-oiled mechanism in place via which the regime could profit from that aid. Humanitarian assistance in

Syria was turned into a business model by President Assad and his cronies, and ultimately into a circular system of money-laundering. The regime also established a hybrid commercial-charity structure with the aim of channelling international money paid to so-called charities back into regime-controlled entities and in particular to friends of the Assad dynasty.

Over the years, criticism has intensified from the media but also from advocacy groups, think tanks and donor countries about at least parts of the UN having become an accomplice of the regime's practices, willingly or unwillingly. The main points of criticism against the UN work in Syria include:

- placing unnecessarily strong emphasis on Syrian state sovereignty with implications for IL, IHL and the government's political posturing.
- individual leading staff in Damascus identifying too strongly with the government as a problematic and abusive partner.
- UN local partners being chosen carelessly at best. Some were fake charities linked to regime militias or persons with a record of collaboration with the Syrian intelligence agencies. Some UN partners were on US and EU sanctions lists.
- procurement practices that favoured organizations working closely with, or being part of, the wider regime.
- employment *during* the conflict of close relatives of important government decision-makers. The government interfered in recruiting processes in UN and other agencies.
- the government interfering in the formulation of UN reports and in the assessment of the crisis and humanitarian needs. The UN and other humanitarian organizations were restricted in their movements and had little first-hand monitoring and intelligence capacities.
- the path of least resistance being chosen all too often in the trade-off between reaching a maximum number of needy and the neediest.
- unclear handling of sensitive information, such as the de-confliction mechanism.
- improper calculation of real needs and thus a destruction of fragile but intact local economies.
- incoherence and turf wars among different UN agencies, leading to distorted outcomes.
- insufficient implementation of internal guidelines and lessons learned.

The long list of complaints against the UN that surged in the media were not unique but occurred perhaps in a condensed way in the Syrian context. They bring to mind the conclusions of the 2000 Brahimi Report. Experts had scrutinized UN peacekeeping performance in the 1990s and made the point that the UN displayed reluctance to distinguish victim from aggressor and thus became an accomplice of evil. Thirty years later, not much seems to have changed. In parallel, respect for the UN has slipped to a dismal low. The world body has become a punchbag for competing powers and an arena for denial. President Assad himself openly conceded his contempt for the United Nations. His allies Russia and Iran called all the evidence collected by UN experts on chemical weapons use or human rights abuses against the Syrian regime simply fake. UN expert work was discredited as either sloppy or biased, and the UN itself slandered in the process. It became the scapegoat in an ever-widening gulf between the major powers and their irreconcilable positions, and the victim of national disinformation campaigns which portrayed it as a tool in the hands of Western powers. However, all this rhetoric has not kept Russia, China and also Syria from using the UN platform for their own purposes, whenever suitable.

Concerning the deep humanitarian quagmire in which the UN found itself in Syria, some voices called for a complete withdrawal. Of course, this would have been one radical option to avoid the Neutrality Trap. But such a step comes with a high human and political cost. The legalistic camp would hold that it comes with a legal cost, too. Such a bold political move would also challenge both the firewall and the legal stability approaches. Moreover, if the alternative to humanitarian presence in a state is supposed to be cross-border activity only, that may not be possible without a political and/or military cover and a commitment from at least parts of the international community to shield such assistance from the host country and its allies. Whether this option is feasible, therefore, depends to a large extent on the individual constellations, circumstances and power relationships in a crisis. Another radical option would be to flatly admit that under such adverse conditions the delivered assistance is not (any longer) humanitarian; or that perhaps it remains so in motivation but becomes impossible in practice. But all this does not solve the underlying problem that not enough people in need get assistance or that the wrong people profit from it.

In any case, with regard to the scope and intensity of abuse that occurred in Syria, the push to reconsider current practices has become stronger. Business as usual would be the worst of all options. Six principle arguments in favour of change are:

1. The *need-based argument*: Under such conditions, humanitarian assistance does precisely not arrive at the most needy and does not reach enough of the needy.
2. The *IHL-based argument*: Legal opinion does support alternative forms of humanitarian cooperation, like cross-border deliveries in extreme situations against the consent of the respective state and, if necessary, also without the consent of the UN Security Council.
3. The *value-based argument*: Diverted and abused humanitarian assistance may strengthen unscrupulous regimes who commit large-scale violations of those human rights that are an integral part of a universal value system.
4. The *mediation-based argument*: A stronger party of the non-international armed conflict may become even more powerful by profiting from the abuse of humanitarian assistance. The increasing asymmetry makes a mediated solution more difficult, which may prolong the conflict and the humanitarian suffering.

5. The *credibility-based argument*: The UN has failed to achieve a mediated political solution to practically all ongoing major conflicts of our recent times, and moreover it has provoked heavy criticism of how it has handled humanitarian assistance. This has left its marks on the organization's credibility, which shapes part of the vicious circle within a general crisis of multilateralism.

6. The *economically-based argument*: Diverted and abused humanitarian resources may drown millions in a war economy that keeps the conflict going and strengthen a predatory regime that may (have to) be a potential partner in later efforts such as post-war reconstruction.

The withdrawal of numerous NGOs from cooperation with the UN in Syria and the series of public denunciations sent shockwaves through the UN system. Not only was the UN unable to mediate a political solution to the conflict, but its remaining task of curing the symptoms came under fire as well. Syria, with its extraordinarily challenging operating environment, became a litmus test for the UN in a crucial period of increased withdrawal of important member states from multilateral ideas and engagement.

The UN reacted to the allegations with internal investigations and a move by the political department in New York to remind its own staff and agencies of the traditional humanitarian principles of impartiality and neutrality with the publication of the Parameters and Principles of UN assistance in Syria in 2017. This document conditioned aid not only on humanitarian consistency but also further-reaching assistance on progress in the political process. And it has become a diplomatic reference point for like-minded donors. However, donor countries have criticized the fact that the promised UN Inter-Agency Task Force that was supposed to monitor the Parameters and Principles has not yet even met and started its work. Several forces worked against rolling out the Parameters and Principles in practice and tried to water them down or even obstruct them. One such force was the UN country team in Damascus itself in an internal struggle about the interpretive authority of UN activities on the ground. Some UN officials toed the line from Damascus more than others in the organization felt was right, and some intended to shift UN activities further towards rehabilitation and reconstruction without any political, human rights or humanitarian concessions in return. A prominent opponent to the established guideline was obviously Assad's ally Russia, which intervened with UN Secretary-General Guterres. He gradually lost interest in the matter, something that disillusioned even high-ranking UN officials.

Disappointed donors reacted with a partial diversification of funds away from the classical instrument and practice of UN humanitarian assistance and towards more bilateral cross-border funding. States like the US came up with political initiatives that were supposed to curb the perceived UN's practice of accommodating the Assad regime ('Stop UN Support for Assad Act' of the US Congress in 2019). A group of like-minded Western donors listed the worst transgressions of humanitarian principles by UN practice in Syria but were not sure of how to use these findings in the smartest way. Targeting the UN head-on at a very senior level in such difficult times could further undermine its credibility and damage its overall work. That said, turning a blind eye did not look like an option either. The issue had not been resolved when this book went to print.

Since radical moves such as a complete humanitarian withdrawal remained risky and unlikely given the power constellations in the UN system and in the Security Council, recommendations of how to improve the UN's work under real life conditions have been discussed in this book. Some of the core demands of NGOs and advocacy groups were for more transparency in procurement and recruiting processes, more diligence and transparency in choosing local partners, and a stronger stance in negotiations with the government by forming alliances and consortiums between international organizations and NGOs on the ground. Assistance offers should be largely pooled, packaged and conditioned. They should be handed over as a take-it-or-leave-it option. This would counter the government's divide-and-rule strategy. Increased negotiation leverage could also be achieved through better coordination among UN agencies themselves and through a stronger formulation of – and insistence on – red lines. Also, the willingness to withdraw temporarily or altogether should remain as a serious option on the table. Some donor countries have also pointed to the need for a more diversified, more committed and more professional staff to lead UN humanitarian assistance efforts in Syria and beyond. They should also be better trained in humanitarian negotiations and dilemma situations.

One of the sad conclusions of this book is that key structural deficits the UN displayed in Syria were anything else but novelties. As we have seen from looking at other cases, and what we read in evaluations that the UN itself commissioned, many similar problems keep occurring. This was the case, for example, after the Brahimi Report as a consequence from Bosnia and Rwanda or after the report about UN failure in Sri Lanka. Unfortunately, the UN's learning curve remained flatter than the authors of such reports had hoped. Structural deficits within the system still account for a lack of accountability among senior staff. When they rotate to new roles, they often commit the same mistakes without being held accountable, and then they are rotated again. So it is by far not only the staff in the field but also senior officials that need better training, proper evaluations and a human resources department that draws the right conclusions. Short-term contracts, frustrations and job insecurity account for a lack of accountability, too. All this causes a deficit in outspokenness creating apathetic behaviour with regard to strong counterparts. It also creates a groupthink culture in which valuable information gets lost and an internal dynamic prevails over facts.

However, no matter how much awareness and training are improved, state bullying will always occur. This is why even well-intentioned staff on the ground need the support of well-coordinated donors. Only such collective action can exert the necessary political pressure. Moreover, donors should not spare efforts to look deeper into the UN system, to question reports, wordings and procedures. In their own ministries, donors' decisions on funding should not be influenced by the law of least resistance or organizational behaviour. An auditing authority may be satisfied to see large sums being channelled to the UN but may ask inconvenient questions when smaller NGOs are chosen as alternatives. And indeed, smaller entities may have to learn first how to handle such sums and report them appropriately in their accounts. Still, this may become a necessary extra mile for a bureaucracy to go if the donor strives to deliver more principled humanitarian assistance, depending on the circumstances. Even a high-ranking former UN official conceded: "Donors are going to have to be far more diligent in monitoring the end use and make it clear that the UN will not be the chosen means of delivery, if the neutrality trap means that those doing the killing are the primary beneficiaries of the assistance."

Frustration and disillusion with the Syrian case has grown high within the UN at many levels. Maintaining the famous firewall between politics and humanitarianism is a hard and constant endeavour. And even harder is the insight that the firewall, under extreme circumstances, may be an obstacle to the purpose for which it was originally built. When humanitarian purity is lost behind the firewall, the wall must be torn down at times so that all parties widen their horizon and readjust, before the veil of ignorance – and humanitarian innocence – can be raised up again for operational purposes.

Given the additional challenge of the coronavirus, the humanitarian situation has often become worse in areas re-taken by the Syrian government; many NGOs no longer find secure enough conditions to operate under regime control, and the government itself moved in with military force but no state services. And the more the regime has been consolidating, the bolder its attempts have become to interfere with the implementation of humanitarian assistance. As a matter of principle, Damascus is still convinced that it can get away without any substantial reforms of its political system in the long run.

The Syrian government and wider regime will remain a very difficult partner for any assistance that may be granted to improve the country's stability or to restore minimum standards of IHL and IHRL. Conditions will remain adverse for non-humanitarian and broader development efforts in a stabilization phase with early recovery measures, reconstruction and refugee return. Since the regime has tried to corrupt the system of international humanitarian assistance, it will do the same with other investments in a post-conflict scenario. So far, the government has not shown any inclination to signal its readiness to cooperate. In fact, it has been trying to tighten its grip and to formalize its control over international and national actors of humanitarian and developmental programmes.

This does not mean that such measures are not urgently needed if many Syrians are to escape their current miserable plight. Education must be one of the priorities for an otherwise lost generation. But at the same time, such measures would again relieve a predatory regime from a duty and burden, feeding its war economy and a ruling circle that will not flinch from continued violations of basic human rights against citizens under their tutelage. They will not even shy away from causing further humanitarian disasters if opportune. Furthermore, unconditioned assistance will cement the forced resettlement of populations and the deprivation of many Syrian citizens of basic civil rights or any prospect of returning safely to their home country in the first place. Therefore, formulating post-conflict policies vis-à-vis the Assad regime represents yet another tough policy dilmmea for diplomatic and political decision-makers. As was the case during the Arab Spring, they will need to weigh old-school stability against human rights.

With or without stronger and unconditioned 'humanitarian plus' engagement, the overall outlook for Syria remains bleak. The conflict constellations display all the attributes of a fragmented, unstable, badly governed or almost failed state for a long time to come. External actors will continue to hedge their claims facing a weak prey. Human suffering and human rights violations will continue. Adequate economic, social and cultural rights that Syrians are entitled to – as any other people – under today's wider IHRL will remain a distant dream. Moreover, from a donors' perspective, the described policy dilemmas will drag on for years. The Syrian crisis has shown everyone that not everything is by nature neutral and impartial just because it carries the label 'humanitarian'; and not everything that was funded from a humanitarian budget and sent out with a humanitarian label ends up according to humanitarian principles at its final destination. In Syria, this distortion has produced a well-oiled machinery of give-and-take that may have been politically and militarily decisive in favour of a regime that has been killing its own citizens at massive scale. Should Assad stay in power, there is no reason why he would change this profitable practice except under pressure from an external ally or by a radically changed negotiation and pooling strategy of the humanitarian donor community.

The Syrian example brings home several bitter lessons. They are not necessarily new but they deserve a refreshed and wider debate. Diplomats and humanitarians will be confronted by similar challenges in future crises. The debate is all the more necessary because of the severity of what happened in Syria and because of the signals it sends beyond this conflict. At the same time, this debate should not turn into a blame game placing humanitarians on the receiving end only. In their daily work they have been stuck with intractable policy dilemmas under immensely difficult circumstances. The Syrian war has laid bare the double deficiency of a highly challenged and partly flawed humanitarian practice *and* the lack of concerted political action against massive human rights violations, in particular those by a state actor. The international failure to boldly invest in a political solution supporting moderate elements at the very beginning of the crisis has led to a protracted conflict, traumatizing brutality and the radicalization of possible political alternatives. This has destroyed policy options for peaceful change and long-term stability. Political failure translated into an immense humanitarian challenge, and not vice versa.

Jamal Suleiman, one of Syria's most famous actors and intellectuals, half Alawite and half Sunni by descent, and vice-president of the Syrian opposition in the political process in Geneva, summarized the dilemma in his own words: "Neutrality killed many in Syria and has left us exiled for eight years now. It killed us softly with silk rope."[2]

NOTES

Chapter 1

1 Syrian Network for Human Rights, 'On the 9th Anniversary of the Popular Uprising,...', (2020).
2 On my use of 'regime' versus 'government' while referring to the power centre(s) in Damascus: the Syrian Government itself, in an effort to uphold its claim to absolute sovereignty, condemned in particular those Western actors that referred to them as a 'regime' (and often meant it in a derogatory way). Within the United Nations, above all, all representatives are protagonists of governments while 'regime' has a derogatory undertone of that of a rogue state or banana republic. This is why the Syrian government strongly insisted it be referred to as such within an international, political and legal framework, suggesting eye level with all other states in the UN, regardless of its behaviour.

   However, I would like to explain my specific use of 'government' versus 'regime' in this book as follows: this is not a normative use of terms but rather an academic attempt to distinguish the different scope and functions of the animal discussed. The Syrian government is referred to with regard to the state's institutions and the functionaries of the Presidency and the government in the fullest sense of the word: cabinet of ministers, ministries, administration. 'Regime' is used when reference is made to this government plus important other structures and players attached to it such as the oppressive apparatus, the powerful secret services (*mukhabarat*), the military and, increasingly, the militias. So when a regime acts, all these connotations and actors are at play. When the delegation from Damascus arrived in Geneva for talks, for example, this was clearly the 'government delegation'. But when we talk about the involvement of *mukhabarat*, military and militias responsible for military activities and oppression, this is the Syrian regime as a wider web of actors. Apart from that, the real 'government' – its cabinet– has almost no power in Syria, and it was the 'regime' that responded to the popular protests and led the war with all its actors, tools and means.
3 http://sn4hr.org/blog/2018/09/24/civilian-death-toll/
4 http://sn4hr.org/blog/2019/10/21/54362/
5 http://sn4hr.org/blog/2018/09/24/record-of-arbitrary-arrests1/
6 'Syria a "torture-chamber", U.N. says in call to free detainees', Reuters, 14 March 2017.
7 Numbers range from 6.6 million (UNHCR: www.unhcr.org/syria-emergency.html) to 9 million (SNHR: http://sn4hr.org/blog/2020/03/15/54765/).
8 Interview with the author in Berlin, 30 January 2020.
9 Interviews by the author; see also: 'UN pays tens of millions to Assad regime under Syria aid programme', the *Guardian*, 29 August 2016.
10 Human Rights Watch (2019).
11 Interview with the author in Geneva, 9 March 2020.
12 Norwegian Refugee Council (NRC) and Oxfam (2020), 2.
13 Thépaut, in: *Foreign Policy*, 24 June 2020.

14 Thépaut, in: *Foreign Policy*, 24 June 2020.
15 For example: Ajami (2012); Balanche (2018); van Dam (2017); Gerlach (2015); Hashemi & Postel, eds (2013); Haj Saleh (2017); Helberg (2018); , Hinnebusch & Zintl, eds (2015); Hokayem (2013); Kerr & Larkin, eds (2015); Lesch (2013); Lister (2015); McMurray & Ufheil-Somers, eds (2013); Phillips (2016); Wieland (2012).
16 Assad in an interview with *Paris Match*, 4 December 2014: 'We cannot say that we regret fighting terrorism since the early days of this crisis. However, this doesn't mean that there weren't mistakes made in practice. There are always mistakes.'

Chapter 2

1 Donini (2012), 3.
2 Rieff (2002), 71.
3 Smillie, in: Donini, (2012), 17.
4 Simms & Trim (2011), 366.
5 Ibid., 3.
6 Ibid., 386–7.
7 Hopgood (2013), 1.
8 Ibid., 20.
9 Ibid., 23.
10 Cunningham (2018), 2ff.
11 Cunningham & Kahn (2013).
12 Hopgood, (2013), 183.
13 Donini, (2012), 247, 248.
14 In the following paragraphs, I draw insights from conversations with and from a research paper by Kristoffer Lidén, senior researcher on ethical dilemmas at the Peace Research Institute Oslo (PRIO). Here, see also: Grace, in: *Journal of International Humanitarian Legal Studies* (2020); Acuto (ed.) (2012); Magone, Neuman & Weissman (2011); Hilhorst & Jansen, in: *Development and Change* (2010).
15 CCHN Field Manual on Frontline Humanitarian Negotiation (2019).
16 'Rescuing Victims Worldwide from the "Depths of Hell"', *New York Times*, 10 July 2004.
17 Slim (2015), 163–7.
18 Barnett (2011); Donini (ed.) (2012); Acuto (ed.) (2012); Duffield (2019); de Lauri (2016); Hoffman & Weiss (2018); Barnett & Weiss (2008).
19 An excellent overview of this dilemma's development can be found in: Donini (ed.) (2012).
20 Leenders & Mansour, in: *Political Science Quarterly* (2018), 254.
21 Pérouse de Montclos, in: *Africa Development* (2009), 71–2.
22 A short overview in: Pérouse de Montclos, in: *Africa Development* (2009), 75ff.
23 De Waal (1997), quoted in: Pérouse de Montclos, in: *Africa Development* (2009), 75.
24 Operation Lifeline Sudan (1996), 2.
25 Ibid., 3.
26 Labonte, in: *Third World Quarterly* (2013), 48–51; Young, in: Donini (2012), 89–108; Loeb (2013); Cunningham (2018), 128ff.
27 Labonte, in: *Third World Quarterly* (2013), 43–5; Young, in: Donini (2012), 235–7.
28 Slim (2015), 18. He also partly refers to Keen, in: *Conflict, Security and Development* (2014).
29 Interview with the author, 10 October 2020.
30 Report of the Secretary-General's Internal Review Panel on United Nations Action in Sri Lanka (2012).

31 Internal UN report dated 2017 by Charles Petrie obtained by the author.

32 Rosenthal (2019), 10–14.

33 Rieff (2003), 135.

34 'Most Relief Operations in Bosnia are Halted by U.N. Aid Agency', *New York Times* (1993); 'Statement by Mrs. Sadako Ogata, United Nations High Commissioner for Refugees, at the Information Meeting of the Executive Committee of the High Commissioner's Programme (ExCom)' (1993); Cutts (1999), 5.

35 Labonte, in: *Third World Quarterly* (2013), 46–8; see also: de Waal (1991).

36 Donini, in: Donini (2012); Rieff (2003), 231–66.

37 Maxwell, in: Donini (2012), 204ff; Bradbury & Maletta, in: Donini (2012), 109ff; Donini, in: Donini (2012), 67ff.

38 'UN to Reduce Aid to Houthi-Controlled Yemen', *Voice of America*, 9 February 2020.

39 Niland, in: Donini (2012), 239.

Chapter 3

1 Bothe (2013), 10.

2 Nowak, in: Clapham & Gaeta (2014), 388.

3 Nowak, in: Clapham & Gaeta (2014), 396.

4 Nowak, in: Clapham & Gaeta (2014), 390.

5 Nowak, in: Clapham & Gaeta (2014), 406.

6 This was promoted by the UN Special Rapporteur on Torture, Manfred Nowak. Nowak, in: Clapham & Gaeta (2014), 391.

7 Convention (IV) relative to the Protection of Civilian Persons in Time of War. Geneva, 12 August 1949. David, in: Clapham (2014), 354–5, lists the further rules applicable to non-international armed conflicts that exist today:

- Article 19 of the 1954 Hague Convention for the Protection of Cultural Property
- The 1977 Additional Protocol to the 1949 Geneva Convention
- Article 2 , paragraph 2 (c–f), of the Statute of the International Criminal Court adopted in Rome on 17 July 1998
- Article of the Hague Protocol of 26 March 1999
- The 1980 UN Convention on Prohibitions or Restrictions on the Use of Certain Conventional Weapons Which May be Deemed to be Excessively Injurious or to Have Indistrimate Effects, as amended on 21 December 2001 with the result that its five Protocols are now applicable to non-international armed conflicts for the states parties which have accepted the amendment made in 2001.
- The majority of customary IHL rules defined and published by the ICRC study (Doswald-Beck/Henckaerts (2005).

8 David, in: Clapham & Gaeta (2014), 370.

9 David, in Clapham & Gaeta (2014), 372.

10 Riedel, in: Clapham & Gaeta (2014), 441ff, also: Jinks, in: Clapham & Gaeta (2014), 673.

11 ICRC, Operational Update (17/07/2012), see also ICRC, Annual Report (2012), 444, Bothe (2013), 14.

12 Nowak, in: Clapham & Gaeta (2014), 406.

13 Cassese, in: Clapham & Gaeta (2014), 9.

14 Riedel, in: Clapham & Gaeta (2014), 454.

15 Montevideo Convention on the Rights and Duties of States, Montevideo 1934.

16 Jellinek (1900).
17 Riedel, in: Clapham & Gaeta (2014), 461–2.
18 Bianchi & Naqvi, in: Clapham & Gaeta (2014), 583–4.
19 YouTube video, *TNT EXCLUSIVE #ASSAD_LEAKS*, 2019 (https://www.youtube.com/watch?fbclid=IwAR3EJ0XsEzi_xIM9CHGAftKeYFTNFTKcsbdoA3U6KLS4vAB0jeqk_H71E&v=Dy1hW-7xM2c&app=desktop).
20 Melzer, in: Clapham & Gaeta (2014), 307.
21 Jinks, in: Clapham & Gaeta (2014), 657 (original italics).
22 Clapham, in: Clapham & Gaeta (2014), 793.
23 https://www.ohchr.org/EN/HRBodies/HRC/Pages/NewsDetail.aspx?NewsID=26237&LangID=E.
24 UN Resolution 46/182.
25 UNHCR Humanitarian Principles (https://emergency.unhcr.org/entry/44765/humanitarian-principles) (my emphasis).
26 Code of Conduct for the International Red Cross and Red Crescent Movement and Non-Governmental Organizations (NGOs) in Disaster Relief (1994) (my emphasis).
27 For example, UN OCHA (https://www.unocha.org/sites/dms/Documents/OOM_HumPrinciple_English.pdf).
28 Müller (2013), 246.
29 Ibid.
30 Fleck, in: Clapham & Gaeta (2014), 220.
31 Müller (2013), 248ff.
32 Müller (2013), 253.
33 Ibid., 251.
34 Ibid., 252–3.
35 Dallaire, in: Donini (2012), xvii–xviii
36 Interview with the author on 10 October 2020.
37 Bothe (2013), 2.
38 Ibid., 255.
39 Ibid., 240–1.
40 Ibid., 245.
41 Ibid., 255–6.
42 Ibid., 256.
43 Ibid., 257ff.
44 Ibid., 259.
45 Ibid., 260–1.
46 Ibid., 264.
47 Interview with a German diplomat in Berlin on 17 January 2020; see also: Breaking Ghouta, *The Atlantic Council*, Washington D.C. 2018, 11–12.
48 Müller (2013), 268–9.
49 Robertson (2002), 430.
50 Donini (2012), 251.

Chapter 4

1 Blair, Tony: Speech to the George Bush Senior Presidential Library, 7 April 2002; see also: Simms & Trim (2011), 371.
2 Robertson (2002), 484.

3   van Dam (2017).
4   Scharf, Sterio & Williams (2020) have focused specifically on the Syrian conflict's impact on international law.
5   A good and concise up-to-date summary can be found in: Arnault (2019), 1ff or Clapham (2012), 1ff.
6   Cali (2015), 15.
7   Kumm, in: *The European Journal of International Law* 2004, 112ff.
8   Ibid., 914.
9   Ibid., 915.
10 Interview with the author in Geneva, 9 March 2020.
11 Ibid.
12 Hopgood (2013), 168.
13 In an exchange with the author, 22 October 2020.
14 'France's Macron says sees no legitimate successor to Syria's Assad', *Reuters*, 21 June 2017.
15 Primarily represented by Georg Jellinek (1851–1911).
16 The Vienna School and Hans Kelsen (1881–1973).
17 This criticism has been put forward by the Critical Legal Studies and the New Approaches to International Law.
18 Cali (2015), 15.
19 Represented by John Austin (1791–1859) and Max Weber (1864–1920).
20 Represented i.a. by Hans Morgenthau (1904–1980).
21 New Haven School (Myres McDougal, Harold Lasswell et al.).
22 Represented by Georges Scelle (1878–1961).
23 Clapham (2012), 53.
24 See also Arnauld (2019), 6, Puglierin (2009), 41.
25 Clapham (2012), 77ff.
26 Ibid., 80.
27 Ibid., 81.
28 Ibid., 83.
29 Cali (2015), 10.
30 Ibid., 10–11.
31 Riedel, in *EJIL* (1991), 64. See also: Clapham (2012), 74.
32 A good overview over the history of state sovereignty can be found in: Clapham (2012), 7ff. See also: Kimminich (1997), 64ff.
33 Clapham (2012), 17.
34 Ibid., 23ff.
35 Ibid., 43.
36 Ibid., 44.
37 Menzel, in: *Jahrbuch für internationales Recht* (1971).
38 Simms & Trim (2011), 381–3.
39 Quoted according to: Robertson (2002), 433, see also: 437ff.
40 Robertson (2002), 433.
41 Ibid., 448.
42 Beck, in: *Blätter für deutsche und internationale Politik* (1999), 987 (original italics); see also: Münkler (2002), 223.
43 For more details, see: Romano, in: Kingston/Spears (2004).
44 Murithi, in: *African Security Review* (2007), 15.
45 Simms & Trim (2011), 367.

46 Bothe (2013), 42.
47 Report of the Panel on United Nations Peace Operations ('Brahimi Report'), New York 2000.
48 Fleck, in: Clapham & Gaeta (2014), 214.
49 Murithi, in: *African Security Review* (2007).
50 Fleck, in: Clapham & Gaeta (2014), 215.
51 Simms & Trim (2011), 392.
52 Fleck, in: Clapham & Gaeta (2014), 216.
53 Kuperman, in: *Foreign Affairs*, March/April 2015.
54 UNSCR 1970 (http://unscr.com/en/resolutions/doc/1970).
55 UNSCR 1973 (http://unscr.com/en/resolutions/doc/1973).
56 'Expressions like "crusades" unacceptable with respect to situation in Libya – Medvedev', Interfax, 22 March 2011.
57 On the dilemma of military intervention in the earlier years of the conflict in Syria, see: Hashemi & Postel (2013).
58 Leenders & Mansour, in: Political Science Quarterly (2018), 227.
59 Leenders & Mansour, in: *Political Science Quarterly* (2018), 228. They refer to: Tilly, C. (1978), 191; Krasner, in: Krasner (2001), 6; Kalyvas (2007), 417.
60 UN minutes of Mohammed Sabra in an official session of the HNC with the UN Special Envoy, Staffan De Mistura, and his team in Geneva, 27 March 2017.

Chapter 5

1 Cassese, in: Clapham & Gaeta (2014), 9.
2 'Des Teufels Oberst', in: *Der Spiegel*, 23 April 2020 (author's translation). Raslan, who received refugee status in Germany after his defection and engagement for the opposition, was indicted for crimes against humanity in front of a German court in April 2020. The allegation that he had participated in torture earlier remained a crime that overshadowed the political fact that he defected and supported opposition members subsequently.
3 Clapham & Gaeta (2014), 27ff.
4 Bianchi & Naqvi, in: Clapham & Gaeta (2014), 588, 598ff, Dörrmann, in: Clapham & Gaeta (2014), 605ff; Robertson (2002), 473ff.
5 Riedel (2010), 242.
6 Quoted according to Riedel (2010), 263.
7 Ibid., 264.
8 'Aboard Air CIA', in: *Newsweek*, 28 February 2005. The Syrian cases involve a Canadian of Syrian descent, Maher Arar, who was intercepted by US authorities on a flight in New York and shipped to Syria where he was tortured. The same is true for Mohammed Haydar Zammar, a German citizen, who was brought to Syria at the end of 2001 and interrogated there by German officials in summer 2002, which is against German law ('A Tale of Extraordinary Renditions and Double-Standards', in: *spiegel online*, 21 November 2005).
9 Cassese, in: Clapham & Gaeta (2014), 8.
10 Dörrmann, in: Clapham & Gaeta, 623.
11 Bianchi & Naqvi, in: Clapham & Gaeta (2014), 583–4.
12 Melzer, in: Clapham & Gaeta (2014), 307ff.

13 Bianchi/Naqvi, in: Clapham & Gaeta (2014), 586, also: Gandhi, in: *ISIL Year Book of International Humanitarian and Refugee Law* (2001).
14 Bianchi & Naqvi, in: Clapham & Gaeta (2014), 574ff.
15 Santos (2016).

Chapter 6

1 Interview with the author, 27 November 2019.
2 According to an internal paper obtained by the author, written by cooperation partners on the ground, outlining the government's strategy.
3 Businessmen who intend to conduct trade with the regime had to:

   a) support the establishment or financing of militias or aid organizations;
   b) take over the payment of state salaries in certain areas;
   c) pay for basic services offered to entire settlements.

   Often, these businessmen are also asset managers for regime figures or relevant loyalists. According to estimates from sources on the ground, money transfers through loyalist businessmen reach several hundred million US dollars each year. Some have reported that President Assad set up a secret bank account through which these transfers are channelled and the war is financed to a large extent.
4 'UNHCR on Aid to Syria: What's Important is to Deliver', in: *The National*, 15 July 2019.
5 Haid (2019), 15.
6 'Breaking Ghouta, The Atlantic Council, Washington DC (2018), 11.
7 According to reports from several sources from the ground.
8 Human Rights Watch (2019).
9 Haid (2019), 19.
10 Human Rights Watch (2019).
11 Leenders & Mansour, in: *Political Science Quarterly* (2018), 237.
12 Haid (2019), 6; Lund (2016).
13 The Syria Campaign (2016), 4, see also: WFP, Emergency Food Assistance to the People Affected by Unrest in Syria (2016), UNSC Report of the Secretary-General on the Implementation of UN Security Council Resolutions 2139, 2165, 2191 and 2258 (2016), paragraph 48.
14 Lund (2016).
15 For a good summary of incidents and challenges, see: Human Rights Watch (2019) and Haid (2019).
16 Gutman, in: *Foreign Policy* (2016); Leenders & Mansour, in: *Political Science Quarterly* (2018), 235–6; Haid (2019), 8.
17 OCHA Syria Evaluation Report, UN-OCHA (2016), 6. See also: Sida, Tormbetta & Panero (2016); Haid (2019), 9..
18 Interview with the author, 3 December 2019. Barabandi referred to official name lists from the governor of Tartous and Lathakia that were made available to him.
19 Omar Abdelaziz Hallaj in an interview with the author, 5 January 2020.
20 Leenders & Mansour, in: *Political Science Quarterly* (2018), 238.
21 According to a senior humanitarian functionary in a church-based NGO. Interview with the author, 13 February 2020.
22 Interview with the author, 27 November 2019.

23 Interview with a local humanitarian UN staff by the author, 27 November 2019.
24 The incident can be watched on: https://www.youtube.com/watch?v=o2vs10Mtlz8.
25 Interview with the author, 5 January 2020.
26 OCHA Syria Evaluation Report, *UN-OCHA* (2016), p.4 (italics added)
27 Interview with the author in Berlin, 16 December 2019.
28 Ibid.
29 'Syria Kicks Out 2 U.N. Staffers Trying to Arrange Aid Deliveries', *AP*, 27 February 2015.
30 Interview with the author, 27 November 2019.
31 Ibid.
32 Amnesty International (2017).
33 Norwegian Refugee Council (2016); Baumann (2019); Human Rights Watch (2019). Particularly controversial has been 2018's Law No. 10, as described in more detail in these publications also..
34 Interview with a Western diplomat based in Beirut, 12 February 2020.
35 Niland, in: Donini (2012), 223.
36 Ibid., 224.
37 Interview with a Western diplomat based in Beirut, 12 February 2020.
38 Human Rights Watch (2019).
39 'Syrian FM urges Int'l Red Cross to avoid politicization of humanitarian work', *Xinhua*, 10 March 2020.
40 For a legal reference on Syria's security system: Yazigi, *Syria Report*, (2019).
41 Amnesty International Report (2011), 22.
42 Ibid., 4ff.
43 Syria Justice and Accountability Centre Report (2019).
44 Interview with the author, 27 November 2019.
45 Human Rights Watch (2019).
46 Haid (2019), 10.
47 For more on the siege in Eastern Ghouta, see: 'Breaking Ghouta', The Atlantic Council (2018).
48 Interview with the author, 28 January 2020.
49 Interview with the author, 3 March 2020.
50 Interview with the author in Berlin, 22 January 2020.
51 'Unschuldige Menschen zahlen den Preis des Krieges in Syrien', Dr. Attar, Präsident des Syrischen Roten Halbmonds im Interview.
52 'The Syrian Arab Red Crescent refutes allegations it is not working in a neutral and impartial manner', ICRC (2012).
53 http://sarc.sy/words-sarc-president-dr-abdul-rahman-attar/
54 'Syria: gambling making a quiet comeback', the *Guardian*, 2 January 2011.
55 Interview with the author in Berlin, 17 January 2020.
56 Interview with the author in Berlin, 30 January 2020.
57 Interview with a German diplomat with long-term experience on the humanitarian Syrian file, 30 January 2020.
58 Interview with the author in Berlin, 21 January 2020.
59 Interview with the author in Geneva, 9 March 2020.
60 Donini (2012).
61 Interview with a German diplomat in Geneva, 9 March 2020.
62 Bothe (2013), 3 (italics added).
63 Ibid.

64 Ibid., 4

65 Ibid.

66 Ibid.

67 Figures on Mercy Corps deliveries compared to UN, for example. See: Leenders & Mansour, in: *Political Science Quarterly* (2018), 247.

68 Interview with the author, 16 January 2020.

69 See also: 'The Political Role of Local Councils in Syria', OMRAN, July 2016; Hajjar et al. (2017).

70 Interview with the author, 18 February 2020.

71 Statement by the Regional Director Dr Ahmed Al-Mandhari on COVID-19 in the Eastern Mediterranean Region, *WHO*, 27 March 2020.

72 'Wash Our Hands? Some People Can't Wash Their Kids for a Week', *New York Times*, 19 March 2020.

73 @hadialbahra, 24 March 2020.

74 Statement by the Regional Director Dr Ahmed Al-Mandhari on COVID-19 in the Eastern Mediterranean Region, *WHO*, 27 March 2020.

75 'Syria's Kurdish northeast had its first Covid-19 death. The case was news to the Kurds', *New York Times*, 17 April 2020.

76 Interview with the author, 13 February 2020.

77 Interview with Till Küster from *medico international*, 10 February 2020.

78 Human Rights Watch (2019).

79 UNHCR Syria Factsheet 2018 but also in factsheets from previous years (https://reliefweb.int/report/syrian-arab-republic/unhcr-syria-factsheetq1-january-march-2018).

80 UN Humanitarian Needs Assessment 2019. Interview with the author, 16 January 2020.

81 Interview with the author, 16 January 2020.

82 Interview with the author, 28 January 2020.

83 Haid (2019), 3.

84 Norwegian Refugee Council (NRC) and Oxfam (2020), 2.

85 https://www.un.org/press/en/2014/sc11473.doc.htm

86 Bothe (2013), 23. Resolution 67/262 of 15 May 2013, OP 15. Emphasis added.

87 S/PRST/2013/15, 02.10.2013, para. 13 (c); Bothe (2013), 23.

88 United Nations Monitoring Mechanism (UNMM) (https://response.ochasyria.org/unmm/?)

89 Interview of a high-ranking OCHA representative by the author in Geneva on 31 October 2019.

90 Interview with the author, 28 January 2020.

91 Interview with a high-ranking OCHA staff member in Geneva, 9 March 2020.

92 https://www.un.org/press/en/2020/sc14074.doc.htm

93 'UN says "no plan B" to Syria cross-border aid system', *AFP*, 7 January 2020.

94 'U.N. renews Syria cross-border aid operation but halves crossings, length of time', *Reuters*, 11 January 2020.

95 'UN Council Members Point Fingers Over Syria Aid Crossings', *Associated Press*, 29 January 2020.

96 'Al-Ja'afari: Improving humanitarian situation in Syria requires lifting economic coercive measures imposed on its people', *SANA*, 12 January 2020.

97 Lund (2019).

98 'On fifth attempt, U.N. Security Council renews Syria aid via Turkey', *Reuters*, 11 July 2020.

99 'Nach wochenlangem Streit hat der UN-Sicherheitsrat sich auf einen gefährlichen Kompromiss für Hilfslieferungen nach Syrien geeinigt. Deutschlands Botschafter lieferte sich einen hitzigen Schlagabtausch mit Vertretern Russlands und Chinas', dpa, 11 July 2020.

Chapter 7

1　Brahimi Report (2000), ix, 9–10 (italics added).
2　Robertson (2002), 524.
3　Ibid., 525.
4　Brahimi Report (2000), 45
5　Interview with the author, 10 October 2020.
6　Leenders & Mansour, in: *Political Science Quarterly* (2018), 227.
7　Ibid., 249.
8　'In the Line of Fire: The War Against the UN in Syria', *Syria Comment*, 4 July 2016. Also: Mazen Gharibeh in an interview with the author, 18 February 2020.
9　Interview with the author in Berlin, 11 February 2020.
10　Interview with the author, 3 December 2019.
11　Interview with the author in Berlin, 30 January 2020.
12　'UNHCR on Aid to Syria: What's Important is to Deliver', *The National*, 15 July 2019.
13　Interview with the author, 5 February 2020.
14　Interview with the author in Berlin, 11 February 2020. See also: Human Rights Watch (2019).
15　Human Rights Watch (2019).
16　See also: Sparrow, in: *Foreign Policy* (2018) and 'UNHCR on Aid to Syria: What's Important is to Deliver', in: *The National*, 15 July 2019.
17　Interview with the author, 2 December 2019.
18　'Mother Agnes Aid Contracts', *Syria in Context* (2019). According to this information, between 2017 and 2019 the Monastery of St James the Mutilated was one of the United Nation's local partner organizations delivering projects under the Humanitarian Response Plan (HRP) for Syria. Social media posts and project plan documents show them partnering with UNHCR, UNFPA, UNICEF, UNDP, OCHA, and at least one Damascus-based INGO during this period.
19　'UN pays tens of millions to Assad regime under Syria aid programme', in: the *Guardian*, 29 August 2016.
20　'UNHCR on Aid to Syria: What's Important is to Deliver', in: *The National*, 15 July 2019.
21　'UN pays tens of millions to Assad regime under Syria aid programme', in: the *Guardian*, 29 August 2016; see also: 'UNHCR on Aid to Syria: What's Important is to Deliver', in: *The National*, 15 July 2019.
22　Human Rights Watch (2019); see also: Haid (2019), 9ff.
23　Ibrahim Olabi in an interview with the author, 2 December 2019, see also: 'UN pays tens of millions to Assad regime under Syria aid programme', in: the *Guardian*, 29 August 2016; 'UNHCR on Aid to Syria: What's Important is to Deliver', in: *The National*, 15 July 2019; Leenders & Mansour, in: *Political Science Quarterly* (2018), 240ff.
24　US 'Stop UN Support for Assad Act' of 2019; non-public document of like-minded states of 2019.
25　'UN pays tens of millions to Assad regime under Syria aid programme', in: the *Guardian*, 29 August 2016.

26 Leenders: 'Why the UN's Excuses For its Aid Fiasco in Syria Fail to Convince', in: *Syria Comment* (2016).

27 Leenders: 'Why the UN's Excuses For its Aid Fiasco in Syria Fail to Convince', in: *Syria Comment* (2016).

28 Interview with the author, 28 January 2020.

29 Sparrow: 'Aiding Disaster: How the United Nations' OCHA Helped Assad and Hurt Syrians in Need', in: *Foreign Affairs* (2016); Haid (2019), 8.

30 Interview with the author, 9 October 2020.

31 'UN hires Assad's friends and relatives for Syria relief operation', in: the *Guardian*, 28 October 2016.

32 Leenders & Mansour, in: *Political Science Quarterly* (2018), 235, list more examples from different sources like Yahya Abuzo, employed as senior policy manager by the WHO in Damascus, who, as Syrian sources report, is working for the secret police; Maria Rumman, the IOM's chief of mission in Syria for more than a decade, who is friends with Asma al-Assad and acted as board member of al-Amal, another of the first lady's NGOs.

33 Interview with the author, 10 October 2020. See also: Lynch, in: *Foreign Policy* (2019).

34 'Aid groups suspend cooperation with UN in Syria because of Assad "influence"', in: the *Guardian*, 8 September 2016.

35 Lund: 'The UN Enters Syria's Moral Labyrinth', in: *Diwan*, 9 September 2016.

36 Interview with the author, 3 December 2019.

37 'The U.N. Tried to Save Hospitals in Syria. It Didn't Work', *New York Times*, 29 December 2019.

38 Interview with the author, 16 January 2020.

39 'The U.N. Tried to Save Hospitals in Syria. It Didn't Work', *New York Times*, 29 December 2019.

40 'Some UN deconfliction system's facilities in Syria used by terrorists – Russian envoy', *Tass*, 29 June 2020. See also: 'UN humanitarian affairs office should discuss deconfliction directly with Syria – Moscow', Tass, 4 July 2020.

Chapter 8

1 In an interview with the author, 5 December 2019.

2 Ban Ki-moon: 'Renewing our commitment to the peoples and purposes of the United Nations'(2013).

3 Parameters and Principles of UN Assistance in Syria (2017) (italics added).

4 In an exchange with the author, 23 September 2020.

5 Non-publicized diplomatic paper available to the author.

6 Interview with the author, 29 April 2020.

7 Stop UN Support for Assad Act, 2019.

8 Interview with the author, 3 December 2019.

Chapter 9

1 Donini, in Donini (2012), 87 (original emphasis).

2 Chandler & Coaffee (2016).

3   Interview with the author in Berlin, 30 January 2020.
4   Talmon, in: *Chinese Journal of International Law* (2013): 219–53.
5   Interview with the author, 3 March 2020.
6   Interview with the author in Berlin, 17 January 2020.
7   Interview with the author in Berlin on 16 December 2019
8   EU Regional Trust Fund in Response to the Syrian crisis (https://ec.europa.eu/
    trustfund-syria-region/content/our-mission_en)
9   See also the discussion in: Barnes-Dacey, *ECFR*, April 2020.
10 Asseburg (2020), 7, Barnes-Dacey, *ECFR*, April 2020, 4
11 Asseburg (2020), 110.
12 Haid (2019), 3.
13 On the dilemma of early recovery and reconstruction measures in Syria, see: Asseburg
    & Oweis (2017); Asseburg (2020); Said & Yazigi (2018); 'The Political Economic Context
    of Syria's Reconstruction: A Prospective in Light of a Legacy of Unequal Development',
    Middle East Directions (2018); 'War Continued Through Other Means: How
    Reconstruction Risks Perpetuating Violence in a Post-war Syria', *syriadirect* (2019)
14 Asseburg (2020).
15 Barnes-Dacey (2020).
16 Favier & Kostrz (2019).
17 Al-Alou (2017).
18 Rosenthal (2019), 13.

Chapter 10

1   Interview with the author, 3 December 2019.
2   Interview with the author, 9 October 2020.
3   Interview with the author, 22 January 2020.
4   Interview with the author, 3 December 2019.
5   Thépaut, in: *Foreign Policy*, 24 June 2020.
6   In an exchange with the author, 22 October 2020.
7   Smillie, in: Donini (2012), 19.
8   Dallaire, in: Donini (2012), xviii.
9   Rieff (2002), 23.
10 Rieff (2002), 56.
11 Russian planes also bombed civilian targets themselves as investigations have shown,
    such as in: 'A Civilian Camp in Syria Was Bombed. Here's How We Traced the Culprit',
    New York Times, 2 December 2019.
12 Established in 2016 by General Assembly Resolution 71/248.
13 'ABC's Barbara Walters' Interview With Syrian President Bashar al-Assad', *ABCNews*,
    6 December 2011.

Chapter 11

1   Interview with Omar Abdelaziz Hallaj, 5 January 2020.
2   Haid (2019) 11ff; Human Rights Watch (2019), 56ff; Norwegian Refugee Council and
    Oxfam (2020), 3.

3   UN-OCHA (2016), 7.

4   Haid (2019), 15

5   Strategic Steering Group, Relief Web (2019).

6   Haid (2019) 14.

7   In an exchange with the author, 23 September 2020.

8   Rosenthal (2019), 11.

9   One recent contribution is Clements (2020).

10 Oliver Müller, head of Caritas Internationalis, in a panel discussion at the Centre for Humanitarian Action in Berlin, 22 September 2020.

11 In an exchange with the author, 22 October 2020.

12 In an exchange with the author, 23 September 2020.

Chapter 12

1   Rosenthal (2019), 11.

2   Jamal Suleiman, in a message to the author, 5 April 2020.

BIBLIOGRAPHY

Academic publications

Abouzeid, Rania. *No Turning Back: Life, Loss, and Hope in Wartime Syria*. New York: Oneworld, 2018.

Acuto, Michelle, ed. *Negotiating Relief: The Dialectics of Humanitarian Space*. London: C. Hurst & Co., 2012.

Ajami, Fouad. *The Syrian Rebellion*. Stanford, CA: Hoover Institution, 2012.

Al-Alou, Sokrat. 'The Arab Socialist Baath Party: Preparing for the Post-War Era', *Arab Reform Initiative* (ARI), 8 August 2017 (https://www.arab-reform.net/wp-content/uploads/pdf/Arab_Reform_Initiative_en_the-arab-socialist-baath-party-preparing-for-the-post-war-era_2976.pdf?ver=14de8736fe094c12032431867f96edd6)

Allen, Tim, Anna Macdonald and Henry Radice. *Humanitarianism: A Dictionary of Concepts*. London: Routledge, 2005.

Amnesty International. 'Health Crisis: Syrian Government Targets the Wounded and Health Workers', London 2011. (https://www.amnestyusa.org/wp-content/uploads/2017/04/mde240592011en_22.pdf)

Amnesty International. 'Human Slaughterhouse: Mass Hangings and Extermination at Saydnaya Prison, Syria', London 2017. (https://www.amnesty.org/download/Documents/MDE2454152017ENGLISH.PDF)

Asseburg, Muriel. 'Wiederaufbau in Syrien: Herausforderungen und Handlungsoptionen für die EU und ihre Mitgliedstaaten', *SWP Studie*, Berlin, April 2020.

Asseburg, Muriel, Wolfram Lacher and Mareike Transfeld. 'Mission Impossible? UN-Vermittlung in Libyen, Syrien und dem Jemen', *SWP Studie*, July 2018.

Asseburg, Muriel, and Khaled Yacoub Oweis. 'Syria's Reconstruction Scramble: In a Game Fraught with Political Risk, Europe Should Aim for Long-term Stabilization', *SWP Comment*, Berlin, 51, 2017.

Balanche, Fabrice. *Sectarianism in Syria's Civil War: A Geopolitical Study*. Washington DC: The Washington Institute, 2018.

Barber, Martin. *Blinded by Humanity: Inside the UN's Humanitarian Operations*. London: I.B. Tauris, 2015.

Barnes-Dacey, Julien. 'Society Max: How Europe Can Help Syrians Survive Assad and Coronavirus', European Council for Foreign Relations (ECFR), April 2020. (https://www.ecfr.eu/page/-/society_max_how_europe_can_help_syrians_survive_assad_and_coronavirus.pdf)

Barnett, Michael. *Empire of Humanity: A History of Humanitarianism*. Ithaca, NY: Cornell University Press, 2011.

Barnett, Michael, and Thomas Weiss. *Humanitarianism in Question: Politics, Power, Ethics*. Ithaca, NY: Cornell University Press, 2008.

Baumann, Hannes. 'Reclaiming Home: The Struggle for Socially Just Housing, Land and Property Rights in Syria, Iraq and Libya', Friedrich Ebert Stiftung, Tunis 2019. (http://library.fes.de/pdf-files/bueros/tunesien/15664.pdf?fbclid=IwAR0IEmZ6oWFCSgelF9HXsCbJetGFg1ySWqKF0IHYIwfdK62DQVRLOsKyBtA)

Beck, Ulrich. 'Über den post-nationalen Krieg', *Blätter für deutsche und internationale Politik*, no.8 (1999).

Bianchi, Andrea, and Yasmin Naqvi, 'Terrorism'. In *The Oxford Handbook of International Law in Armed Conflict*, edited by Andrew Clapham and Paola Gaeta. New York: Oxford University Press, 2014.

Bothe, Michael. Access for Relief Operations in Syria: Legal Expert Opinion. Frankfurt am Main: 2013

Bradbury, Mark, and Robert Maletta. 'When State-building Fails: Famine, Counterterrorism, and the Politicization of Humanitarian Action in Somalia'. In *The Golden Fleece: Manipulation and Independence in Humanitarian Action*, edited by Antonio Donini. Boulder, CO: Lynne Rienner Publishers, 2012.

'Breaking Ghouta', The Atlantic Council, Washington DC, 2018. (https://www.publications. atlanticcouncil.org/breakingghouta/wp-content/uploads/2018/09/20180924_ breakingghouta_web.pdf)

Bruch, Elisabeth M. *Human Rights and Humanitarian Intervention: Law and Practice in the Field*. London, Routledge: 2016.

Cali, Başak. *The Authority of International Law: Obedience, Respect, and Rebuttal*. Oxford: Oxford University Press, 2015.

Cannizzaro, Enzo. 'Proportionality in the Law of Armed Conflict'. In *The Oxford Handbook of International Law in Armed Conflict*, edited by Andrew Clapham and Paolo Gaeta. New York: Oxford University Press, 2014.

Cassese, Antonio. 'Current Challenges to International Humanitarian Law'. In *The Oxford Handbook of International Law in Armed Conflict*, edited by Andrew Clapham and Paolo Gaeta. New York: Oxford University Press, 2014.

CCHN field manual on frontline humanitarian negotiation, 2nd ed. Geneva: Centre of Competence on Humanitarian Negotiation (CCHN), 2019. (https://frontline-negotiations.org/cchn-field-manual/)

Chandler, David, and Jon Coaffee. *The Routledge Handbook of International Resilience*. London: Routledge, 2016.

Chetail, Vincent. 'Armed Conflict and Forced Migration: A Systemic Approach to International Humanitarian Law, Refugee Law, and Human Rights Law'. In *The Oxford Handbook of International Law in Armed Conflict*, edited by Andrew Clapham and Paolo Gaeta. New York: Oxford University Press, 2014.

Chinkin, Christine, and Mary Kaldor. *International Law and New Wars*. Cambridge: Cambridge University Press, 2017.

Clapham, Andrew, and Paola Gaeta, eds. *The Oxford Handbook of International Law in Armed Conflict*. New York: Oxford University Press, 2014.

Clapham, Andrew. 'Focusing on Armed Non-State Actors'. In *The Oxford Handbook of International Law in Armed Conflict*, edited by Andrew Clapham and Paolo Gaeta. New York: Oxford University Press, 2014.

Clements, Ashley Jonathan. *Humanitarian Negotiations with Armed Groups: The Frontlines of Diplomacy*. London: Routledge, 2020.

Crawford, James. *The Creation of States in International Law*. 2nd ed. New York: Oxford University Press, 2007.

Cunningham, Andrew J. *International Humanitarian NGOs and State Relations: Politics, Principles and Identity*. London: Routledge, 2018.

Cunningham, Andrew J., and Clea Kahn. 'Introduction to the Issue of State Sovereignty and Humanitarian Action'. *Disasters, Special Issue: State Sovereignty and Humanitarian Action*, Vol. 37, No. s2 (October 2013)

Cutts, Mark. 'The Humanitarian Operation in Bosnia, 1992–95: Dilemmas of Negotiating Humanitarian Access.' UNHCR working paper, Geneva, May 1999. (https://www.unhcr.org/research/working/3ae6a0c58/humanitarian-operation-bosnia-1992-95-dilemmas-negotiating-humanitarian.html)

Dagher, Sam. *Assad Or We Burn the Country: How One Family's Lust for Power Destroyed Syria*. Boston: Little, Brown, 2019.

Daher, Joseph. 'The Political Economic Context of Syria's Reconstruction: A Prospective in Light of a Legacy of Unequal Development.' *Middle East Directions*, December 2018.

Dallaire, Roméo. 'Foreword.' In *The Golden Fleece: Manipulation and Independence in Humanitarian Action*, edited by Antonio Donini. Boulder: Lynne Rienner Publishers, 2012.

van Dam, Nikolaos. *Granaten en minaretten: Een diplomaat op zoek naar vrede in de Arabische en islamitische wereld*. Amsterdam: Prometheus, 2020.

van Dam, Nikolaos. *Destroying a Nation: The Civil War in Syria*. London: I.B. Tauris, 2017.

Daoudy, Marwa. *The Origins of the Syrian Conflict: Climate Change and Human Security*. Cambridge: Cambridge University Press, 2020.

David, Eric. 'Internat (Non-International) Armed Conflict.' In *The Oxford Handbook of International Law in Armed Conflict*, edited by Andrew Clapham and Paolo Gaeta. New York: Oxford University Press, 2014.

De Waal, Alexander. 'Evil Days: 30 Years of War and Famine in Ethiopia.' Human Rights Watch, September 1991.

De Waal, Alexander. *Famine Crimes: Politics and the Disaster Relief Industry in Africa* London: James Currey, 1997.

Donini, Antonio, ed. *The Golden Fleece: Manipulation and Independence in Humanitarian Action*. Boulder: Lynne Rienner Publishers, 2012.

Donini, Antonio. 'Afghanistan: Back to the Future.' In *The Golden Fleece: Manipulation and Independence in Humanitarian Action*, edited by Donini, Antonio. Boulder: Lynne Rienner Publishers, 2012.

Dörrmann, Knut. 'Unlawful Combatants.' In *The Oxford Handbook of International Law in Armed Conflict*, edited by Andrew Clapham and Paolo Gaeta. New York: Oxford University Press, 2014.

Doswald-Beck, Louise, and Jean-Marie Henckaerts. *Customary International Humanitarian Law*. 3 vols. Cambridge: Cambridge University Press.

Duffield, Mark. *Post-humanitarianism: Governing Precarity in the Digital World*. Medford: Polity Press, 2019.

Favier, Agnès, and Marie Kostrz. 'Local elections: Is Syria Moving to Reassert Central Control?' Research project report at European University Institute, San Domenico di Fiesole 2019. (https://cadmus.eui.eu/bitstream/handle/1814/61004/MED_RR_2019_03.pdf?sequence=4&isAllowed=y)

Ferris, Elisabeth G., Kirişci, Kemal. *The Consequences of Chaos : Syria's Humanitarian Crisis and the Failure to Protect*. Washington, D.C., Brookings Institution Press 2016

Fleck, Dieter. 'The Law Applicable to Peace Operations.' In *The Oxford Handbook of International Law in Armed Conflict*, edited by Andrew Clapham and Paolo Gaeta. New York: Oxford University Press, 2014.

Franck, Thomas M. *The Power of Legitimacy Among Nations*. New York: Oxford University Press 1990.

Franck, Thomas M. *Fairness in International Law and Institutions*. Oxford: Oxford University Press, 1995.

Franck, Thomas M. *The Empowered Self: Law and Society in an Age of Individualism*. New York: Oxford University Press, 2000.

Gaeta, Paola. 'War Crimes and Other International "Core" Crimes. In *The Oxford Handbook of International Law in Armed Conflict*, edited by Andrew Clapham and Paolo Gaeta. New York: Oxford University Press, 2014.

Gandhi, M. 'Common Article 3 Of Geneva Conventions, 1949, In The Era Of International Criminal Tribunals.' In *ISIL Year Book of International Humanitarian and Refugee Law*, 2001 (www.worldlii.org/int/journals/ISILYBIHRL/2001/11.html)

Gerlach, Daniel. *Herrschaft über Syrien: Macht und Manipulation unter Assad*. Hamburg: Edition Körber, 2015.

Grace, Rob. 'The Humanitarian as Negotiator: Developing Capacity Across the Aid Sector.' *Negotiation Journal*, Vol. 36 No. 1 (2020).

Grace, Rob. 'Humanitarian Negotiation with Parties to Armed Conflict.' *Journal of International Humanitarian Legal Studies*, March 2020 (https://doi.org/10.1163/18781527-01101003)

Gutman, Roy. 'How the U.N. Let Assad Edit the Truth of Syria's War.' *Foreign Policy*, 27 January 2016 (https://foreignpolicy.com/2016/01/27/syria-madaya-starvation-united-nations-humanitarian-response-plan-assad-edited/)

Haid, Haid. 'Principled Aid in Syria: A Framework for International Agencies.' Chatham House, London, July 2019. (https://www.chathamhouse.org/sites/default/files/2019-07-04-PrincipledAidSyria.pdf)

Haines, Steven. 'The Developing Law of Weapons: Humanity, Distinction, and Precautions in Attack.' In *The Oxford Handbook of International Law in Armed Conflict*, edited by Andrew Clapham and Paolo Gaeta. New York: Oxford University Press, 2014.

Haj Saleh, Yassin. *The Impossible Revolution: Making Sense of the Syrian Tragedy*. London: C. Hurst & Co., 2017.

Hajjar, Bahjat, Corinne von Burg, Leila Hilal, Martina Santschi, Mazen Gharibah and Mazhar Sharbaji, 'Perceptions of Governance: The Experience of Local Administrative Councils in Opposition-held Syria.' swisspeace, January 2017.

Hallaj, Omar Abdulaziz. 'The Internal Legal and Institutional Framework for Reconstruction in Syria: A Brief Note for Discussion.' Unpublished discussion paper, February 2019.

'Hard Lessons: Delivering Assistance in Government-held Areas of Syria.' Norwegian Refugee Council (NRC) and Oxfam, July 2020. (https://www.nrc.no/globalassets/pdf/briefing-notes/syria-joint-bp/bp-hard-lessons-syria-access-150720-en.pdf)

Hashemi, Nader, and Danny Postel, eds. *The Syria Dilemma*. Cambridge, MA: The MIT Press, 2013.

Helberg, Kristin. *Der Syrien-Krieg: Lösung eines Weltkonflikts*. Freiburg and New York: Herder, 2018.

Hilhorst, Dorothea, and Bram J. Jansen. 'Humanitarian Space as Arena: A Perspective on the Everyday Politics of Aid.' *Development and Change*, Vol. 41, No. 6 (2010).

Hinnebusch, Raymond, and Tina Zintl, eds. *Syria: From Reform to Revolt. Vol. I*, New York: Syracuse University Press, 2015.

Hinnebusch, Raymond and William Zartman. 'UN Mediation in the Syrian Crisis: From Kofi Annan to Lakhdar Brahimi.' International Peace Institute, March 2016.

Hof, Frederic C. 'Syria at Seven.' Atlantic Council, March 2018. (https://www.atlanticcouncil.org/blogs/syriasource/syria-at-seven-part-one/)

Hoffman, Peter J., and Thomas G. Weiss. *Humanitarianism, War, and Politics: Solferino to Syria and Beyond*. Lanham, MD: Rowman and Littlefield, 2018.

Hokayem, Emile. *Syria's Uprising and the Fracturing of the Levant*. London: Routledge, 2013.

Hopgood, Stephen. *The Endtimes of Human Rights*. Ithaca, NY: Cornell University Press, 2013.

Housing Land and Property (HLP) in the Syrian Arab Republic. May 2016. (https://www.nrc.no/globalassets/pdf/reports/housing-land-and-property-hlp-in-the-syrian-arab-republic.pdf)

Hurd, Ian. 'Saving Syria: International law is not the answer.' Al-Jazeera, 27 August 2013. (https://www.aljazeera.com/indepth/opinion/2013/08/2013827123244943321.html)

'Inside the Syrian Arab Red Crescent.' Syria Justice and Accountability Centre, Washington DC, 8 August 2019. (https://syriaaccountability.org/updates/2019/08/08/inside-the-syrian-arab-red-crescent/)

Jellinek, Georg. *Allgemeine Staatslehre*. Berlin, Häring, 1900.

Jinks, Derek. 'International Human Rights Law in Time of Armed Conflict.' In *The Oxford Handbook of International Law in Armed Conflict*, edited by Andrew Clapham and Paolo Gaeta. New York: Oxford University Press, 2014.

Kapila, Mukesh. *Against a Tide of Evil: How One Man Became the Whistleblower to the First Mass Murder Of the Twenty-First Century*. London: Sharpe Books, 2019.

Kalyvas, Stathis N. *The Logic of Violence in Civil War*. Cambridge: Cambridge University Press, 2007.

Keen, David. '"The Camp" and the "Lesser Evil": Humanitarianism in Sri Lanka.' *Conflict, Security and Development*, Vol. 14 No. 1 (2014).

Kellenberger, Jakob. 'The Role of the International Committee of the Red Cross.' In *The Oxford Handbook of International Law in Armed Conflict*, edited by Andrew Clapham and Paolo Gaeta. New York: Oxford University Press, 2014.

Kennedy, David. *The Dark Sides of Virtue: Reassessing International Humanitarianism*. Princeton, NJ: Princeton University Press, 2004.

Kerr, Michael, and Craig Larkin, eds. *The Alawis of Syria: War, Faith and Politics in the Levant*. Oxford and New York: Oxford University Press, London 2015.

Kimminich, Otto. *Einführung in das Völkerrecht*. 6th ed. Tübingen/Basel, A. Francke: 1997.

Krasner, Stephen D. 'Problematic Sovereignty.' In *Problematic Sovereignty: Contested Rules and Political Possibilities*, edited by Stephen D. Krasner. New York: Columbia University Press, 2001.

Kumm, Matthias. 'The Legitimacy of International Law: A Constitutionalist Framework of Analysis.' *The European Journal of International Law*, Vol. 15 (2004).

Kuperman, Alan J. 'Obama's Libya Debacle: How a Well-Meaning Intervention Ended in Failure.' *Foreign Affairs*, March/April 2015. (www.foreignaffairs.com/articles/libya/2019-02-18/obamas-libya-debacle)

Labonte, Melissa T., and Anne C. Edgerton. 'Towards a Typology of Humanitarian Access Denial.' *Third World Quarterly*, No. 1/34, February 2013.

de Lauri, Antonio. *The Politics of Humanitarianism: Power, Ideology and Aid*. London/New York: I.B. Tauris, 2016.

Leenders, Reinoud. 'Why the UN's Excuses For its Aid Fiasco in Syria Fail to Convince.' *Syria Comment*, 3 September 2016. (https://www.joshualandis.com/blog/uns-excuses-aid-fiasco-syria-fail-convince-reinoud-leenders/)

Leenders, Reinoud, and Khouloud Mansour. 'Humanitarianism, State Sovereignty, and Authoritarian Regime Maintenance in the Syrian War.' *Political Science Quarterly*, 19 June 2018.

Lesch, David. *Syria: The Fall of the House of Assad*. 2nd ed. New Haven: Yale University Press, 2013.

Lister, Charles. *The Syrian Jihad: Al-Qaeda, the Islamic State and the Evolution of an Insurgency*. London: C. Hurst & Co., 2015.

Loeb, Jonathan. 'Talking to the other side: Humanitarian engagement with armed non-state actors in Darfur, Sudan, 2003–2012.' *Humanitarian Policy Group (HLP)*, August 2013.

Lund, Aron. 'The Failure to Stop Starvation Tactics in Syria.' *Diwan, Middle East Insights from Carnegie*, 31 March 2014. (https://carnegie-mec.org/diwan/55172)

Lund, Aron. 'Let Them Eat Bombs: The Cost of Ignoring Syria's Humanitarian Crisis.' *Diwan, Middle East Insights from Carnegie*, 17 October 2014. (https://carnegie-mec.org/diwan/56958)

Lund, Aron. 'The UN Enters Syria's Moral Labyrinth.' *Diwan, Middle East Insights from Carnegie*, 9 September 2016. (https://carnegie-mec.org/diwan/64524)

Lund, Aron. 'Diplomats battle over key Syria aid resolution.' *The New Humanitarian*, 16 December 2019. (https://www.thenewhumanitarian.org/analysis/2019/12/16/Syria-UN-United-Nations-Security-Council-aid-Russia)

Lundgren, Magnus. 'Mediation in Syria: Initiatives, Strategies, and Obstacles 2011–2016.' *Contemporary Security Policy*, Vol. 37 No. 2 (2016).

Lynch, Colum. 'The Alleged War Criminal in the U.N.'s Midst.' *Foreign Policy*, 3 May 2019. (https://foreignpolicy.com/2019/05/03/the-alleged-war-criminal-in-the-u-n-s-midst/)

Magone, Claire, Michael Neuman and Fabrice Weissman. 'Humanitarian Negotiations Revealed.' The MSF Experience, London 2011.

Maxwell, Daniel. '"Those With Guns Never Go Hungry": The Instrumental Use of Humanitarian Food Assistance in Conflict.' In *The Golden Fleece: Manipulation and Independence in Humanitarian Action*, edited by Donini, Antonio. Boulder: Lynne Rienner Publishers, 2012.

Maxwell, Daniel, and Kirsten Gelsdorf. *Understanding the Humanitarian World*. London: Routledge, 2019.

McMurray, David, and Amanda Ufheil-Somers, eds. *The Arab Revolts: Dispatches on Militant Democracy in the Middle East*. Bloomington, IN: Indiana University Press, 2013.

Melzer, Nils. 'The Principle of Distinction Between Civilians and Combatants.' In *The Oxford Handbook of International Law in Armed Conflict*, edited by Andrew Clapham and Paolo Gaeta. New York: Oxford University Press, 2014.

Menkhaus, Ken. 'Leap of Faith: Negotiating Humanitarian Access in Somalia's 2011 Famine.' In *Negotiating Relief: The Dialectics of Humanitarian Space*, edited by Michelle Acuto. London: C. Hurst & Co., 2012.

Menzel, Eberhard. 'Die militärischen Einsätze der Vereinten Nationen zur Sicherung des Friedens.' *Jahrbuch für internationales Recht*, 15/1971.

Minear, Larry. 'Humanitarian Action and Politicization: A Review of Experience Since World War II.' In *The Golden Fleece: Manipulation and Independence in Humanitarian Action*, edited by Donini, Antonio. Boulder: Lynne Rienner Publishers, 2012.

Moodrick-Even, Hilly Khen, Nir T. Boms and Sareta Ashraph, eds. *The Syrian War: Between Justice and Political Reality*. Cambridge: Cambridge University Press, 2019.

Müller, Amrei. *The Relationship Between Economic, Social and Cultural Rights and International Humanitarian Law: An Analysis of Health-related Issues in Non-International Armed Conflicts*. Leiden/Boston, Martinus Nijhoff, 2013.

Münkler, Herfried. *Die neuen Kriege*. Hamburg, Rowohlt, 2002.

Murithi, Tim. 'The Responsibility to Protect, as Enshrined in Article 4 of the Constitutive Act of the African Union.' *African Security Review*, September 2007.

Niland, Norah. 'Protection and Instrumentalization: The Contemporary Solferino?' In *The Golden Fleece: Manipulation and Independence in Humanitarian Action*, edited by Donini, Antonio. Boulder: Lynne Rienner Publishers, 2012.

Nowak, Manfred. 'Torture and Other Cruel, Inhuman, or Degrading Treatment or Punishment.' In *The Oxford Handbook of International Law in Armed Conflict*, edited by Andrew Clapham and Paolo Gaeta. New York: Oxford University Press, 2014.

Operation Lifeline Sudan. 'A Review.' July 1996.

Oweis, Khaled Y. 'Local Dynamics in the Syrian Conflict: Homegrown Links in Rebel Areas Blunt Jihadist Ascendency.' *SWP Comments*, July 2016.

Pérouse de Montclos, Marc-Antoine. 'Humanitarian Aid and the Biafra War: Lessons not Learned.' *Africa Development*, Vol. XXXIV, No. 1 (2009).

Phillips, Christopher. *The Battle for Syria: International Rivalry in the New Middle East.* London: Yale University Press, 2016.

Phillips, David L. *Frontline Syria: From Revolution to Proxy War.* London: I.B. Tauris, 2020.

'The Political Role of Local Councils in Syria.' OMRAN, July 2016.

Puglierin, Jana. *John H. Herz: Leben und Denken zwischen Idealismus und Realismus, Deutschland und Amerika.* Berlin: Duncker & Humblot, 2009.

Riedel, Eibe. 'Standards and Sources: Farewell to the Exclusivity of the Sources Triad in International Law?' *European Journal of International Law (EJIL)*, 2/1991.

Riedel, Eibe. 'Quo Vadis Europe: The EU Treaty Reforms, Human Rights, Rule of Law and the Fight against Terrorism.' *31 Adel. L. Rev.* 241 (2010).

Riedel, Eibe. 'Economic, Social, and Cultural Rights in Armed Conflict.' In *The Oxford Handbook of International Law in Armed Conflict*, edited by Andrew Clapham and Paolo Gaeta. New York: Oxford University Press, 2014.

Rieff, David. *A Bed For a Night: Humanitarianism in Crisis.* New York: Vintage, 2002.

'Rigging the System: How GoS co-opts aid funding in Syria.' *Human Rights Watch*, Washington DC, 2019. (https://www.hrw.org/report/2019/06/28/rigging-system/government-policies-co-opt-aid-and-reconstruction-funding-syria)

Robertson, Geoffrey. *Crimes Against Humanity: The Struggle for Global Justice.* 2nd ed., London: Penguin, 2002.

Romano, David. 'Safe Havens as Political Projects: The Case of Iraqi Kurdistan.' In *States within States*, edited by Paul Kingston and Ian S. Spears. New York: Palgrave Macmillan, 2004.

Rowe, Peter. 'Members of the Armed Forces and Human Rights Law.' In *The Oxford Handbook of International Law in Armed Conflict*, edited by Andrew Clapham and Paolo Gaeta. New York: Oxford University Press, 2014.

Said, Salam, and Jihad Yazigi. 'The Reconstruction of Syria: Socially Just Re-integration and Peace Building or Regime Re-consolidation?'. Friedrich Ebert Stiftung, December 2018.

Santos, Juan Manuel. 'Peace in Colombia: From the Impossible to the Possible.' 10 December 2016. (www.nobelprize.org/prizes/peace/2016/santos/lecture/)

Schabas, William A. 'The Right to Life.' In *The Oxford Handbook of International Law in Armed Conflict*, edited by Andrew Clapham and Paolo Gaeta. New York: Oxford University Press, 2014.

Scharf, Michael P, Milena Sterio and Paul R. Williams. *The Syrian Conflict's Impact on International Law.* Cambridge: Cambridge University Press, 2020.

Semenov, Kirill. 'Who Controls Syria? The Al-Assad family, the Inner Circle, and the Tycoons.' Russian International Affairs Council, February 2012.

Sida, Louis, Lorenzo Tormbetta and Veronica Panero. 'Evaluation of OCHA Response to the Syria Crisis.' OCHA, March 2016. (https://www.unocha.org/sites/dms/Documents/OCHA)

Simms, Brendan and D.J.B. Trim, eds. *Humanitarian Intervention: A History*. Cambridge: Cambridge University Press, 2011.

Slim, Hugo. *Humanitarian Ethics: A Guide to the Morality of Aid in War and Disaster*. Oxford and New York: Oxford University Press, 2015.

Smillie, Ian. 'The Emperor's Old Clothes: The Self-Created Siege of Humanitarian Action.' In *The Golden Fleece: Manipulation and Independence in Humanitarian Action*, edited by Donini, Antonio. Boulder: Lynne Rienner Publishers, 2012.

Sparrow, Annie. 'Aiding Disaster: How the United Nations' OCHA Helped Assad and Hurt Syrians in Need.' *Foreign Affairs*, 1 February 2016. (https://www.foreignaffairs.com/articles/syria/2016-02-01/aiding-disaster)

Sparrow, Annie. 'Hypocritic Oath: How WHO and other international agencies aid Assad's war against Syria's civilians.' *Foreign Policy*, 9 February 2018. (https://foreignpolicy.com/2018/02/09/hypocritic-oath/)

'Taking Sides: The United Nations' Loss of Impartiality, Independence and Neutrality in Syria.' The Syria Campaign, July 2016. (http://takingsides.thesyriacampaign.org/)

Talmon, Stefan. 'Recognition of Opposition Groups as the Legitimate Representative of a People.' *Chinese Journal of International Law* (2013), 219–53.

Thépaut, Charles. 'How to Aid Syria Without Aiding Assad.' *Foreign Policy*, 24 June 2020. (https://foreignpolicy.com/2020/06/24/how-to-aid-syria-without-aiding-assad/#)

Tilly, Charles. *From Mobilization to Revolution*. Reading, MA: McGraw-Hill, 1978.

Tomuschat, Christian, ed. *Modern Law of Self-Determination*. 2nd ed. Heidelberg: 1993.

Tomuschat, Christian. *Human Rights: Between Idealism And Realism: The Collected Courses of The Academy of European Law*. 3rd ed. New York: Oxford University Press, 2008.

'Walls Have Ears: An Analysis of Classified Syrian Security Sector Documents.' Syria Justice and Accountability Centre, April 2019. (https://pro-justice.org/en/news_views/research/walls-have-ears-an-analysis-of-classified-syrian-security-sector-documents.html)

'War Continued Through Other Means: How Reconstruction Risks Perpetuating Violence in a Post-war Syria.' *syriadirect*, February 2019. (https://syriadirect.org/news/%E2%80%98war-continued-through-other-means%E2%80%99-how-reconstruction-risks-perpetuating-violence-in-a-post-war-syria/)

Wieland, Carsten, Adam Almqvist and Helena Nassif. 'The Syrian Uprising: Dynamics of an Insurgency.' St. Andrews Papers on Contemporary Syria, Fife, 2013.

Wieland, Carsten. *Syria: A Decade of Lost Chances: Repression and Revolution from Damascus Spring to Arab Spring*. Seattle: Cune Press, 2012.

Wieland, Carsten. سورية – الاقتراع أم ارصاص؟ الديموقراطية و الإسلامية و العلمانية في المشرق. Beirut: Riad El-Rayyes Books, 2011.

Wieland, Carsten. 'Assad's Lost Chances.' *Middle East Research and Information Project*, 14 April 2011.

Wieland, Carsten. 'Syrian Scenarios and the Levant's Insecure Future.' *Orient*, III/2011.

Wieland, Carsten. 'Between Democratic Hope and Centrifugal Fears: Syria's Unexpected Open-ended Intifada.' *International Politics and Society*, 4/2011.

Wieland, Carsten. Syria at Bay: Secularism, Islamism, and 'Pax Americana'. London, Hurst, 2006.

Wieland, Carsten. *Syria: Ballots or Bullets? Democracy, Islamism, and Secularism in the Levant*. Seattle, Cune Press, 2006.

Wolfrum, Rüdiger, and Volker /Röben, eds. 'Legitimacy in International Law.' *Beiträge zum öffentlichen Recht und Völkerrecht, Max Planck Institut für ausländisches öffentliches Recht und Völkerrecht*, Vol. 194. Berlin/Heidelberg/New York 2008.

Wolfrum, Rüdiger. 'Legitimacy in International Law.' *Beiträge zum ausländischen öffentlichen Recht und Völkerrecht*, Vol. 194. Heidelberg 2010.

Yazigi, Jihad. 'Syria's Security Sector: A Legal Handbook.' *Syria Report*, March 2019. (https://www.syria-report.com/sites/all/libraries/ckfinder/userfiles/files/SR_Legal%20 Handbook_Web.pdf)

Young, Helen. 'Diminishing Returns: The Challenges Facing Humanitarian Action in Darfur.' In *The Golden Fleece: Manipulation and Independence in Humanitarian Action*, edited by Donini, Antonio. Boulder: Lynne Rienner Publishers, 2012.

Journalistic articles

'A Civilian Camp in Syria Was Bombed. Here's How We Traced the Culprit', *New York Times*, 2 December 2019. (https://www.nytimes.com/2019/12/01/reader-center/syria-russia-bombing-video-investigation.html)

'ABC's Barbara Walters' Interview With Syrian President Bashar al-Assad', *ABCNews*, 6 December 2011. (https://abcnews.go.com/International/transcript-abcs-barbara-walters-interview-syrian-president-bashar/story?id=15099152

'Aid groups suspend cooperation with UN in Syria because of Assad "influence"', *Guardian*, 8 September 2016. (https://www.theguardian.com/world/2016/sep/08/aid-groups-un-syria-concern-assad-united-nations)

'Al-Ja'afari: Improving humanitarian situation in Syria requires lifting economic coercive measures imposed on its people', SANA, 12 January 2020. (https://www.sana.sy/en/?paged=2075)

'Colombia's ELN rebels call ceasefire over coronavirus', BBC, 30 March 2020. (https://www.bbc.com/news/world-latin-america-52090169)

'Des Teufels Oberst;', *Der Spiegel*, 23 April 2020. (https://www.spiegel.de/politik/ausland/koblenz-prozess-gegen-geheimdienstoffizier-anwar-raslan-aus-syrien-des-teufels-oberst-a-f2127ff5-99ea-4fe0-8ccd-a2c1edaa7fc6?sara_ecid=nl_upd_1jtzCCtmxpVo9G AZr2b4X8GquyeAc9&nlid=ik1qu50j)

'Expressions like "crusades" unacceptable with respect to situation in Libya – Medvedev', Interfax, 22 March 2011. (http://www.interfax-religion.com/?act=news&div=8298)

'In the Line of Fire: The War Against the UN in Syria', *Syria Comment*, 4 July 2016. (https://www.joshualandis.com/blog/line-fire-war-un-syria/)

'Mother Agnes Aid Contracts', *Syria in Context*, 26 November 2019. (https://tande.substack.com/p/syria-in-context-weekly-briefing-be6)

'Nach wochenlangem Streit hat der UN-Sicherheitsrat sich auf einen gefährlichen Kompromiss für Hilfslieferungen nach Syrien geeinigt. Deutschlands Botschafter lieferte sich einen hitzigen Schlagabtausch mit Vertretern Russlands und Chinas', dpa, 11 July 2020.

'On fifth attempt, U.N. Security Council renews Syria aid via Turkey', Reuters, 11 July 2020. (https://www.newsbreak.com/news/1598924571543/on-fifth-attempt-un-security-council-renews-syria-aid-via-turkey

'Rescuing Victims Worldwide from the "Depths of Hell"', *New York Times*, 10 July 2004. (https://www.nytimes.com/2004/07/10/world/the-saturday-profile-rescuing-victims-worldwide-from-the-depths-of-hell.html)

'Some UN deconfliction system's facilities in Syria used by terrorists – Russian envoy', *Tass*, 29 June 2020. (https://tass.com/politics/1172955)

'Syria: gambling making a quiet comeback', *Guardian*, 2 January 2011. (https://www. theguardian.com/world/2011/jan/02/syria-gambling-makes-comeback-casino)

'Syria a "torture-chamber", U.N. says in call to free detainees', *Reuters*, 14 March 2017. (www.reuters.com/article/us-mideast-crisis-syria-un/syria-a-torture-chamber-u-n-says-in-call-to-free-detainees-idUSKBN16L0SF)

'Syria Kicks Out 2 U.N. Staffers Trying to Arrange Aid Deliveries', *Associated Press*, 27 February 2015 (http://mashable.com/2015/02/27/syrian-kicks-out-2-un-staffers/#FjZuXbG_NEqC)

'Syria's Kurdish northeast had its first Covid-19 death. The case was news to the Kurds', *New York Times*, 17 April 2020. (https://www.nytimes.com/2020/04/17/world/coronavirus-news-updates.html)

'Syrian FM urges Int'l Red Cross to avoid politicization of humanitarian work', *Xinhua*, 10 March 2020. (http://www.xinhuanet.com/english/2020-03/11/c_138863962.htm)

'UN Council Members Point Fingers Over Syria Aid Crossings', *Associated Press*, 29 January 2020. (https://apnews.com/8b62d6e82571d9c595790244d68a8db0)

'UN hires Assad's friends and relatives for Syria relief operation', *Guardian*, 28 October 2016. (https://www.theguardian.com/world/2016/oct/28/un-hires-assads-friends-and-relatives-for-syria-relief-operation)

'UN humanitarian affairs office should discuss deconfliction directly with Syria – Moscow', *Tass*, 4 July 2020.

'UN pays tens of millions to Assad regime under Syria aid programme", *Guardian*, 29 August 2016. (https://www.theguardian.com/world/2016/aug/29/un-pays-tens-of-millions-to-assad-regime-syria-aid-programme-contracts)

'U.N. renews Syria cross-border aid operation but halves crossings, length of time', *Reuters*, 11 January 2020. (https://ca.reuters.com/article/idCAKBN1Z92HE)

'UN says "no plan B" to Syria cross-border aid system', *AFP*, 7 January 2020 (https://www. arabnews.com/node/1609606/middle-east)

"UN to Reduce Aid to Houthi-Controlled Yemen", *Voice of America*, 9 February 2020 (https://www.voanews.com/extremism-watch/un-reduce-aid-houthi-controlled-yemen)

'UNHCR on Aid to Syria: What's Important is to Deliver', Khaled Y Oweis, *The National*, 15 July 2019. (https://www.thenational.ae/world/mena/unhcr-on-aid-to-syria-what-s-important-is-to-deliver-1.886179)

'Unschuldige Menschen zahlen den Preis des Krieges in Syrien, Dr. Attar, Präsident des Syrischen Roten Halbmonds, im Interview', *Euronews*, 14 December 2015. (https:// de.euronews.com/2015/12/14/unschuldige-menschen-zahlen-den-preis-des-krieges-in-syrien-dr-attar-praesident)

'The U.N. Tried to Save Hospitals in Syria. It Didn't Work', *New York Times*, 29 December 2019. (https://www.nytimes.com/2019/12/29/world/middleeast/united-nations-syria-russia.html)

'Wash Our Hands? Some People Can't Wash Their Kids for a Week', *New York Times*, 19 March 2020. (https://www.nytimes.com/2020/03/19/world/middleeast/syria-coronavirus-idlib-tents.html)

Documents and statements

'Al-Jaafari calls for stopping the politicization of humanitarian affair in Syria', Mission of the Syrian Arab Republic to the United Nations, New York, 14 December 2018.

(www.un.int/syria/statements_speeches/al-jaafari-calls-stopping-politicization-humanitarian-affair-syria)

Ban Ki-moon. 'Renewing our commitment to the peoples and purposes of the United Nations', New York, 22 November 2013. (https://www.un.org/sg/en/content/sg/speeches/2013-11-22/renewing-our-commitment-peoples-and-purposes-united-nations-scroll)

Blair, Tony. Speech at the George Bush Senior Presidential Library, 7 April 2002. (https://www.theguardian.com/politics/2002/apr/08/foreignpolicy.iraq)

Charter of the United Nations, New York 1945 (www.un.org/en/charter-united-nations/)

Code of Conduct for the International Red Cross and Red Crescent Movement and Non-Governmental Organizations (NGOs) in Disaster Relief, Geneva, 31 December 1994. (www.icrc.org/en/doc/assets/files/publications/icrc-002-1067.pdf)

EU Regional Trust Fund in Response to the Syrian crisis (https://ec.europa.eu/trustfund-syria-region/content/our-mission_en)

'Humanitarian Needs Overview', Strategic Steering Group, *Relief Web*, March 2019. (https://reliefweb.int/report/syrian-arab-republic/2018-humanitarian-response-monitoring-report-january-june-2018)

ICRC Operational Update, Geneva, 17 July 2012. (www.icrc.org/eng/resources/update/2012/syria-update-2012-07-17.htm)

ICRC, Annual Report, Geneva 2012.

ICRC, 'The Syrian Arab Red Crescent refutes allegations it is not working in a neutral and impartial manner', Geneva, 28 February 2012. (https://www.ifrc.org/en/news-and-media/news-stories/middle-east-and-north-africa/syria/the-syrian-arab-red-crescent-refutes-allegations-it-is-not-working-in-a-neutral-and-impartial-manner-/)

Montevideo Convention on the Rights and Duties of States, Montevideo 1934 (www.jus.uio.no/english/services/library/treaties/01/1-02/rights-duties-states.xml)

'Most Relief Operations in Bosnia are Halted by U.N. Aid Agency', *New York Times*, 18 February 1993.

OCHA Syria Evaluation Report, UN-OCHA, New York 2016. (https://www.unocha.org/sites/dms/Documents/OCHA)

'On the 9th Anniversary of the Popular Uprising, the Deaths of 226,247 Civilians Have Been Documented, including 14,391 Due to Torture, along with the Enforced Disappearance of 100,000, and the Displacement of 15.2 Million Syrians', Syrian Network for Human Rights, 15 March 2020. (http://sn4hr.org/wp-content/pdf/english/On_the_ninth_anniversary_of_the_popular_movement_documenting_the_killing_of_226247_civilians_en.pdf)

Parameters and Principles of UN Assistance in Syria (internal UN document), New York, October 2017. (https://www.voltairenet.org/article202706.html?)

Report of the Panel on United Nations Peace Operations ('Brahimi Report'), New York, 2000. (www.un.org/ruleoflaw/files/brahimi%20report%20peacekeeping.pdf)

Report of the UN Secretary General on the Protection of Civilians in Armed Conflict, New York, 29 May 2009. (https://digitallibrary.un.org/record/1477249)

Report of the Secretary General's Internal Review Panel on United Nations Action in Sri Lanka, New York, November 2012. (https://digitallibrary.un.org/record/737299)

The Responsibility to Protect: Report of the International Commission of Intervention and State Sovereignty (ICISS), December 2001. (http://responsibilitytoprotect.org/ICISS%20Report.pdf)

Resolution of the 33rd International Conference of the Red Cross and Red Crescent: Bringing IHL Home: A Road Map for Better National Implementation of International

Humanitarian Law, Geneva, 2019. (https://rcrcconference.org/app/uploads/2019/12/33IC-R1-Bringing-IHL)

Rosenthal, Gert. A Brief and Independent Inquiry into the Involvement of the United Nations in Myanmar from 2010 to 2018, New York, 29 May 2019. (https://www.un.org/sg/sites/www.un.org.sg/files/atoms/files/Myanmar%20Report%20-%20May%202019.pdf)

Statement by Mrs. Sadako Ogata, United Nations High Commissioner for Refugees, at the Information Meeting of the Executive Committee of the High Commissioner's Programme (ExCom), Geneva, 26 February 1993. (https://www.unhcr.org/admin/hcspeeches/3ae68fcd14/statement-mrs-sadako-ogata-united-nations-high-commissioner-refugees-information.html)

Statement by the Regional Director Dr Ahmed Al-Mandhari on COVID-19 in the Eastern Mediterranean Region, WHO, 27 March 2020. (http://www.emro.who.int/media/news/regional-director-covid-19-statement.html)

Stop UN Support for Assad Act of 2019, 28 October 2019. (https://www.congress.gov/bill/116th-congress/house-bill/4868/text)

UN Commission of Inquiry on Syria: No clean hands – behind the frontlines and the headlines, armed actors continue to subject civilians to horrific and increasingly targeted abuse (https://www.ohchr.org/EN/HRBodies/HRC/Pages/NewsDetail.aspx?NewsID=26237&LangID=E)

UN General Assembly Resolution 46/182, New York, 1991. (https://www.ifrc.org/Docs/idrl/I270EN.pdf)

UN Humanitarian Needs Assessment 2019 (https://reliefweb.int/report/syrian-arab-republic/syrian-arab-republic-2019-humanitarian-response-plan-january-december-0)

UN Monitoring Mechanism pursuing UNSCR 2165 (https://response.ochasyria.org/unmm/?)

UN OCHA Humanitarian Principles (https://www.unocha.org/sites/dms/Documents/OOM_HumPrinciple_English.pdf)

UN Security Council: Report of the Secretary General on the Implementation of UN Security Council Resolutions 2139, 2165, 2191 and 2258, New York, 21 January 2016. (https://reliefweb.int/report/syrian-arab-republic/implementation-security-council-resolutions-2139-2014-2165-2014-2191-31)

UN Security Council Resolution 1970 (http://unscr.com/en/resolutions/doc/1970)

UN Security Council Resolution 1973 (http://unscr.com/en/resolutions/doc/1973)

UN Security Council Resolution 2165 (https://www.un.org/press/en/2014/sc11473.doc.htm)

UN Security Council Resolution 2504 (https://www.un.org/press/en/2020/sc14074.doc.htm)

UNHCR Humanitarian Principles, New York (https://emergency.unhcr.org/entry/44765/humanitarian-principles)

UNHCR Syria Factsheet 2018 (https://reliefweb.int/report/syrian-arab-republic/unhcr-syria-factsheetq1-january-march-2018)

United Nations Monitoring Mechanism (UNMM) (https://response.ochasyria.org/unmm/?)

WFP: 'Emergency Food Assistance to the People Affected by Unrest in Syria', April 2016 (https://reliefweb.int/report/syrian-arab-republic/syria-emergency-food-assistance-people-affected-unrest-syria-april-2016)

INDEX